WHITE COLLAR BIKER

WHITE COLLAR BIKER

Rediscovering Life, America, and Love

by

Robert McPherson

Copyright © 2014 by Robert McPherson

All rights reserved. This book or any portion thereof may not be reproduced or used in any manner whatsoever without the express written permission of the publisher except for the use of brief quotations in a book review.

Printed in the United States of America

First Printing, 2016

ISBN 978-1542567381

For all stroke survivors

Since the writing of *White Collar Biker*, Rob suffered a stroke on January 7, 2014. Rob was a healthy 51-year-old with no prior history.

Rob has made great strides in his recovery and his drive and determination are remarkable.

Rob's accomplishment of writing *White Collar Biker* has been a lifetime dream. His journey in the book and through life encouraged me to put the final touches on bringing this book to print. I realize, now more than ever, the importance of fulfilling dreams. I hope you enjoy!

– Ann Marie, loving wife

Proceeds from this book are going to *YoungStroke, Inc.*, a non-profit 501(c)3 organization based in Conway, South Carolina, which serves as an advocacy organization benefitting young adult stroke survivors under 65 and their caregivers. Through research and education, *YoungStroke* aims to raise awareness, increase knowledge, and share good practices to improve their quality of life.

www.youngstroke.org

Heartfelt thanks to my four amazing children, Ryan, Christopher, Eliot, and Emily; and my loving wife Ann Marie of 27 years.

Special thanks to Megan McPherson for her tireless hours of editing, designing the book jacket, and continued support, which was instrumental in getting the book to print.

Many thanks to Karen Venable, Mark Bone, and Laurie Salatto for their contribution of editing and support.

Contents

Prologue	1
Part I: Getting Ready	7
Part II: Riding Out Day 1: I Can Do This	33
Day 2: Into the Abyss	47
Day 3: On to the Promised Land	83
Part III: Riding Around Day 4: Hard Lessons	113
Day 5: Black Cloud Returns	139
Day 6: A Parallel Universe	165
Day 7: Uneasy Feeling	197
Part IV: Riding Back Day 8: Starting to Lose It	213
Day 9: Scorched Earth	231
Day 10: Through the Demilitarized Zone	249
Day 11: Guardian Angels	265
Part V: Aftermath	283

Prologue

I wasn't exactly dealt a great hand as a teenager—I was skinny and athletically challenged, and growing up in suburban Maryland surrounded by ragweed fields gave me crippling asthma and hay fever. My outlet, my way to cope, was to pour my energies into learning about engines and cars. By the time I was twelve I could identify nearly every American car produced between 1960 and 1972, including their engine options and corresponding power outputs. When I was able to start working, at fourteen, I used my earnings to buy and fix up minibikes and go-carts. My first go-cart could hit 50 mph with only a five horsepower lawnmower engine and a single gear. It had no brakes. I couldn't afford to add them, so I made a bunch of wooden slats for the front bumper and whenever I had to stop quickly I just plowed into something and broke one. Speed mattered a whole lot more than lumber.

My parents and just about everyone who knew me dreaded the day I got my driver's license because they all knew what it meant. The entire Washington DC area was at risk. I'm not sure what the betting line was, but whoever predicted that I'd get my first ticket within two weeks was spot on.

I'd decided to skip school and drive out to see one of my sisters at her college in Harrisonburg, Virginia. Taking the back way, across the foothills of the Appalachian Mountains, I merged onto State Route 211 and started hauling as fast as I could. It's an interesting road, two lanes on either side with a steep crown and almost no shoulders, so it takes a good deal of concentration and skill to "keep it between the ditches." Mile after mile, flying down the declines and leaping over the crests of the upgrades, grinning uncontrollably, I did.

Of course, the one thing a clueless sixteen-year-old kid never thinks of is checking the rear view mirror. Just as I was reaching the bottom of a long hill, probably going as fast as I'd ever gone up to that point, I glanced at it. He was about two car lengths behind me in a silver and blue Plymouth Fury with its high beam headlights on. The single red bubble light on the roof was already rotating. Panic-stricken, I looked down at my speedometer and noticed that it was better than three-quarters of the way around. It maxed out at 120 mph. The speed limit on Route 211 was 55 mph. I was in deep shit.

When I finally pulled over on the soft grass abutting the right lane, heavy wet snow had started to fall. About as nervous as I'd ever been, I got out of my car and loitered by the door, shivering in the cold. He had to be a foot taller than me and at least twice my weight and his dark, Smokey Bear Trooper hat, now rimmed with melting snowflakes, made him look even meaner.

Taking his time, he walked over, grabbed my license and said in a thick, mountain man drawl, "Buoi, ya know ya were doin' bettah den nine-dee-two mile-an-hour goin' down that heeill?"

I tried to think of some credible excuses but nothing came to mind, so I started stammering about visiting my sister. He listened for a moment, sizing me up, but just as quickly, and with some notable irritation, pointed towards his cruiser.

"Geeit in the caarh Rah-burt," was all he said.

After a long silence broken only by an occasional squelch from his police radio, he grabbed his ticket book and spoke up.

"You know Rah-burt . . . doin' ovuh seventy-fahive in Vir-gin-ya is reckliss drivin'. And bein' that yuh'r un-duh eighteen. I'm gonna have to take you back to the station, lock ya up, set bail, and wait fo' your parents to come to geeit-cha."

Utterly dumbfounded, I thought about my chances. My parents had just been through a nasty divorce. My stepfather didn't care much for his own kids, still less my mom's, and my dad spent his days at the office and his nights drinking with girlfriends. So with a hint of humor, I turned towards him and said what I believed to be the God's honest truth.

"They won't come."

Trying to suppress a smile, he turned back towards his ticket book and started writing. I was pretty sure by that point that he was going to cut me a break, but I had no idea where on the spectrum of warning to a bad ticket he was going to land.

Finally, when he was just about finished, he handed me back my license and said, "OK Rah-burt. I'll tell ya what I'm gonna do. I'll put ya down fo' doin' seventy-fo'hr in a fiftee-fahive. That'll keep ya out of reckless drivin'." And then, with a kind of exasperated astonishment, he ripped the ticket off, handed it to me and added, "But *buoi* . . . , daaht was the slowest you was *EV-VUH* goin'."

And so it was, through high school, college, and even into my first career. By the time I was twenty-five I'd almost been kicked out of two states (Maryland and Virginia). During one six-month stretch alone I picked up not only two reckless driving tickets, but an irresponsible *boating* citation as well. The guys in the wardroom of my submarine loved the last one. They all wanted me to get a pilot's license so the FAA could cite me for reckless flying (which they knew, of course, would come). It would be a perfect "trifecta."

But over time I settled down. Learning to drive an attack submarine and properly run its nuclear power plant satisfied my intellectual curiosity while marriage and the kids that came afterward—quicker than we'd planned—forced me to rapidly mature. By the time I left the Navy as a twenty-nine-year-old Lieutenant, I was down to one classic car and wood-paneled Buick station wagon that was so slow we had to turn off the air conditioning and mash the throttle to just merge onto a highway.

Determined to be a good provider, husband, and father, I poured everything I had into my second career. I'd picked up a Master of Business Administration degree during my Pentagon assignment by taking evening classes at a nearby university. I had the ticket necessary for entry into what was, at least at that time, one of the hottest careers in business: management consulting. As it turned out, I had a knack for it. Management consulting is really just analytical problem-solving (which engineers are good at) applied to the business, coupled with good storytelling—in PowerPoint. Throw in some Wall Street level suits and a little chutzpah, and you can do well. Within eight years of starting, I made full partner at one of the big firms.

By the time I was in my late thirties, however, I was starting to feel the pressure of all the conformity. It's been said that the sum of a man's vices is constant, and at least at that point, I didn't have any. I didn't drink booze (OK, a lot of wine, but still responsibly), chase women, gamble, smoke, golf, tailgate, or do almost anything that wasn't with my family. I'd even sold my last classic car and bought a "yuppie" mobile, one of those mid-nineties Volvo sedans that were all the rage. It was killing me.

So one day I floated the idea of buying a motorcycle. We had a lake cottage in Laconia, New Hampshire, the site of the one of the major annual rallies, and it seemed like a lot of fun. Realizing that I needed an outlet, my wife slowly gave in.

Of course, I was never a *real* biker—one of the guys with tricked-out machines, tattoos, and leather jackets with club affiliations. I dabbled on weekends, mostly riding alone, always when the weather was good, and doing it, as best as I could, responsibly. I wore proper protective gear, rarely sped, and never rode recklessly or after drinking alcohol. The risk of riding was enough for me at that point; I still had a family and didn't need to push it.

After spending ten years as a partner, then cashing out and moving to South Carolina, I was ready to take another big risk: a cross-country motorcycle trip to the annual rally in Sturgis, South Dakota. My brother-in-law had talked me into it, but since he lived in Pennsylvania we couldn't travel together. Like most other attendees, he and the other riders in his group were either flying out and shipping their bikes, or driving out in four-wheeled vehicles, towing their bikes in attached trailers. If I decided to ride the whole way—nearly two thousand miles and back—the total trip would take about two weeks: four days out, six days at the rally, and four days back.

It would have to be a solo trip because my wife wasn't going with me. When I started riding back in New Hampshire, she'd made it clear that she would never ride with me while any of our kids were still at home. Over the last decade, she pretty much has kept that promise. I've only been able to coax her into riding with me twice for short trips of no more than twenty minutes each: one on my first motorcycle, and the other on my current bike. It isn't that she doesn't like it. She just worries incessantly about the risk. It's all very logical. We have four kids, and if there were ever a terrible accident while we were both riding, they'd be alone. She also isn't into the culture, thinking, like a lot of folks I suppose, that bikers aren't the kind of people that suburban moms with kids should hang out with. Just for fun after our first ride together, I bought her a Harley leather jacket and a pair of riding boots. They're still in her closet gathering dust.

I'd also never taken an "alone" vacation in my entire married adult life. With a crazy job, a wife, a family, a house, and so many other time-consuming commitments it was a luxury I could only dream about. Even with all of my business travel, during the most hectic and stressful periods of our life together, I'd never been away from my wife and children for more than a week at a time. But I'd made a decision: if I was going to attend, I was going to ride the whole way out and back. "No guts, no glory," a business mentor of mine had always said. There was no middle ground.

Everyone I knew who cared about me didn't want me to do it, and that's being kind. When I'd mention my plans to the women in my life, including my wife, mother, sisters, relatives, and friends, whether younger or older, the reaction was always the same. They'd quickly slap their hands on their cheeks and gasp that riding out and back, alone, for that distance was a horrible idea. The guys would listen and smile, most of them saying something like, "Dude, you're crazy." My father said I was an idiot. It wasn't that they didn't trust me or think that I was wholly inexperienced or a bad rider. On the contrary, my family and friends knew by now that I was a very safe rider, probably the most boring, risk-averse middle-aged male rider on the planet. But there was some history in our family that multiplied the tensions and anxiety by an order of magnitude. My wife, while not saying that I couldn't go, pleaded with me up until the hour I left to fly and ship my bike.

In many ways, the story of my eleven-day Sturgis trip is unremarkable. I didn't fall in with a biker gang linked to the drug rackets and "break bad," and no one tried to kill me (well, at least *deliberately*). I didn't get involved in any raucous bar fights or run off with a stripper. I didn't get lost in the wilderness and have to hack off a leg with a dull pocketknife to survive. No, it's just the story of a washed up executive who rode an open motorcycle on a cross-country trip that he was ill-prepared to take, to a place he really didn't belong. In a way that was entirely unscripted, I learned along the way a lot about the art of riding a motorcycle, the stunning beauty of this country, and what it means to really *love*.

Part I: Getting Ready

The idea to go to Sturgis was hatched by my brother-in-law Jim and some of the guys in his Harley riding club north of Philadelphia. For many folks it's a once in a lifetime event—the kind of vacation that gets put on your bucket list of life and you know that at some point, before you die, you have to do. But it's expensive and time-consuming, especially if you live far away. Flights to and from Rapid City, South Dakota from the East Coast are rarely under $800. Shipping a bike a distance of two thousand miles round trip can easily cost $1,000 each way. The hotels in and around Sturgis, for hundreds of kilometers in either direction, charge their maximum allowable rates the week of the rally. An average Holiday Inn room can cost over $300 a night. Of course there's also food, booze, entertainment, gas, parking, and merchandise—no one goes back empty-handed—and gambling if you're so inclined. For the average guy who ships his bike, even traveling solo, it can easily be a $5,000 commitment. Couples who both ride their own bikes and want to live well can drop five figures. There are, of course, cheaper ways to do it. A lot of people decide to stay in recreational vehicles (RVs). During rally week, you see every kind imaginable, from luxurious bus chassis, rigs with satellite television dishes and internet pods, to Class Cs, fifth wheels, and pop-up trailers. Some of the more rugged types stay in pup tents, renting spots on the lawns of local residents who parcel them out for a little extra cash. As my father likes to say, "Where there's a will, there's a way," but no matter how you slice it, it's likely to be an expensive adventure.

It also takes at least a full year to plan if you want to stay in a hotel or a house, as reservations for each successive rally are usually made right after the last one. Given all of these complexities, planning for the trip began as early as the fall of 2009, almost two years before the actual event. Jim simply mentioned that he and his friends were thinking about it as a "turning fifty" milestone indulgence and if they were able to put it together, would I want to go. I said, "Sure," not really thinking that it would ever come together or that I'd actually attend. The chances that our vacation schedules would align, at best, would be minimal. I was just happy that he'd asked.

Jim is, however, a very methodical planner, and every couple of months I'd receive an email highlighting how it was coming together. About a year out, it was time to put a substantial deposit down on where we were going to stay. They'd decided on a house to the northwest of Sturgis close to another town called Deadwood. It was a rental lodge, tucked in a ridge high on a canyon that overlooked the main road and the surrounding Black Hills. It was perfectly designed to host biker parties—with four bedrooms and baths, two large indoor living areas, a fully equipped kitchen, and a spacious outdoor deck with a hot tub below. To manage the cost, they planned to stuff it to capacity with twelve people, so there'd be three to each room. I'd have to bunk with others, which was a real bummer.

I honestly didn't pay much attention to the emails. We just sent him money when he asked, usually late because I was still struggling with whether or not I really wanted to go. It was the fall of 2010, and as a family we were still recovering from the physical and emotional damage stemming from my son Chris's accident in late July of the year before. Before that fateful day, I thought that Chris might be able to come with us. But, unfortunately, that wasn't going to happen.

It all started in the winter of 2009 shortly after his seventeenth birthday. He wanted a motorcycle; he wanted to ride. We brushed it off at first. My wife would just say, "Not happening," with a flash of emotion. I'd try to make logical arguments, like that it was dangerous. There weren't a lot of safe roads for riding in Northern Virginia (where we lived at the time), and he didn't have a job yet to help pay for it. But he wouldn't let it go. When I'd bring up the roads issue, he'd respond that he'd never ride it on the beltway during or near rush hour, or approach any congested areas like Tyson's Corner. When I mentioned safety, he'd bring up that his driving record so far had been perfect, with no accidents or tickets, which was true. He was an A student and co-captain of his high school tennis team. He'd just secured a part-time job.

"Come on Dad," he kept saying, "I won't let you and Mom down. I'll be a safe rider like you. I'm not an idiot."

Sometime in March, he opened the first crack. I was cleaning my bike, getting it ready for the season, and he wandered into the garage.

After some small talk, he said, "You know in Virginia you have to ride with an adult when you're under a permit, so you could ride with me and teach me. All I need to do for now is take the beginner rider course. Can I just do that?"

I added some more polish to the cloth. My heart pounded and I was about to cave. The truth was I was lonely. I didn't have the time to join a local riding club that would require the commitment of predictable time blocks. Only one of my friends rode, a fellow executive at my company. In the four years that we had worked together, we'd only been able to ride together once. I had always been alone. It was selfish, but I wanted a riding buddy.

So with very mixed emotions I quietly said, "OK, I'll square taking the course with your mother."

Each step along the way, we'd lay down some ground rules and he'd quickly accept. He'd have to pay for the gas and expenses associated with going to the beginner rider course. No problem. He'd have to keep his grades up and stay out of trouble. No problem. I had complete veto power over the choice of his first bike and he'd have to pay for half of it. No problem. The toughest part was working on Mom, a job that now fell to me. It wasn't easy. I worked on her a step at a time, using some of the same arguments that Chris had used on me: I was a very safe rider and I'd be teaching him. He wasn't going to ride it to school, at night, or to any practices or tournaments. He was a good kid; he wasn't stupid. It was an emotionally exhausting three-month running gun battle, but we slowly brought her on board.

Finally, in June, having kept all of his commitments and with $3,000 saved from work and accumulated gifts, it was time to purchase his first bike. I tried to steer him towards a used Harley, maybe a Fat Boy with loud pipes, but he wasn't interested. It had to be a sports bike. I was against it at first. After doing some research, we found a few models that seemed to be good starter bikes for young men—easy to ride and maintain, easy to see (dazzling colors with good lighting), and not too powerful (600 cc engines mostly). We agreed on the list and Chris scoured the internet every day looking for potential candidates. A few weeks later, a sports bike dealer close to us announced a year-end closeout special on Kawasaki Ninja 600s at a very attractive price. I met Chris there after work late one weekday afternoon and we checked them out, presumably just for fun. They had two left, one Neon Green, and one Red. Chris loved the Neon Green model and I was suitably impressed, so we started negotiating. Though out of our target price range, they'd throw in a five years extended warranty, free maintenance, and discounts on other riding gear. We worked a deal.

Before we picked up his bike the following week, we went back to the dealer to shop for riding gear. He wanted a full-faced helmet, which I would have insisted on anyway, but he didn't have the money for a top-of-the-line job. I said I'd pay the difference. The owner of the dealership helped us. She was a very sweet woman about my age with powerful, veiny arms, and a face bronzed from years of riding experience. Over the course of the next hour or so, with her expert help, we picked out boots, gloves, and finally, a jacket. The jacket was by far the most expensive single piece of gear, but I insisted on a good one with body armor in the shoulders, back, and elbows. I liked the one we ultimately picked out for him so much that I bought a similar one, figuring I'd score points with my wife for being so practical.

A few days later, riding together on my bike, we picked his up. It took about fifteen minutes to go through the walk-through spiel that nobody actually listens to, and when the young man giving it was finished, I looked at Chris and said, "Ready?"

He nodded and took a deep breath. I'm not sure who was more nervous.

The ride back to our house took about thirty minutes because I led him through mostly back roads, constantly looking in my mirrors to see that he could handle the bike and was making the right decisions. His bike stalled once, but otherwise he never faltered. When we pulled into our garage and finally parked, he was beaming. Within seconds, he was snapping photos and texting his friends. It was, I'm sure to him at that time, the single greatest accomplishment of his life.

His training began that weekend on one of my favorite local rides—a loop around the Potomac River that consisted of riding out to Leesburg. Taking a ferry across to the Potomac Highlands, riding down River Road back to the beltway, crossing again, and winding along a road that cut through thick woods back to our house. The only tricky part was the beltway portion, but it was short. You could stay in the right lane the entire time. The weather was perfect, a beautiful late spring day, and we had a great time together shooting the breeze on the ferry and stopping occasionally to check out the local Civil War history. I could tell his riding technique was also rapidly improving. His shifts were smoother and his stops were more natural, without the foot skipping that new riders do when they slow to a full stop.

Later that week, Jim called me and said that he, his wife Theresa, and a bunch of his club members were riding to Gettysburg for the Fourth of July weekend. Since it was only about an hour and a half from me, he suggested that I join them for a nice day ride. I mentioned that I was training Chris, and we debated whether or not it would be a good idea to bring him along. It would be a great learning opportunity, but it would take all day, there was always the possibility of thunderstorms, and while showing great promise, he was still pretty inexperienced. My wife was against it at first, but knowing that both Jim and I would be there to guide him was comforting. As long as the weather held, we'd give it a shot.

We left relatively early in the morning on a Sunday so that traffic heading west on Route 7 would be light. The air was humid and warming rapidly; the sky obscured by an opaque haze, particularly towards the east.

Before long, we passed the outlet malls in Leesburg, crossed the Potomac River, found Route 15 North, and in what seemed like no time, we were on our way to Gettysburg. Within another hour, we found the hotel where Jim and Theresa were staying. By the time we shut down, we were bitching like all riders do about what we had encountered—the heat, the dozens of empty soda cans we had to dodge that some idiot had dumped on the highway, the gas station we'd stopped at with half of its pumps out of order.

Jim, Theresa and a friend of theirs, a guy named Larry, greeted us. He was Jim's age, tanned and tough looking, with a thick chest and leathered hands. He was riding a surgically clean, metallic blue Harley Road King Classic and took an instant liking to my bike.

In short order, Jim described what he was planning for the day. We were going to a road rally type of ride where they give you clues and you have to figure out each successive leg. Since Chris was with us, however, we agreed that we didn't care in the least about winning. We'd just take it very easy and finish when we finished. It would be Theresa's job, riding on the back of Jim's bike, to figure out the clues. All we had to do was follow.

There were a lot of other motorcycles around, but hour after hour, leg after leg, we rode along without incident, Jim leading, me following, with Chris on my wing. We were even able to sample the culture a little bit, stopping at a local rider hangout to watch a bikini bike wash. Later, we stumbled into one of those random chance moments that I loved so much about unscripted riding, the kind where you ask yourself, "What are the chances of this?" It was at a local, entirely forgettable restaurant we'd stopped at for a late lunch. The type with oak paneled walls, an array of lacquered wood tables, a small dance floor, and a dark red carpet that was probably chosen to hide dirt. A large party sat a few tables away from us, dressed a step above what the restaurant deserved. I figured they'd probably come there after some kind of church social.

As we waited for lunch, the laughter and banter from the large table increased and some of the people started to chant, "Song! Song! Song!"

A young woman rose and began moving towards the dance floor and two staff members quickly followed her. One removed a tarp from a karaoke machine and the other pulled down a projector screen. "Oh God," we all thought, "We're going to have to listen to this." We weren't the only ones—a quick scan of the restaurant revealed a lot of rolling eyes. She was tall, blonde, and cute, with smooth skin, healthy curves, and beautiful teeth—probably a former high school cheerleader working her way through a local college. I don't remember the song, but when she started singing, the collective conversation in the room began to trail off. Heads turned and people starting adjusting their chairs to face the dance floor. Soon the entire restaurant was captivated. The patrons stared at her and then back at each other with a kind of puzzled awe. As she sang, I wondered what it must have been like for people to hear Loretta Lynn, Jewel, or Avril Lavigne sing at their first bar gigs, if they knew they heard greatness. It was all we could talk about as we left.

At the end of the day, as we were gearing up to ride back, Jim pulled me aside and told me that he and the guys had been very impressed with Chris. For a new rider, he was doing great. He was a natural, a good stick. The ride back reinforced that perception. We ran into a little rain, his first, and he handled it like a pro.

In the meantime, as the summer progressed my wife began making plans for Chris's college-hunting trip. Over the past year, we'd helped him refine his target list. Fortunately, all of the schools were located in a corridor from Pennsylvania to Massachusetts. This would make the trip relatively easy and inexpensive. We could drive and stay in hotels where we needed to, but also stay with friends, particularly in the Boston area where we once lived. One of us would stay behind with the other kids, and one of us would go. We both wanted to take a week off so we flipped a coin to make the decision. I won.

The idea to take the motorcycles was mine. It would be a great father-son trip—a once-in-a-lifetime adventure that would bring us even closer together. We'd take the back way through Pennsylvania and lower Connecticut, bypassing the sprawl of Philadelphia and New York City. The weather would be perfect, with azure blue skies, moderate temperatures, and low humidity, and with the scents of summer flowers, field grasses, and cow manure filling our nostrils. We'd stop at random restaurants and hotels along the way, share some mediocre meals, and talk about life. Rain, thunderstorms, hail, crosswinds, animals, horrible traffic, bad road surfaces, flying truck tire treads, or crazy drivers would never materialize, and, of course, we'd come back unharmed. We'd talk about it for years afterward, and Chris would mention it to me on my deathbed.

"I'll never forget that trip," he would say, squeezing my hand. "It was the best time I ever spent with you."

My wife was solidly against it. She had an ill feeling—too much could go wrong. I put up a spirited defense, only considering the positive vision of the trip. "You're overcautious," I said. "You can't live life risk-free. We can manage it."

Chris stayed out of it, but for the next two weeks it was a constant source of tension between us. Eventually, she acquiesced.

The morning we left, my wife pleaded with me one last time to take the car, but it was different this time, even more anguished. She dreamed that night that it was going to be a terrible mistake. I asked Chris to step outside and worked on her one last time.

Taking her hand, with genuine resolution, I said, "It'll be OK. We're going to take it slow. It's all back roads and we have plenty of time . . . I won't let you down," I said.

She pushed me away, but the definitive "No!" never came.

The ride into Connecticut, the first leg, was just as I had envisioned. The weather was perfect, the ride through Pennsylvania especially invigorating. I'd decided to take I-81 to Scranton and then head East on I-84, a bypass route around the New York City area that I'd never tried before. It was a rare find: a relatively new, lightly traveled interstate that cut its way through undulating hills topped with granite outcroppings and summer wildflowers. We spent the night in a hotel near Waterbury and had dinner at a quiet nearby restaurant, thoroughly enjoying our Father-son time.

The ride to Westford, Massachusetts the next day was similarly uplifting and we arrived at our friend's house unscathed. We spent a few days catching up, sizing up how everyone had changed and laughing about old times.

Thinking ahead, I made a reservation for a hotel in Cambridge for Sunday night. We'd leave in the afternoon to ensure that traffic was light, allowing plenty of time to arrive before the check-in time at four o'clock. My plan was to take a back way in through Carlisle and Concord, a route I knew well, and then reach Route 2. Then we'd loop around to the northeast on Route 128 and take I-93 into Boston. The only tough part would be the last couple of miles snaking our way through the city after exiting the interstate.

We left around half-past two in the afternoon. It was a perfect New

England summer day, about eighty degrees with a sky so cloudless and brilliantly blue that the contrails of passing planes hung like pictures. So beautiful, in fact, that within five minutes of leaving, while staring at the oscillating shadows formed by the bright sun and the overhanging oak and maple trees, I missed the turn to Concord. But it wasn't a big deal. I knew that Route 225 intersected with Route 4, the road to Bedford, and Route 4 also intersected with Route 128 a few miles further to the north. It might even be shorter.

After we'd turned onto Route 4, just to be sure, I pulled over to check the maps in my Harley Touring Handbook. I smiled at the sight of the quaint cedar shingle houses that lined the street—it was so New England. I told Chris what I was doing and he just smiled. He was taking it in too. After a few minutes, I figured out that we were indeed on a road that would lead us to Route 128. Contented, I restarted my bike and pulled into a line of steadily thickening traffic. Chris waited for the right moment to follow, and correctly choosing to be cautious, let a few cars go by before falling in. I noticed immediately that he wasn't directly behind me but wasn't overly concerned. He'd have plenty of chances to catch up and if he didn't, I'd just slow, pull over, and let the cars in front of him pass by.

Up ahead at the intersection of a road that led to a post office on the left and a shopping center on the right, a seventy-two-year-old grandmother impatiently waited to make a left turn. Her eyes squinted to block out the steadily lowering afternoon sun. She was a local resident, probably in the middle of making Sunday dinner; she might have run out of some ingredient or spice and just had to dash into the grocery store for a few minutes. As the light grew brighter, she slowly inched into the intersection, carefully watching the line of traffic, looking for a gap. After more traffic had passed, she saw the unmistakable triple front light combination of a Harley-Davidson motorcycle followed by two other vehicles, what seemed to be a gap and more cars. Chris was riding in the gap.

In all of his training up until that moment, I'd forgotten to teach him a valuable riding tip regarding how to be seen in a line of traffic. If someone is waiting to make a left turn ahead, you ride on the left side of the lane. Almost on the lane line so they can pick up your headlight and the row of traffic looks unbroken. If someone is waiting to make a right turn ahead from across the street or parking lot, you ride to the right for the same reason. Instead, Chris rode in the center of the lane increasingly close to the vehicle ahead, a large minivan, sensing that the light might turn. He was completely hidden.

As soon as I entered the intersection the light turned yellow. Sensing that Chris might not make it, two vehicles back, I eased off the throttle and drifted to the right to let the cars following me pass. Surely, I figured at least one of them would proceed through, probably both. As I slowed, I looked in my side mirrors and saw that no one was following me. "I guess they all stopped," I said to myself, registering no concern.

Sure enough, the vehicles ahead of Chris, after noticeably increasing their speed, both decided to stop. The grandmother, still waiting, her left signal monotonously blinking, saw their front ends nosedive and decided to turn before she got trapped in the intersection. Chris, still hidden by the minivan, had to either brake hard or go around. He jerked left around the minivan, briefly crossed the double line and then cracked the throttle wide open to try and make it through the intersection before the light turned red. It was a mistake I didn't think he was capable of making.

The grandmother, now turning, her eyes focused on the entrance to the parking lot, never saw him coming, but Chris knew as soon as he passed the minivan that he was in deep trouble. The light had turned red and a car was turning in front of him. Instinctively, he dipped as hard as he could to the right and tried to serpentine around it.

He didn't make it.

He plowed into the right front fender of her car just forward of the passenger side door. No match for the 3,400 pound Acura, the bike rapidly collapsed and came to an almost immediate halt. Still traveling at 40 mph, with nothing to restrain him, Chris's groin slammed into the heavily sloped gas tank just forward of the bike's main saddle, splitting the sack surrounding his right testicle. An instant later, he was airborne. Rising almost fifteen feet into the air, he flipped a full 360 degrees and then 60 degrees more. His helmet hit the pavement first, just over his left eye, with a deafening crack, followed immediately by his right hand as he tried to break the fall. Absorbing the full momentum of his body weight and velocity, his right wrist collapsed, pushing every bone in it almost a perfect inch backward. The next thing to hit was his right knee.

It hyper-extended upon impact, tearing the two critical ligaments connected to the kneecap while the soft meniscus tissue behind it shredded into gelatinous goo.

A half a football field ahead, still slowing, I heard the crash. It was shockingly loud, like a sledgehammer hitting a car door amplified a thousand times more. So loud, in fact, that my first thought was to ponder how it was even possible. The sound had come from behind me, a considerable distance away, and I was wearing a helmet that covered my ears with an inch of foam. How could it have been that loud? I stopped, shut off my bike, dismounted, and turned back to scan the intersection. Two cars were stopped at the light, abreast, and a third car, a silver-gray mid-sized sedan, was stopped in the front of them at an angle. A motorcyclist was lying on the ground. It still hadn't hit me.

In the bright sun, now even lower, the helmet of the motorcyclist was throwing off mirror-like reflections so I couldn't see what it looked like. It seemed at first to be a uniform color, maybe white, so I thought, wow, another motorcyclist who must have been behind us just crashed. Instinctively walking back towards the intersection, I dipped my head and placed my left hand on my brow to try and see a little better. I picked up hints of a bright green color shimmering back from the helmet. I also finally caught sight of the bike. It was laying on its right side and leaking gasoline onto the pavement. And, with a chilling horror, I recognized something else—the color of the gas tank. It was Neon Green.

In the next ten seconds or so I ran what was probably the fastest fifty-yard dash of my life, saying to myself, over and over, "Please God, please God, please God." I was so panicked I couldn't even think of a proper prayer. When I arrived at the intersection, I calmed myself and took a quick medical triage of the situation. He was conscious and moving. All of his limbs were attached and none of them were cocked at odd angles. There were no exposed bones and there was no blood. Though screaming in pain, he was lucid, his eyes bright and full of fire.

The only visible injury, at least to me at that point, was his groin. He was holding his crotch and twisting his legs and screaming in a guttural, bear-like roar, "My Baaaalls! My Baaaaalls!"

Always the optimist, I thought he might have just been severely cracked. I put my hand on his arm and looked straight into his eyes. "You'll be alright," I said. "Don't worry, I'm here."

A few seconds later, just as I was wondering if anyone had called for help, or how I'd do so, a City of Bedford police officer gently tapped me on my shoulder. As luck would have it, he was several cars back in the line of traffic and heard the crash.

"You know the rider?" he asked evenly.

"Yes, he's my son. We were riding together. His name is Chris."

The officer's presence was immediately calming and he worked rapidly to stabilize the situation, all the while telling me that Chris was going to be fine. Within minutes, an ambulance arrived and the paramedics quickly reaffirmed that it didn't look that bad, even going so far as to say that maybe he'd just suffered a severe racking, as I had initially hoped. Nonetheless, they were appropriately cautious, avoiding any movements that could exacerbate possible injuries. After a few more minutes getting things ready, we worked together to place him on a wooden transfer board and carefully moved him into the ambulance. Seeing that he was stable, the officer walked with me over to Chris's bike. Both of the front forks were broken at jagged angles, the front wheel was bent, and the main fairing was shattered. The instrument cluster had also popped off and was lying lifelessly by the curb. The officer kicked it as hard as he could onto a grassy area, saying only, "The bike's junk."

He was heavyset with a pale complexion and an advancing five o'clock shadow—probably towards the end of his shift. We simultaneously opened the doors to his cruiser and slumped into the seats. He introduced himself and handed me his card. Having not seen Chris's attempt to run the light, he started off by saying that he thought it was her fault, a classic case of making an improper left turn in front of another vehicle. I handed him Chris's license and the bike's registration. After a few moments, I sensed that something was wrong. He was studying Chris's license particularly carefully, the hint of a frown forming on one side of his mouth. Finally, he spoke.

"He's under a permit?"

"Yes," I replied, nervously.

After another awkwardly long silence, he inhaled deeply and said,

"You can't ride a motorcycle with an out-of-state learner's permit in Massachusetts."

My heart skipped a beat, but I honestly replied that I had no idea that it would be an issue and told him what we were doing, an abbreviated version of the father-son college hunting trip story. He smiled and said he'd overlook the permit issue, but he was going to give Chris a written warning for failing to stop at a red signal. It was a gift, a compassionate gesture, and I told him I really appreciated it.

He smiled and said, "It'll be punishment enough for him to lose his bike." He added, with a smirk on his face, "and I suspect you're going to be punished pretty hard by his mother."

"Smart cop," I thought.

The paramedics talked to me next. They were going to take Chris to one of the best trauma centers in the Boston area, the Lahey Clinic in Burlington. It was only fifteen minutes away and I could follow them on my bike. A towing company would take care of removing what was left of Chris's motorcycle.

When we arrived at the hospital, the emergency room (ER) team went straight to work. Initial X-rays showed that his right wrist was broken and he'd sustained a groin injury that would require surgery. There were also injuries to his right knee, but the extent of them was unclear. He'd require an orthopedic specialist and perhaps another set of surgeries. They also wanted to do a complete CT scan to make sure that there wasn't any head trauma.

Once they had painkillers into him, Chris relaxed a bit and the banter in his ER suite turned more lighthearted. They treated him like a rock star. I'd never seen so many doctors and nurses and residents fawning over a patient. One, in particular, caught our eye. A short, young female doctor with piercing blue-gray eyes, close-cropped light brown hair and what were probably spectacular curves lurking beneath her hospital garb. She introduced herself and explained the nature of Chris's wrist injury. She told us that she might be able to press it all back into position without surgery, assuring me, after detecting a skeptical look, that she'd done it many times before.

In the next twenty minutes or so, I watched in astonishment as she performed an "open reduction" on Chris. It looked like she was kneading his wrist, one push at a time with increasing intensity, all the while trying to gain leverage by adjusting her body and the sling she'd tied around his arm. At one point she was actually kneeling on his bed, pulling and pushing so hard that I thought she might dislodge his arm from its shoulder socket. The combination of the painkillers, most likely her looks, and continued joke-making by Dad and the other staff kept Chris calm, but I knew it had to hurt like hell.

After she had finished, they took another set of X-rays. An hour later, after conferring with a more experienced orthopedic specialist, she came back in, smiling broadly.

"It worked!" she said, "He won't require surgery or any pins."

I was stunned.

Some time after this, with at least some positive news in hand, I made the phone call I'd been dreading. I began with a tentative, "Hi," followed closely with, "Houston, we have a problem . . ." and then described what had happened.

She yelped at first like a wounded puppy, but her training quickly took over. She'd been a critical care nurse in her twenties with plenty of ER experience, so to her, the to-dos were apparent. She wanted to know who the doctors were. She wanted me to call one of her best friends in Westford who was also a nurse to get recommendations from others. She wanted me to get a suite at the Residence Inn. She and the kids were leaving in the morning and they'd be in his hospital room by four o'clock the next day. Knowing that the only correct answer was "Yes dear," I dutifully copied down the orders and waited for the start of what I figured would be a devastating retribution. It never came.

Her only dig at the end was, "This is it, right?"

I knew she meant riding for Chris; I didn't find out if I was included in the ban.

Around eight o'clock that night, they rolled Chris into surgery for his groin. It was a tricky tear but within an hour the doctor strolled into the waiting room with a broad smile on his face. It had gone very well. He'd fixed the tear, and while he wasn't completely out of danger yet, it appeared that his testicle would be okay.

By midnight he was in the room he'd stay in for the next two days, quietly sleeping. I sat on a small couch that had been converted into a cot and stared at the tubes in his arms, the catheter running from his groin. The large yellow foam block that had been placed on his right arm (converted into a SpongeBob look-alike by the staff) and the knee brace on his right leg. The only sounds were the periodic soft whirring of the catheter pump, the beeping of the monitors, and the airflow from the ventilation registers. The room was bland, as they tend to be, with only a single picture on the wall and a small vertical whiteboard presumably for use by the nurses. I'd drawn a diagram of the accident on it, complete with a stick figure likeness of Chris and a jagged "whammo" callout to mark the point of impact. The staff loved it.

As the hospital quieted even further, I was flooded with memories. More than any of my kids, he loved bedtime stories. As soon as the trucking ritual would start, he'd be the first one to ask.

"Story! Story! Story!" he'd blurt.

"Well," I'd say, "give me a beginning."

Smiling mischievously, he'd respond with a giggle, "There once was a boy named *Poop*."

And then I'd take a deep breath, think of some rhyming words, and dive in.

". . . Who had a dog named Droop . . . that sat out on a stoop . . . and slobbered a lot . . . with great gobs of snot?"

Before long, I'd dump the rhyming scheme and just let my imagination run with the most random series of story fragments I could think of, from torpedo evasions to alien abductions. But always, somehow, steer the story back to the same ending: three little boys getting tickled to death. They *loved* it. One night he giggled so hard he actually sweated through his jammies.

But the memory that actually started it was how he got his family nickname. As a toddler, he was a bed jumper. Each night before bedtime he'd bounce around like he was on a pogo stick, giggling like crazy. My wife was, of course, concerned about the safety of it. One night, he actually lost control and split one of his eyelids open on a footboard, but he wouldn't let up. So we started calling him "Bumble." Because as anyone who's ever watched the Christmas TV-show *Rudolph the Red-Nosed Reindeer* knows—Bumbles *bounce*.

Only this time, he didn't.

And with that thought, I lost it. It wasn't an out of control wailing, just a soft gulping kind of sob, but I couldn't stop and I wondered why. A combination of things, I supposed: Chris had been badly hurt and might not ever be the same again; I'd been selfish and stupid; but mostly, after all of my promises, I'd let my wife down. She was the one who'd have to bear the brunt of it. Nursing him back to health at home and shuttling him back and forth to physical therapy, all the while enduring the disapproving head shakes and snickers of the other moms in our town. They'd all be outwardly sweet of course and ask how Chris was doing. Most would be thinking the same thing: that they'd have never let their own sons ride; that she was a terrible mother. I wondered if she'd ever forgive me.

The outpouring of support from the staff at the clinic, our friends, and our family over the next two days was only remarkable. During the quiet times, when his mother was out of the room, we'd talk about the accident and what we'd learned. Aside from the obvious point of not gunning it to try and make it through an intersection while someone is waiting to make a left turn, we talked a lot about proper riding technique and safety equipment. One thing was clear: while we'd made a lot of dumb decisions leading up to the accident, the decisions we made in the Kawasaki dealership the day we selected his riding gear probably saved his life. The full-faced helmet had protected his head and neck and spared his face from horrible life altering injuries. The jacket had protected his upper body including his shoulders, back, torso, arms, and elbows. The gloves had protected his hands—they didn't have a scrape. The boots had protected his feet and ankles. Quite naturally, the proper protective gear worked.

We also made some promises to each other. I made him promise that he wouldn't bug us to ride again until he was through high school (His mother would later extend that ban to "through college"). He made me promise that I would buy a full-faced helmet and always wear my jacket with body armor (not the Harley leather job I also owned). It wasn't the father-son time I'd envisioned before leaving, but, strangely enough, it brought us even closer together.

Within a few days he was ready to be discharged. He'd require follow-up visits with an orthopedic specialist in Virginia for his knee, and probably surgery, but the prognosis for his groin was for a full recovery. I agreed to ship my bike back, knowing full well that riding it home, at this point, was not an option. It was even possible, I thought, that I'd never ride again.

About two months later, after Chris's surgery and the start of his physical therapy, my bike finally arrived from Massachusetts and I quietly pushed it into our garage. Though my wife had calmed a great deal since the accident and Chris was steadily recovering, we hadn't talked at all about her feelings regarding me continuing to ride. Late in the fall, around Thanksgiving, it was time to store my bike for the winter. As part of the preparation ritual, I needed to take it to the dealership to get the oil changed and the state inspection updated. It would be the first test, post-accident, to see how she really felt.

She knew something was up the morning of my service appointment, probably sensing (as only wives can) that I was unusually furtive about something. The tip-off was when I walked into the kitchen wearing my riding boots and jeans. I obviously wasn't going to the office that day.

"You riding your bike today?" she asked.

"Yes," I replied, "I'm taking it to the dealership to get it serviced."

After an awkward pause, hoping to score a few points for being practical, I added, "When I'm there, I'm going to buy a full-faced helmet. They're safer."

Cocking her head with a sly smile, as if she was about to catch me in a lie, she asked, "How are you going to ride home with two helmets?"

Thinking on my feet, I replied, "I can tie my old helmet onto the passenger seat with bungee cords."

Though I'd probably screw it up and leave it bouncing along the road somewhere, I was proud of myself. It actually made sense.

And it was enough. With a sarcastic "uh huh," she turned and walked away. I had her approval—however shaky—to ride again.

When fall came, with Chris fully recovered and off to college, the emails from Jim regarding the Sturgis trip began arriving more frequently. It was time to place a large deposit on the lodge we were going to rent. Despite what had happened, I figured my wife wouldn't put her foot down and say no because her brother was leading the trip. On the other hand, I had severe reservations. I didn't know any of the people that I'd be staying with except for Jim, his wife Theresa, and Larry (who we'd met that day in Gettysburg). I didn't really know anything about Sturgis or the surrounding area. I also had to be honest about the sum of my experience as a rider. In ten years, I only had about five thousand miles under my belt. I still hadn't taken the advanced rider course and I'd never even attempted an emergency maneuver. I hadn't ridden through any kind of bad weather. Though reasonably skilled because I rode mini-bikes as a kid, I wasn't anything close to a real Harley road warrior. Riding to Sturgis would require three to four days of consecutive five to six hundred mile rides in the unpredictable summer weather, and, when I got there, I'd have to dodge more than a quarter of a million other motorcycles. Then, to get home, I'd have to ride two-thirds of the way across the country again. It seemed nuts.

I went ahead and sent Jim the money he asked for, thinking that despite the risks, I wanted to ride the whole way. Through the winter and into the spring of 2011, my wife kept asking if I'd make flight reservations and arrangements to ship my bike. Each time I deflected her inquiries, saying only that I was focused on other things. The truth was that I was stalling so, in effect, with no time left to arrange for shipping my bike, I'd only have two choices: ride there and back, or cancel. To hedge my bet, I made sure that my calendar was cleared for the two weeks in August necessary to make the trip but deferred any other severe planning.

I did, however, make one other preparation: I started to alter my daily shaving habits. I tried starting a goatee a few times, usually during vacation periods. Unfortunately, my wife always asked me to shave it off. She didn't like the way it felt on her skin and she thought it made me look older. I always liked how it looked, but I never had the guts to keep it when I went back to work. It just didn't look right on a guy who was supposed to be a "polished business executive." This time, however, I figured I had a pretty solid excuse. I needed to "man up" a little if I was going to a hardcore motorcycle rally and my options were somewhat limited. I wasn't a member of a riding club and didn't have a jacket with a respectable crest and the right smattering of patches. I didn't have bulging chiseled muscles, a shaved head, nasty scars, or any tattoos or body piercings. Other than being pretty fit, I wasn't in the least bit threatening. The goatee definitely helped. A couple of my lady friends confirmed that it made me look rougher. One even went so far as to say that it was scary and she liked "corporate Rob" better. So against my wife's objections, I kept growing it.

Sometime in June, with less than two months to go, we finally had it out. I was going, and I was riding there and back. There was no time to arrange for shipping or flights, and even if there was, I wasn't taking that approach. It was a once-in-a-lifetime opportunity before I turned fifty to see the country by motorcycle, and I was going to take the chance. We had the money and I had the time blocked off. She pleaded with me again but knew that there was no changing my mind. In the end, she only asked me to make sure that things were set up so she'd know what to do if I didn't come back.

I winked and said, "Either way, you'll win. If I come back, it'll be no harm, no foul. If I get killed, you'll get an excellent life insurance payout."

She chuckled playfully and asked, "How much again?"

With the wife at bay, at least for the time being, I started a punch list of things I had to do before leaving: pay the personal property taxes and get the car registrations renewed; pay the kids college bills and make sure she had enough money in the checking account; assemble and check my riding gear, purchase any needed items, and have the bike serviced; and more. She had her own list as well, which, of course, took precedence, but one by one, I started to check the collective items off.

About ten days before leaving, I rode to the Harley-Davidson in Savannah to address some punch list items. My plan was to accomplish three things: have the first, five thousand mile service completed for my bike; replace the standard horn with Harley's new air horn accessory for an added measure of safety (much louder); and buy a pair of riding pants or chaps to fill a gap in my riding gear inventory. When I arrived, I quickly completed the service check-in. It would take four hours to do the work. With plenty of time, I wandered back to the clothing section of the dealership and found a rack of chaps. Trying to look cool, like I belonged, I slowly flipped through the collection and pulled out a pair that might fit. A lovely young lady walked up to me, a store employee, and asked if she could help. I told her that I was looking for either a good pair of riding pants or chaps for myself.

She smiled and said in a low voice that was not meant to embarrass me, "Well then we probably ought to start with the men's chaps and not the ladies."

"Great," I thought, "I've been here for ten minutes and I've already made a complete fool of myself."

Dispensing with all pretenses that I knew what I was doing, we walked over to the men's rack of chaps and riding pants. I checked out the riding pants first, but they were intimidating. I'd never seen so many pockets, compartments, zippers, and layers. They probably came with a military-style tech manual that was thicker than a phone book. It would take me a week just to figure out how to put them on. We moved to the chaps next and I found a pair in my size range. She helped me try them on, and soon enough, she had a sale. The only problem was I still had three and a half more hours to kill.

As it turns out, in a brilliant marketing stroke, somebody decided to build a Hooters restaurant next to the dealership. The two businesses actually share a parking lot. I wandered over and took a table towards a back wall overlooking the kitchen. Soon enough, a young waitress walked over and asked me if I wanted a drink. She was petite with a pug nose and oversized eyes but well suited for the standard miniskirt uniform that all Hooters girls wear. I ordered a beer and told her that I would be squatting at the table for a while to kill time. She said, "No problem," but badgered me nonetheless to order some food. Her nagging worked. I ordered a piece of cheesecake and turned my thoughts to the trip.

Using the Google Maps application on my iPhone, I entered my home address and Deadwood, South Dakota. It came back with 1,835 miles. The route was nearly all interstates, beginning with I-95 in South Carolina. Then I-16 to Macon Georgia, then I-75 to Atlanta and Chattanooga, Tennessee. Then I-24 through Nashville, Southwestern Kentucky, and Illinois, then I-57 and I-64 to St. Louis, reaching I-70. I-70 West would then take me to Kansas City where I'd pick up I-29, which would lead me north, through Iowa and into Sioux Falls, South Dakota. The final leg would be I-90 West all the way to Rapid City, South Dakota where I'd finally pick up the roads to Sturgis and Deadwood.

The only problem was, like most riders, I wasn't crazy about interstates. They're a double-edged sword. On the one hand, they're typically well paved, have wide shoulders and smooth turns and, of course, they're faster. If you really need to make miles in a limited amount of time, they're the only way to go. They also have a lot of truck traffic which causes all kinds of problems, including major air turbulence, water wash (if it's raining), and truck tire tread remnants which can be extremely hazardous.

The other problem with interstates, particularly in the summer, is road construction. They're always doing something, and while mostly an inconvenience to automobiles and trucks because it slows traffic down, construction sites can be an order of magnitude more nerve-rattling to motorcyclists. Jersey barriers, especially ones placed very close to inner and outer lane lines, make you jumpy—there's no room for error. Road surface transitions are common and sometimes they purposely leave seams within a path that run along with it. Two-wheelers hate seams, particularly if they run parallel to the direction of travel. In any event, I vowed to try and find some alternate routes before leaving. My new 2011 Harley Touring Handbook had arrived in the mail a month before and was lying on my desk. When I got home, I'd scour it to find some better recommendations.

My thoughts then turned to the rally. I didn't really know anything about it. In fact, I had never participated in a motorcycle rally in my life. The closest I ever came was when we had a summer cottage in Laconia, New Hampshire, at the base of Lake Winnipesaukee. We made the mistake of going up for a long weekend during rally week. What I remembered the most was the noise and the partying. Bikers were doing burnouts all over the place and the roads and hotel parking lots were lined with scores of cheering revelers. Every now and then women would lift their shirts up to amplify the mood. We slept with our windows open, like most people do in New England cottages, listening to the sounds of full throttle races that went on all night. It was borderline out of control.

I wasn't scared of having a fun time. I liked doing an occasional full throttle speed run as much as anybody else. At the same time, I didn't want to go there and get hammered every night and sleep off hangovers during the day. I wanted to ride and see the area. Jim and I had talked about this a few times, and he had assured me that his intention was to ride every day.

The easiest part of the trip, of course, would be my brother-in-law Jim. The tallest of my wife's brothers with the most prominent Van Buren "hook nose," riding was Jim's main escape from a life that never seemed to deal him superb cards. They'd started their family in Rochester, New York, which turned out to be about the only community in the U.S. to not see any price appreciation during the last real estate boom. Then he sold out and took a new job working for his wife Theresa's brother in a small business. They bought a home in a quiet town north of Philadelphia in 2006, right at the peak of the housing bubble. He also had been diagnosed and treated for a mild form of prostate cancer, and his wife, Theresa, had been through a nastier bout of breast cancer. The combination of not making any money on real estate and the medical bills had strained their finances. Jim, always the solid citizen, soldiered on, managing not only to make ends meet but also to put their two kids through college. He was another big brother to me, with solid-as-a-rock core values and a fantastic, dry sense of humor. I admired him. As long as he and Theresa were going, no matter what happened, we'd be going on day rides. Jim would insist on it. It's what he lived for.

The only other "guest" I knew was Larry, the guy with the sparkling clean electric blue Road King that Chris and I had met at Gettysburg. He seemed harmless enough, a typical fifty-something blue collar Harley guy who loved to ride, particularly fast. Jim had told me about his club once and how a subset of the group liked to travel at speeds that required them to lean into turns so hard their footboards scraped the ground. Jim and Larry had the experience to handle speeds like that, but I didn't. It would be interesting to see how they'd integrate me into the group.

I tried to milk my beer and cheesecake for as long as possible, but my waitress fell back into her badgering mode, asking me again and again if

I wanted something else. Annoyed, I paid the bill and walked back to the dealership. I had spent the last hour before my bike was ready studying the new bikes, especially the ones with fairings (a large plastic piece that surrounds the main headlight). In Harley-speak, they're called "glides." Bikes with fairings are very popular because they deflect an enormous amount of air which reduces turbulence at highway speeds. Road Kings, like mine, are more versatile. You can remove the windshield and turn them into sports cruisers, but they don't have the highway stability of fairing bikes. I wondered if it would matter on a cross-country trip.

When I got home, I grabbed the Harley Touring Handbook on my desk and tried to find recommended roads that would more or less follow the track of the all interstate route. The options were very limited. The few that did lead in the right direction were either well off the interstates which would have required major detours, or they were tightly coiled, winding scenic roads with very low average speeds. The only road that had possibilities was Route 2 in Nebraska, starting at Grand Island. It ran northwest all the way into South Dakota where I could pick up a main road to Sturgis. I'd have to divert on I-29 in Iowa and across the upper Missouri River south of Omaha and run due west for a short period before getting to Grand Island. Once there, I could take the recommended route and bypass I-90 in South Dakota entirely. So my plan was simple: interstates all the way into Iowa and then I'd pick up Route 2, cross into Nebraska, and follow it all the way into South Dakota.

My planned departure date was always Wednesday, August 3rd, three days before the start of our rental lodge lease which covered the period of the rally, August 6-13. Since we couldn't check in before four o'clock in the afternoon on Saturday, August 6th, leaving the Wednesday before would give me four full riding days to get there. The last leg from Nebraska to Sturgis I'd do on Saturday, hopefully arriving around five o'clock.

Still, with only a week to go, I had my doubts. By this time I'd mentioned my trip plans to my family and friends and they universally thought that I was crazy at best—stupid, selfish, and irresponsible at worst. My wife also started to waver, begging me to find a last minute way to fly and ship my bike. I was being inundated with a final chorus of disapproval.

With all of this weighing on my mind, I approached the last days of preparation with only sporadic bursts of energy. I uncovered the tour pack that fits on the bike but didn't mount it. I dug out my large travel bag but couldn't find the smaller one that fits inside the tour pack (eventually I found it). I pulled out my rain gear, which I'd never used, but didn't inspect it or try it on. I washed my bike but spent days lethargically detailing it, one section at a time. When it came time to pack, I barely thought it through, assembling a standard array of jeans and t-shirts but not much else. It was like I was packing for a death march.

To make matters worse, my wife asked me with just a few days to go if I could leave on Thursday instead of Wednesday. One of her best friends from Massachusetts was coming to visit and she was flying into Savannah on Wednesday. They both had wanted a day with me before I headed out. It wouldn't matter if I arrived a day late, she reasoned, there'd still be plenty of time to hook up with Jim and do whatever we were going to do. I agreed to delay my departure for a day to keep the peace, but knew immediately what it meant. Since there was no way I was going to arrive a day late if I didn't absolutely have to, I was going to have to make it to Sturgis in three days, not four. It would test me to the limit.

The Tuesday before "D-Day," in what would become an increasingly obsessive habit, I started watching the national weather carefully. A large front was expected to roll out of the Rocky Mountains and make its way across the Great Plains by the end of the week. The southern tier of states, including Tennessee and Georgia, were projected to be hot and steamy with pop-up afternoon thunderstorms every day. It would be almost impossible to get to South Dakota without riding through the rain.

Wednesday morning, before we had to leave to pick up my wife's friend, I made the final packing decisions and started to load my bike. I wanted to have to do as little as possible once her friend arrived so I could focus on spending time with them. I threw some shorts and a few polo shirts into my big travel bag thinking it would be good to have something to wear around the lodge (I never wore them once). I also had to make some final gear decisions. When I'd purchased my full-faced helmet because I almost never rode in the rain, I'd removed the plastic shield that covers the primary opening. It was lying on a shelf in my garage and I studied it, wondering if I should put it back on. I decided to leave it behind, figuring that the bike's windshield and my glasses would be more than enough to shelter me from any rain. As for riding boots, I had two choices: my waterproof pair of Harley cowboy boots that were pretty worn out, or my newer military style thick lace-up boots that looked outdated but offered better traction and protection. It had to be my cowboy boots. I just couldn't part with them.

Having made most of the final decisions, I moved all of the gear into the garage and started the loading ritual. The first thing I had to load was the small travel bag that fits into the tour pack. I'd decided to take my laptop computer and all of its accessories, so that covered the bottom of the bag. I also wanted to take along my short passenger seat backrest, figuring that as soon as I got there I'd take off the tour pack and convert the bike back into something more sporty looking. Once I stuffed that in, along with a few days' worth of clothes and my bathroom kit, the bag seemed heavier than it had ever been before. I opened the top of the tour pack and noticed that there was a warning sticker inside stating not to exceed a load of twenty-five pounds. The tour pack bag was now probably heavier than that, but I didn't take the time to weigh it. I was an engineer and load ratings were always conservative. I'd be okay.

The next step was to place the large travel bag stuffed with clothes, bug spray and suntan lotion on the passenger seat and secure it with two bungee cords. I'd done this only two other times before, but it came back quickly. They just had to cross.

Finally, I loaded the saddlebags. I stuffed some detailing supplies, a small tool kit, and my rain gear, including the jacket and pants, into the right bag. It wasn't easy, but I was able to get the lid closed. In the left pocket, I dropped in my Touring Handbook, the new pair of chaps, the two extra pairs of gloves I was bringing, two water bottles and, at the last minute, a bottle of Johnny Walker Blue scotch my two older boys had given me for Father's Day. What the hell, I figured—you only live once. I left the jacket, my helmet, and the gloves I was going to wear by my bike. All I had to do in the morning was dress, put on my riding gear, and head out.

Around sunset, just before dinner, I nervously paced around my backyard trying to figure out if I forgot anything. My wife and her friend were outside also, reclining in lounge chairs, talking and laughing, cocktails in hand.

Realizing that the pool level was a bit high, I walked into the pool equipment shed and unrolled the plastic waste tubing, laying it out on the driveway like I'd done a hundred times before. Then I went back inside, turned the main filter valve to waste, and turned the T-handle on the drain pipe. After about five minutes of draining, I started to convert the T-handle on the drain pipe again. About a quarter inch from the full shut position, I felt a pressure surge and heard a loud, distinctive "crack!" that sounded like plastic splitting.

Suddenly, water was shooting from the pump casing everywhere. I felt like I was in a submarine simulator again and shouted, more to amuse myself than anything else, "Flooding in the engine room! Flooding in the engine room!"

A few moments later I reached the central control panel and shut off the pump. Soaking wet, I walked back to where my wife was sitting with a guilty look on my face.

"What did you do now?" she asked.

"I'm pretty sure I blew up the pool pump," I said sheepishly. "You'll have to get it fixed while I'm away."

Part II: Riding Out
Day 1: I Can Do This

After a restless sleep, I woke up before dawn, took a quick shower, and headed into the kitchen for a light breakfast. I strolled back into our bedroom to say a final good-bye, but my wife met me in the foyer. She was trying to be supportive, but I could see it in her eyes—she was really going to miss me. She asked one more time if I really wanted to do this, and I replied with a "Yes." She stroked my chin, now covered with long dark whiskers, and made me promise that I'd shave the goatee when I got back. I gave her a kiss with a gentle nod. It was a last easy concession to make.

When I opened the garage door, I was greeted with a wash of humidity typical of a South Carolina Low Country August morning. The air was warm and thick with scents of pine bark and moldy grasses. To the east, in the predawn light the edges of a bank of small clouds were rimmed with pink and purple. To the west it was still dark, the last stars of the evening steadily dimming. I put on my gear, fired up my bike, and pulled it into the driveway, shutting the garage door behind me.

"This is it," I said to myself.

I wasn't even out of my neighborhood before I noticed that something didn't feel right. The light on Route 278 had turned red and I had to stop before making a left turn. As I slowed and started to put my feet down, the bike wobbled noticeably. It wasn't that bad, but to counteract the forces I had to turn the front fork and plant my feet from side to side more than I was used to. As I waited for the light to change, I tried to rationally analyze the situation. The bike was a little unbalanced and possibly overloaded, but it would only affect me at very low speeds. Stopping and repacking at this point would only cost me time. I had to make at least six hundred miles. So when the light turned green, I took a deep breath, turned left, and accelerated onto the empty highway.

One of the first things that strikes you when you ride a motorcycle is how much more the air temperature affects you than when driving a car. Literally, you can go from feeling shivering cold to boiling hot in the span of fifteen degrees Fahrenheit. A lot depends on how fast you're moving, what's covering your body, the location of the sun in the sky, and cloud cover. But in general, because of evaporative cooling, your body usually feels colder on a motorcycle than it otherwise would in the enclosed cabin of a motor vehicle. If you ride in a t-shirt on a 70°F night at speeds above 30 mph or so, you're going to be cold. On a 60°F night, even with a long sleeve shirt on, a jacket, long pants, and gloves, you're still going to be cold. When the temperature dips into the fifties, if the sun's not out you'll need a long sleeve shirt, a sweatshirt, and a fully lined jacket. It's even worse if there's a cold wind blowing in a direction that increases the relative wind speed across your body. Conversely, when the sun comes out and the temperature rises, you have to rapidly shed layers or you start to overheat.

When I walked outside to check the weather, it was about 75°F—reasonably warm and humid, but the sun hadn't come up yet. I was wearing only a t-shirt and my jacket without the liner. I was cold, but I knew that the sun would be up soon. So like most motorcyclists, I shrugged it off and waited for the change. I knew right then that I'd made a rookie mistake: I hadn't dressed in layers or even packed the gear necessary to do so.

By the time I reached I-95, the sun was rising behind me and rapidly warming the air. I thought about stopping to top off the gas tank and maybe down a quick cup of coffee, but decided to keep rolling instead. Within moments I was heading south at my favorite highway speed (in good weather with decent roads) for my Road King, 72 mph, trying to avoid the long, longitudinal ruts in the asphalt.

Road conditions are another thing that make riding a motorcycle so much more challenging than driving a car or truck. If traveling in the open air amplifies temperature differences by a factor of ten, road surface characteristics increase riding comfort—and dangers—by a similar amount. Dirt and gravel roads are obviously very difficult for road bikes, but even paved highways have characteristics that present frustrating challenges. The right lane of a well-travelled asphalt covered road, for instance, often resembles a *w*. The tires of heavy trucks compact the layers of the road surface directly beneath them, resulting over time in noticeable depressions on each side of the crown. If the asphalt isn't prepared or laid down properly, it can also shear in the spaces between sets of dual truck tires, resulting in breaks that turn into longitudinal ruts. At the same time, oil and fluids that leak from vehicle traffic coat the crown, creating a slippery dome. If you ride on either flat side of the *w*, the longitudinal ruts pull the front tire from side to side creating an annoying wandering effect. If you ride on the dome, over time you'll cover your front and rear tires with a slime that can adversely affect turning and braking. The left lane of a two-lane interstate usually doesn't have the same *w* effect or as much rutting as the right path. But unless you want to get run over, you have to ride much faster. On I-95 in light traffic, if you're doing much less than 80 mph in the left lane, somebody's going to drive right up your rear. A lot of the time, it's simply a game of picking your poison.

When I turned onto I-16 the road surface, thankfully, turned to concrete. Though eighty-five to ninety percent of the roads in the U.S. are covered with asphalt, concrete is still used for heavily traveled highways that support a lot of truck traffic. It's by far my favorite road surface for a motorcycle because it doesn't deform or rut as readily. It's also a lot cooler on hot days, which can be a real blessing in stop-and-go traffic. In any event, I was glad to leave I-95 behind.

After a while, the sun became cloaked behind growing longitudinal bands of grayish clouds, and I started to get a little bored. The crape myrtle trees that had adorned the center median with their purple, red, and white blooms had also vanished, leaving only brownish-green grasses and ragweed. At the same time, homogeneous looking bands of pine trees lined the shoulders. With the sky now occluded and the scenery bland, my head started to involuntarily jerk downward. I scanned the gas gauge and it was nearly empty. It was time to get off.

As it turns out, there aren't a lot of choices for food and fuel in the "lonely stretch" halfway between Savannah and Macon, Georgia. My general rule of thumb for picking places to gas up or fill my stomach when traveling on interstates is that I have to be able to see the establishment from the exit ramp before committing to getting off. Almost out of gas and falling asleep, I finally saw a blue sign that had a single gas station logo on it, but couldn't see any infrastructure through the trees. I veered off, hoping for the best.

Sure enough, about a quarter mile down the road there was a lone, relatively large gas station with an attached restaurant. It didn't look too inviting. The entrance to the parking lot was partially covered with patches of gravel and the blacktop was old, heaved, and broken. The awning over the pumps was noticeably sagging and the paint on the store behind it was faded and peeling. With no other choices, I dodged a few of the gravel patches and stopped in front of one of the pumps.

After filling up, I walked into the store to find a bathroom and buy a cup of coffee. The store was much larger inside than it had looked from the pumps, but was otherwise deserted. I spotted the restrooms and started walking towards them. A few paces later I noticed that a sign had been taped across one of the doors. Printed on a single sheet of 8 ½ x 11-inch white paper in large black and blue letters, it said, "RESTROOMS ARE ABSOLUTELY AND STRICTLY FOR THE USE OF IN-STORE CUSTOMERS ONLY." It was so obnoxious I hesitated for a moment before reaching for the doorknob, wondering if it applied to me. I'd purchased some gas, but that was outside the "store." Were they saying that I had to buy something at the shop to use the restroom? They certainly had a lot of stuff. Dozens of shelves were stocked with every kind of convenience store item imaginable, including groceries, snacks, over-the-counter pharmaceuticals, cleaning supplies, car care items, and even souvenirs. Two of the back walls were completely covered with floor-to-ceiling refrigerators that stocked an incredible array of beverages. There was also a large coffee station and an enormous assortment of tobacco products and lottery games behind the counter. Apparently, they wanted you to buy something. But did I have to make a purchase before using the restroom, or could I wait until afterward? When did you officially become an "in-store customer"? I also wondered who in their right mind would use their bathrooms other than customers. The place was absolutely in the middle of nowhere. There were no tourists and it wasn't the kind of place that would entice anyone to stop if they didn't need something.

Dismissing the warning, I opened the door and walked in. The toilets were on the right. "Out of Order" signs were hanging on all but one of the wooden stall doors and two of the three urinals were covered with green plastic bags that were held in place with sloppily applied duct tape. A single dingy sink without a mirror above it was aligned at an odd angle against the wall. A dirty bucket with cleaning supplies occupied another corner. "Who are you kidding?" I thought. It's not like you're protecting a first-class restroom from vagrants. Even more offensively, the same "restrooms are strictly for in-store customer use only" signs were plastered on every wall of the bathroom and above each urinal. I started to relieve myself in the only functioning one, thinking as I did so that I'd leave directly afterward and skip buying anything. They didn't deserve any more of my money. A few seconds later, however, I lifted my head and saw that someone had scrawled "Fuck You" over the sign. It was one of those moments when somebody unexpectedly captures in graffiti exactly what you're thinking and I just burst out laughing. "Whoever you are," I thought, "you're OK."

In a better mood, I changed my mind and made my way over to the hot beverage station. I grabbed a small cup, filled it with the most robust blend of coffee they offered, and walked over to the counter. A tired looking female clerk was working behind a large Plexiglas safety enclosure.

"Is thaat awwll ya want?" she asked in a thick Georgia drawl.

"Yep, that's it."

Then I pulled out a $5 bill, handed it to her, and gulped the drink while she made the change. It might have been her best sale of the morning.

Just north of Atlanta I stopped, gassed up, downed a quick fast food lunch, and checked my weather applications. There were some rain showers to the north and west, but they were light and heading east. I'd probably be able to dodge any bad weather. I was also faring pretty well physically. The Diet Coke from lunch was keeping me awake and my rear end wasn't hurting too badly, but I could feel the onset of cramping in my hamstrings and hands. Your body, as it turns out, isn't actually designed to sit upright in a lightly padded saddle for hours at a time with your legs cocked at a ninety-degree angle, your arms stretched out ahead of you, and your hands tightly clutching one-and-a-half inch thick, cylindrical grips. The signal that it gives you that "this is abnormal and you ought to stop" is a dull throbbing in your rear end that becomes sharper over time, followed by lower back pain and sporadic cramps in your hands and legs. There are ways to fight it. Stopping and stretching certainly helps, and you can even try some yoga-like exercises while riding. At some point, every rider reaches a level of physical fatigue and mental exhaustion where you can't ride another mile. I wasn't close to this yet, but the preliminary signs were there.

An hour later, I had my first close call. In addition to passing heavy trucks, one of the most dangerous situations for a motorcyclist on an interstate highway is approaching an on-ramp in the right lane when another vehicle is trying to merge into traffic and you can't shift into the left lane. The issue isn't what most people would think, that the other driver might have difficulty seeing you (although that can always happen). On the contrary, from what I've observed, often times the issue is that the driver gets overly nervous about now to handle merging into the path of a motorcycle and hesitates, creating a very dangerous situation towards the end of the ramp.

It typically goes something like this: The driver of the other vehicle sees a motorcycle coming and doesn't want to cut in front of the rider, so the driver doesn't accelerate and cut over as quickly as he or she might do otherwise. The motorcyclist, seeing the car, doesn't want to blow it for fear it might come over at the last second, so the natural inclination is to back off the throttle and slow a bit. This results in the vehicle not accelerating as fast as it should, and the motorcycle slowing probably more than it should. The net effect is the car and the motorcycle wind up with almost zero relative speed, with the bike often trapped in the blind spot of the vehicle. The situation becomes even more dangerous as the on-ramp space runs out. The driver of the car either has to stomp on the brake to avoid running onto the shoulder or accelerate rapidly and cut over in front of the motorcycle. The rider of the bike has the same decision to make, either slow quickly and let the vehicle come over or gun it and get out in front of it.

About halfway between Atlanta and Chattanooga where I-75 narrows back into only two lanes each way, I was rolling along when I spotted a mid-size white sedan accelerating down an on-ramp. I was in the right lane and the left lane was blocked with a line of faster moving heavy rigs. Gauging its speed and assessing that it looked like it'd pass in front of me, I slowly backed off the throttle. It appeared as if the driver saw me and did the same thing and very soon we were riding close to each other, with the car ahead and me slightly behind, at almost no relative speed. The next moment, I saw the car move a little to the right. Taking this as a sign that the driver had seen me and wanted me to pass, I rolled on some throttle. About the instant when I passed the driver's side front door, the vehicle started to come rapidly back over. If I didn't do something fast, it was going to clip me in the rear which is virtually unrecoverable. I tried to reach for the horn button, but like so many times before in near-panic situations, I missed it and hit the left turn signal instead. My next reaction was to floor it. I rotated my right wrist as fast as I could to slam open the throttle. I leaned a little to the left to try and position the bike as close to the left side of the right lane as possible. It was going to be close—real close.

One of the great things about the Harley Screaming Eagle 110 engine is that it has a tremendous amount of torque. Riding a heavy touring bike with this engine is like driving a full-size car with a big block V8 during the muscle car era. The bike with a rider and touring load weighs about 1,050 pounds, so the equivalent weight, if it were a car, would be 4,200 pounds. And as anyone who's ever watched the movie *The Blues Brothers* knows, a 440 cubic inch motor can push around a four thousand pound car surprisingly well. The torque band is also very broad, so if you punch it at highway speed, no matter what gear it's in, it's going to move out crisply. The 110 in my Road King is like this. Even in sixth gear, as long as you're going 60 mph or above when you floor it, the bike leaps forward. You don't need to downshift and bring up the engine rpm.

The torque of the 110, at that moment, might have saved my life. As soon as I cracked the throttle the bike growled and lurched forward. I watched in my mirrors as the car, still shifting rapidly to the left, passed behind me with what appeared to be no more than a yard of clearance. I also saw the reaction of the driver, and it was pretty clear from her thoroughly rattled look that she hadn't seen me. For the next several miles, she stayed well behind me, afraid to approach. I broke out in a mild form of flop sweat and practiced reaching for the horn button. I wasn't going to miss it again.

By the time I reached Chattanooga, the clouds had lowered to the point where they were touching the small mountains surrounding the city. It was a dreary, forlorn kind of summer fog, the type that makes an otherwise charming city look like a tired, run-down industrial mill town. In any event, I didn't have a lot of time to study the area because just north of the city, on the way to Nashville, I quickly realized I had another problem.

Another thing that strikes you when you ride a motorcycle, aside from how much more sensitive you become to differences in temperature, is how much more it seems to amplify your sense of smell. Everything appears to be an order of magnitude either more pleasant or offensive. The difference is even more noticeable since many passenger cars and light trucks now have climate control systems with cabin air filters that reduce pungent odors. On an open motorcycle, however, for better or worse, your nose picks up everything.

Unfortunately, I rolled through the city during the start of the afternoon rush hour and it was confusing—really confusing. Although I only had to stay on one highway through the city (I-24), several other interstates intersect with it (I-440, I-40, and I-65). To remain on the right track, I had to shift from being in the far right lanes to the far left lanes and back again a total of five different times. With light traffic this wouldn't have been a problem, but traffic that day was unusually heavy. It was much harder to see the signs, understand where I needed to be, and change lanes to be in the right position. To make matters worse, right in the middle of the most confusing part (the I-65 splits)—I had my second close call.

The highway at that point was four lanes wide and I was riding in the right center lane surrounded by traffic on all sides. Several on-ramps were dumping even more cars onto the crowded highway and the pace of traffic flow was maddeningly uneven. Vehicles in the left two lanes would rush by and then moments later come to an almost complete stop, while vehicles in the two right lanes would sprint ahead. Several times I was being tailgated so badly that I had to change lanes, only to have to change back again to maintain the right position to stay on I-24 North. Just after I switched back to the right center lane for another time, I saw a slug of SUVs whiz by in the left lane followed closely by a large tractor trailer. Even before I heard or smelled anything, I had a fleeting thought that this seemed unsafe, that the massive rig was going way too fast and following too closely for this kind of traffic. I was maybe three car lengths behind at the time.

The first warning sign was the all-too-familiar smell of burning rubber. It came to me at first as just a whiff, a subtle warning sign that something was about to go very wrong. I probably never would have picked it up if I had been driving a car. In the open air, however, it was strong enough to trigger a reaction in my brain that made my right hand release the throttle. A fraction of a second later the sound came at me, a terrifying, "Bang! Slam! Bang!" followed by the roar of tires hop-skidding and a fast moving mini-cloud of rubber smoke that I knew had to be coming from the big rig just ahead and to my left. I wasn't in a position to run into the back of the truck. My primary concern was that it would swerve to the right into the path of the other vehicles around it and cause them to either brake hard or careen into me. Instinctively I slowed further and made a fast change into the far right lane, watching, as I did so, the trailer of the big rig start to skid at an obtuse angle into the next lane. This precipitated a wild chain reaction of emergency maneuvers by the vehicles around the trailer, culminating in the car that had previously been to my left moving over into the exact same position that I'd been in moments earlier. Incredibly, no one hit anyone and traffic rolled on, but if I hadn't slowed initially and changed lanes when I did, I probably would have been clipped. The extra warning time from the super sensory perception you get on a motorcycle had probably saved me. I raised my head towards the sky, made the subtle sign of a cross, and said to myself, "OK, that makes two." It was just past four o'clock.

By the time I rolled into Kentucky, the sky had almost entirely cleared and the humidity had dropped a notch. It was still hot, but I was down to wearing jeans and a t-shirt so it didn't bother me. In fact, despite a growing throbbing in my rear end from fatigue, I was really starting to enjoy myself. The road was relatively new, with a bright finely grooved concrete surface, broad shoulders, and smooth turns. Traffic was light with few trucks. The scenery was also beautiful. A mixture of pristine, gently sloping corn fields, small dark blue lakes, lazy streams, forests, and state parks that blended together in a way that seemed perfectly orchestrated to please the senses. With my feet up on the highway pegs and my skin slowly tanning from the steadily lowering sun, I decided to try and make a few more hours.

Finally, I saw a sign and a few other advertisements for a town called Paducah about forty miles further up I-24. The fuel remaining function on the trip odometer gave me eighty miles. It would be close, but I could make it. As long as the weather and traffic continued to cooperate, I'd roll off the interstate before seven o'clock.

Named after an American Indian Chief, Paducah, Kentucky was built at the intersection of the Ohio and Tennessee Rivers to support the riverboat commerce and became a major Illinois Central Railroad hub. Captured early during the Civil War, it was a highly prized Union supply depot. The great Ohio River flood of 1937, coupled with the decline of the railroad industry, steadily eroded the prominence of the town. Though several industrial facilities still remain, including a uranium enrichment plant owned by the Department of Energy, Paducah has become more of a cultural and arts center of Southwestern Kentucky. A huge mural was started, for instance, in 1996 on the flood wall that borders the town. A relocation program initiated by the local government in 2000 still draws artists and musicians to the area. Since the flood, much of the downtown area has been restored in a way that's preserved the period correct architecture of the late nineteenth and early twentieth centuries.

I didn't know any of this when I first rolled off the interstate. But, when I made a right turn onto the road that leads to the historic area and the river wall, I was pleasantly surprised. The red brick and gray stone buildings that lined each side of the road had just the right splash of alternating colors, differing roof details, and awning styles to capture my interest. I slowed and carefully studied them, searching for a hotel in the midst of what seemed to be an unbroken line of antique stores, art galleries, boutiques, restaurants, and regional banks. I didn't see any.

Frustrated, I made a series of left turns onto the next block over and continued the search, scanning for anything that resembled a place to stay. I even stopped and used the Around Me application on my iPhone to find hotels, but they all appeared to be back towards the interstate. Exhausted, thirsty, and lacking the energy to start a new navigational challenge, I decided to head back to a hotel by the interstate I'd already passed, a strangely painted Comfort Inn. Ten minutes later I pulled under their portico.

The clerk behind the counter greeted me with a polite, "Hello."

She was young, pale, and rounded, with dark blonde hair and oily skin.

"Do you have any rooms?" I asked.

Before she could respond, I noticed there was a small refrigerator behind the counter fully stocked with water, so I added, "And can I have one of those?"

She reached back, grabbed a sweating sixteen-ounce bottle, handed it to me, and said, "Yes we have rooms and I can give you a splendid rate, only seventy-nine dollars a night."

Before saying anything further, I downed the entire bottle with great, successive gulps. It's one thing that's easy to forget when you're riding a motorcycle in hot weather with exposed skin. You can rapidly get very dehydrated.

Feeling better, I made a half-hearted attempt to suppress a burp and said, "I'll take one."

She stared at me for a long moment wondering, I supposed, why I was so thirsty, but completed the check-in and handed me the key plastic cards.

Hoping I wouldn't have to ride anymore for the day, I asked, "Are there any restaurants within walking distance of the hotel?"

"There's one just up the road, on the other side, but it's pretty straightforward. All the right ones are in the downtown area."

It figures, I thought. Nothing can ever be easy.

Within fifteen minutes, I'd unloaded my bike and was headed back the way I'd just come. The bike felt entirely different, noticeably more stable and easier to handle, confirming what I had first thought when leaving my neighborhood over thirteen hours ago. I'd packed too much stuff and had loaded it improperly.

With so many empty parking spaces along the street it didn't take me long to find a spot that was acceptable. It was about two blocks from the riverfront across from what appeared to be a larger restaurant. I backed in at an angle, like most bikers do, shut off the motor, glanced at the trip odometer, and switched off the ignition. I had clocked 685 miles, a new single-day record—at least for me. For the next ten minutes, I strolled up and down each side of the street checking out the restaurant options. There were quite a few, including a very expensive Italian place with an excellent menu that was just behind where I'd parked the bike. But like just about everything in historic Paducah that night, it was empty. Not wanting to take a chance, I chose the restaurant across the street instead. At least some people were inside.

I walked in through the side door which was close to the bar. The bartender seemed friendly enough, but the stools were all empty except for one middle-aged guy nursing a beer. Before I could decide if I wanted so sit there, a hostess came up to me and asked if I wanted a table. A few small tables were set up in the windows that adjoined the street, perched on a ledge slightly higher than the main floor. I told her I'd take one. It would allow me to continue to scan the downtown area while also providing a panoramic view of the restaurant.

A few moments later my waitress approached. She was about forty with black hair, dark eyes and brownish skin, more Eastern European than Latin.

"Hi, my name's Judy. Can I get you something to drink?"

"How about a beer. Any local recommendations?"

"Oh, we have quite a few."

"Don't bother rattling them off. Just bring me something amber, please. I trust you."

Within minutes, she brought over a tall glass of ale that I'd never heard of and handed me a menu. I could tell she wanted to talk, but I was more interested in the band that had started to play on the lower floor adjacent to the bar.

There were three of them: two guys and a young woman. One of the guys was playing an acoustic guitar and the other one a mandolin. The girl played what looked like a fiddle. They were all respectably dressed. The young men wore tan pants and long-sleeved shirts and the girl, who was easily a foot taller than either of the guys, wore a softly patterned red and white summer dress. The music was delightful, a soft kind of bluegrass that was more uplifting than sad.

When Judy returned, we started to chat again.

"I saw you pull up on your bike. It's nice. You going to a rally?"

"Yeah, Sturgis. The first day on the road."

"I've been there, maybe five years back. Wild place. My boyfriend and I went . . . but I don't ride with him anymore."

I really didn't want to get into her breakup story, so I tried to think of a way to change the subject. It came to me pretty quickly.

"Would you mind taking a picture of me? I'd like to let my family know I'm OK."

"Sure!"

When she handed my phone back, I gave her my food order and blasted the picture out to my family and friends. And as the return texts came back, slowly drinking my beer and listening to the music, my mood rapidly improved.

The trip was going relatively well. I'd had a few close calls, but I'd ridden further on a motorcycle than I ever had before in one day. The weather had cooperated, and I'd found what seemed to be a charming restaurant in a lost city by a sleepy river. I was tired but happy, relaxed and confident.

Day 2: Into the Abyss

Waking up early without the need for an alarm clock, I reached for my phone and tapped on the Radar US application. The major front that had come out of the Colorado Rocky Mountains had progressed into Eastern Kansas. Shaped like the closed end of an apostrophe and several hundred miles long, it was moving east into Missouri across my intended path. The only good news was that the line of the most intensive thunderstorms, the ones that always show up as red or purple blobs on Doppler radar, was relatively thin. If I was moving west at 60 mph and the storms were moving east at half that speed and the line was less than ten miles wide, I'd be through it quickly. Small scattered thunderstorms stretched out in front of the main front for about another hundred miles, spread out like scouts, waiting to coalesce and intensify. It would take a miracle to avoid getting wet.

Betting that at some point I'd have to put on my rain gear, I moved a few of the heavier laptop computer accessories I purchased to my right saddlebag and moved my rain jacket to the top of the small tour pack bag. This would still allow me to get my rain gear relatively quickly while shifting a little more weight lower in the bike. Otherwise, I was still too tired to consider a complete repacking. Already feeling behind for some reason, I decided to head down for a quick breakfast and then head out. I'd already decided before trailing off to sleep the night before that my objective would be to make Grand Island, Nebraska if possible—another seven hundred miles. Then I could sleep in, start a little later, and make the relatively easy, more scenic 460 miles run to Sturgis on Saturday.

After reloading the bike, I walked through the lower level of the hotel to the lobby where the breakfast spread was laid out. I popped a couple of English muffins in the toaster, poured myself a cup of coffee, and found a table next to two older guys who had sat down a few moments before me. They were wearing riding boots, jeans, and t-shirts. Both had near white-gray hair and beards. "You guys on your way to Sturgis?" I asked.

"Yeah," they replied.

"Where are you from?"

"North Carolina," they responded together, without accents.

"Oh. I'm from Hilton Head."

"Never heard of it."

And that was it. Apparently not interested, they turned and walked away. OK, I thought, you've met your first bikers on the way to the rally and they're not very friendly.

Having gassed up the night before, I pulled back onto I-24, crossed the Ohio River and entered Illinois, chuckling at the change in the speed limit as I crossed the border. Somebody thought that 65 mph was safer than seventy. Maybe the politicians in Illinois wanted to save fuel or maybe there was more farm machinery traffic. Maybe they just wanted to be different. In any event, it didn't take me long to formulate another hypothesis. The road surface changed from concrete to asphalt and judging from its condition, I suspected that most of the money in Southern Illinois gets sucked into the maintenance of Chicago area infrastructure. I'd never seen so many longitudinal ruts in a major highway outside of the lake effect snow belt.

By the time I reached I-57 North, the road surface was even worse. The two depressions in the right lane caused by heavy truck traffic looked like long ribbons of pockmarked, crumbling marble. Truck tire tread remnants were everywhere, from the whole thread pieces to tiny shreds that looked like shattered pieces of black fiberglass. Traffic was also heavy and the big rigs were mostly using the left lane, aware, no doubt, as I was, of the horrible surface in the right lane. Annoyed by their noise and air wash, I stayed in the lane nobody else wanted. I moved along at a little over the speed limit, riding on the greasy crown while scanning for potholes and watching the sky. The clouds were getting thicker, lowering and darkening. Small bands of lighter, more vertically oriented cottony clouds were drifting by at noticeably faster speeds. I wondered if the rain would hold off until St. Louis.

After another hour or so I finally saw the sign for I-64 West to St. Louis and departed the worst interstate I'd encounter on the trip. I checked my watch and figured that I'd cross the Mississippi and roll past the famous arch around ten o'clock, missing the Friday morning rush hour.

By the time I reached St. Louis, the sky had become more uniformly gray and the cloud ceiling had descended enough to obscure the tallest skyscrapers. Shortly before the bridge over the Mississippi River, a light rain shower began. Staying in the right lane, I strained my neck to try to catch a view of the water and the famous arch. As soon as I started to cross, however, I had to direct all of my focus to staying upright and positioning for the turnoff to I-70 at the end of the bridge. It's yet another thing that motorcyclists have to contend with: bridges with steel grate surfaces, narrow lanes, and concrete guardrails or barriers. The steel grates become incredibly slippery when wet, and pull your front tire from side to side in a fast, oscillating motion. The walls also make you nervous, and if you don't like heights—and I don't—your body tenses with a creepy sense of anxiety. Still, I did manage to look down at the dark blue-gray water and the arch standing to the north, on the west side of the river bank. It seemed smaller than I imagined, almost like a scale model of the real thing.

As I contemplated how people could even stand up on the top of the arch, traffic began to slow for the turnoff to I-70. Then, without warning, a car cut in front of me from the left. Caught off guard, I grabbed the front brake handle a little harder than I probably should have. I rapidly slowed to less than 10 mph, the speed at which you typically start to move your feet down from the foot boards to the road surface to steady yourself for an eventual stop. Unprepared, my boots hit the pavement a little late and at more of an angle than normal, causing them to slip off of the grated surface at the exact moment when the bike came to an almost complete stop. Still overloaded and top heavy, with no balance lever on either side, the bike started to drop towards the side that was more weighted—the right. I couldn't believe it. I was going down.

Instinctively, I reached out with my right leg a little further, planted my boot on the ground, and heaved with all of my quad and calf strength. Miraculously, the boot held and I stopped the fall. For the next quarter mile or so, with traffic alternately stopping and moving at no more than 10 mph, my boots kept doing the same thing: skipping and slipping along every time I came to a near stop. I'd made a big mistake. They had to go.

Thankfully, after a short time the rain stopped, traffic started to move again, and the slow speed stability problem caused by my boots was behind me. I was finally on I-70 West heading towards Kansas City. About twenty minutes later I pulled into a gas station right off the interstate, filled the tank, and rechecked the weather. The approaching storm front had progressed past Kansas City and the middle part of the apostrophe was right over I-70. Severe thunderstorm warnings were still up for Kansas City and some of the counties to the east. I played the time-lapse version of the radar images several times and figured that the cells were moving at about 30 to 40 mph. If I was back on the road in fifteen minutes and made about 70 mph towards them, somewhere around Columbia Missouri, in about an hour, all hell was going to break loose.

Thinking that I'd been smart to plan ahead, I decided for the first time in my riding career to don my rain gear. I bought it ten years ago as part of the accessory kit they recommended for new riders when I purchased my first bike.

My first decision was whether or not to put them on over my jeans. Though the sun was still mostly occluded, I could see its outline through the opaque cloud cover and the temperature and humidity were rapidly increasing. The black exterior would absorb heat and the PVC interior would retain it. If I wore my jeans, I'd probably bake. But I was outside and I couldn't exactly take them off and stand there struggling to put the pants on in my underwear. They'd have to go over. The foot straps on the legs were similarly puzzling. It would make sense for the pants to slide over my boots so the belt was meant to slide under the heel. But since I was still standing up by a pump with gasoline residue on the concrete, it probably wouldn't be a good idea to remove my boots. At the same time, there wasn't exactly an easy place to change in private. The store attached to the gas station was fairly busy, and the bathroom, which I'd already frequented, was a cramped single toilet job. So I decided to try and put them on without taking off both my jeans and boots.

Standing on my left leg, I carefully lifted my right leg and slid my right boot into what I thought was the right leg of the rain pants. Within a few seconds, it got stuck and I tried to extract it, hopping backward and noticing, as I did so, that I had the front to back orientation wrong. With sweat beads already forming on my forehead, I spun the pants around and tried again, hopping back forward towards the pump. This time my right boot got a little further down the correct pant leg, but was soon stuck at an odd angle. Hopping on one foot again and cursing under my breath, I tried to extract it, lost my balance, and fell backward into a trash can, knocking the plastic lid and a few discarded fast food items onto the ground.

Now self-conscious, I stopped for a moment and scanned the gas station area. A few people by the entrance to the store were staring at me, gently poking each other with their elbows and trying to suppress smiles. I picked up the trash I'd spilled, popped the top back on the garbage can, and walked back to my same starting spot. It was becoming a quest. The damn pants were not going to beat me. Realizing now that my boots had to come off, I draped the pants over the back of my bike, reached down, and tried to remove my right boot with one hand while balancing on my left leg. Within seconds, I was doing another hop dance. It wouldn't budge. Sweating even more, I thought about sitting down but there was no place to do that without getting soiled—other than the sidewalk in front of the store where the small crowd was standing, mocking me. So I lowered into a half squat and tried again, this time using both hands. Finally, I had my first victory. My right boot slid off.

Not wanting to make another snicker-inducing mistake, I stood for a moment, pondering my next move. If I grabbed the pants and slid my right leg into them, I wouldn't be able to remove my left boot without placing my right sock into a large fuel stain. So I looked back at my bike, resting on its kickstand and hatched an idea. I could lay my removed boot on the ground sideways, place my sock on it, and then half sit on the bike's saddle, remove my left boot and do the same thing. Then I could reach back for my rain pants, slide each leg in and put my boots back on one at a time. Reinvigorated with the new plan, I planted my right sock onto my boot but mistakenly placed it on the small, hard rubber heel section rather than on the larger, soft leather shaft. A second later, the heel shifted and I fell clumsily forward, slamming into the gas pump with my right shoulder, stunned.

Increasingly angry and embarrassed, with sweat now pouring from my forehead into my eyes, I leaned in the saddle of my bike again, pulled up both rain pant legs (which were now on), slid on my boots, and lowered the pant legs over both of their shafts. Then I stood up, slipped the suspender straps over my shoulder, snapped the clips shut, tugged the straps tight, and pulled up the zipper. The only step left, other than calming down, was to remove the leg straps under my boot heels. I reached down and tried to do this while standing, but they wouldn't slide over. Steadying myself against the pump, I tried again and again. I couldn't get them to slide over while standing and reaching down, so I slumped onto the fuel pump island with my rear end, cocked my legs one at a time, and pulled them over. Finally, they were on. I glanced back at the store to see if anyone was still watching, but mercifully everyone seemed to have dispersed. Still, I had a sick feeling. Knowing my luck, I thought, someone had probably made a video of the whole thing that would spread like wildfire on YouTube. Titled, "Idiot Doing Rain Pants Dance," it would be the stuff of legend by the time I arrived in Sturgis.

Shrugging off the thought, I gulped some water from one of the bottles in my left saddlebag, pulled my rain jacket from its storage place on top of the tour pack bag, and stuffed my riding jacket into the right one. The rain jacket went on easier; about the only thing I couldn't figure out initially was what to do with the collar around the neck. It had Velcro strips and was meant to be pulled around snugly, but it was lined with heavy felt, probably to keep a rider warm in colder weather. Even though it might result in a little rain water leaking down my neck, I decided to leave it unsecured. It was too hot.

A short time after rolling back onto I-70 West, the sky started to transform again. The opaque bands of white-gray clouds were gone, replaced instead with lower bands of darker, more ominous looking clouds and disorganized light-gray thunderheads. The scenery also changed. Somewhere past the I-64 interchange, where the road narrows again to two lanes on either side, I was treated to my first glimpse of the "big sky" Great Plains. The land seemed to go on forever in all directions, the gently sloping hills interrupted only by minor tree breaks that separated the fields of adjacent farms. The sky also seemed immense, much bigger than the land, a floor to ceiling canvas of light and clouds that even with the sun blocked was hard to study without squinting. As I rolled along, I wondered what the first settlers must have felt like when they left the security of St. Louis in their horse-drawn wagons, heading west. In the agrarian world of the early nineteenth century, when the land was everything, they must have felt like they'd struck gold. There was fertile farmland as far as the eye could see in every direction. No wonder, I thought to myself, they endured so many deprivations and fought so hard to tame it.

Unfortunately, my feeling of new discovery didn't last long. Bookended by two major cities on either side of Missouri, I-70 is one of the most heavily traveled truck routes in the country. When it narrowed back into two lanes on either side, the traffic compressed into a seemingly endless snaking band of heavy trucks in the right lane and faster-moving vehicles in the left lane. I stayed in the right lane but found myself always trapped by trucks that were moving slightly slower than the speed at which I had set my cruise control: 72 mph. Time and time again, I'd move up on one and get buffeted by the swirls of air streaming from the edges of its boxy trailer, or move into the left lane to pass and then get run up on by another fast-moving car or truck before I could make a sensible pass. It was maddening.

Up ahead, the sky kept darkening. A particularly nasty looking, relatively homogeneous dark cloud filled about a quarter of the sky to my immediate left. A few moments later, there was a cloud to ground lightning strike in the distant horizon. To the right, still far away but closer than the preceding lightning strike, a dark band of clouds had blended with the ground in soft, vertical stripes that looked airbrushed. It was already raining there. Imagining that my wife was riding with me, I started to say out loud, over and over again, "It's looking pretty nasty, Ma," thinking that I knew what she'd be doing if she were, in fact, sitting on my passenger seat. She'd be poking me in the back and smacking the side of my helmet, imploring me to get off of the highway and seek shelter. The truth was I was looking forward to it. I'd never ridden through a thunderstorm line before and I was intensely curious. If nothing else it would cool me down, as I was still sweating under my rain gear.

Later I saw unmistakable signs that the show was about to start. Eastbound vehicles were all traveling with their headlights and windshield wipers on, and huge puffs of water vapor trailed behind the trucks. The scary looking cloud to my left had overspread the area from the highway and several more lightning strikes hit the ground much closer to me than before. The right side of my view was also deteriorating. The gray thunderheads were larger and closer to the road and I could see visible rain in the fields. It seemed as if the whole sky was collapsing towards me.

It didn't start as a downpour. Much like the rain shower I'd ridden through in St. Louis, the first drops were light and sporadic, giving me a false confidence to keep going. I slowed a little but otherwise kept rolling, enthusiastically waiting for the next change in intensity, imagining that someone was up there turning a dial, experimenting with me, seeing how much I could take. The first tick to "1" on the thunderstorm meter was meant to tease me, to draw me in. About half a minute later, the dial must have been turned up to "4."

This time the drops were larger and heavier and came at me in undulating sheets that slapped against my windshield, jacket, and helmet. They also started to smack the areas of my body that were still exposed—parts of my face, fingers, and the tops of my hands—and the associated sting surprised me. It really hurt, particularly the drops that hit my face. Just as I was thinking that maybe I was a wimp, that other riders could surely take what I was experiencing, the dial was turned up to "6." The drops were even larger and hit the windshield with "thwats" that resembled bursts of machine gun fire. Instinctively I started to slow from the additional sensations of pain, but visibility was also rapidly becoming a problem. A week earlier when I was detailing my bike, I'd found a small plastic container of Harley windshield water repellent wipes buried deep in a saddlebag. Figuring that treating the windshield might be a good idea, I'd carefully followed the directions, repeating the procedure twice for good measure. Given its treatment, I expected any water that hit the windshield to bead into tiny droplets and rapidly slip off into the air stream, providing a decent view. But it didn't work. Within seconds, the windshield was coated with large droplets that clung to each other like pulsating, living cells. Small streams of water were also running off in every direction. To further complicate matters, my glasses were coated with water and the drops hitting my forehead were running down into my eyes. I made a big mistake leaving my helmet visor behind.

Slowing now to around 50 mph, I tried different approaches to improving visibility. Crouching lower and moving my head forward reduced the stinging pain of the rain, but I couldn't see a thing except the pavement below me. Raising my head slightly above the windshield line momentarily improved the view, but the torrent of water battering my face and my eyes hurt so much that I had to squint to the point of nearly shutting them tight. I thought briefly of removing my glasses, but to do that I'd have to let go of one of the handgrips and find a place to store them in my new, seemingly impervious rain gear. I'd probably just wind up dropping them, causing a larger problem. The only good news was that I could still make out the taillights of the truck ahead of me despite the stream of spray it was generating.

Less than a minute later, the intensity was turned up to "8," the start of the red band on the 1-10 thunderstorm dial, and I lost sight of the truck ahead of me. I slowed further, downshifted, and simultaneously pressed and held both turn signal switches to turn on my hazard flashers. Luckily, the truck ahead of me did the same thing, so I could just make out its taillights again, but the waves of water hitting me now were almost comical. It was like riding through a ring of carefully aimed fire hoses: maybe two trained at me from the rear of the truck ahead, one down from a sky cam riding on a hidden wire, and one on each side from flanking dolly cars. Still, I wasn't getting wet underneath my rain gear. The bike felt amazingly stable, with both tires making good contact despite what had to be at least a half an inch of standing water on the road—and I could still see well enough to keep in the center of the right lane. I also knew that my rear turn signals, which I'd converted a few years ago to additional taillights so they had red lenses, were incredibly bright when flashing. My tombstone shaping the main taillight, which I'd converted to LEDs, was almost as bright. Whatever was behind me, particularly if it had working windshield wipers, should have been able to see me. I managed to smile, thinking for a moment that I just might win this battle with Mother Nature.

Sensing that perhaps I was a little cocky, and just to get even, she quickly cranked the dial to its hard forward stop of "10." The rain intensified even more, but the major difference was the unconstrained fury associated with a real severe thunderstorm cell. All of a sudden, high gusts of wind blew dense clouds of water vapor at me from what seemed to be all directions at once, and multiple claps of thunder boomed like cannon fire, shaking the ground. I couldn't see any lightning strikes, but there were almost continuous flashes of bright light, as if someone had turned on a randomly timed strobe light. It wasn't funny anymore. It was life threatening. I had to find shelter—fast. Slowing down even more and shifting into second gear, I saw an exit sign ahead and quickly glanced to my right to see if there were any buildings that could offer protection. In the distance I could make out one: a gas station with a large overhang over the pumps. That would have been perfect, but when I shifted my head back forward to study the road, I completely lost sight of the solid white lane line that I'd been tracking. In fact, for several long seconds I couldn't see a thing. I was totally blinded. Not wanting to stop altogether for fear or being rear-ended, I rolled slowly on and finally picked up the white line again, but it was straight and not veering off to the right as I'd expected for the exit. I missed it.

"Shit!" I strained my eyes to see as far down the road as I could but saw absolutely nothing that could provide shelter. I thought about pulling over and stopping, but I'd probably be even more vulnerable, so I poked along at 20 to 25 mph, praying for a break. About a minute later, perhaps out of sympathy or because She wanted to save me for some later, even more arduous test, the dial was turned back to level "7." In the distance, about a mile away, I spotted a bridge. It wasn't particularly big—maybe wide enough to accommodate a simple farm road or a train on a single track—but it was sheltered. Carefully, I rolled on a little throttle, upshifted a few times and made for the bridge, thinking along the way that maybe I'd been through the worst of it and could keep rolling. Just before the point of no return, the point when I couldn't have made a safe stop, as if She was helping me now, giving me a sign that I should indeed take the offering of shelter, the intensity was dialed back up to "9."

"OK," I said to myself, "it's time to bail." Being careful to apply the front brake a little harder than the rear, I leaned to the right, downshifted, rapidly slowed and pulled the fattest part of the bridge on the shoulder between the right lane and the bridge abutment. I hit the engine kill switch and dismounted, leaving the ignition on so that all of my lights would remain illuminated.

Without the engine noise of the bike and the water wash associated with its movement, the sound of the thunder was even louder, a growling kind of rumble that was amplified by the bridge overhead into what seemed like a continuously reverberating bass chorus. I looked to the west in the direction that I'd been traveling and saw several cloud to ground lightning strikes. I made the right decision. Back behind me, traffic was still rolling but almost every car and truck had its hazard flashers on and the pace of traffic flow was no greater than 30 mph. I looked overhead and studied the underside of the bridge. It was rusting a little in spots but seemed otherwise to be in decent condition. The drainage of the surface above wasn't working very well, however. Every ten seconds or so, waves of water would spill over the edges and slap noisily down onto the road surface below. My bike was parked a few feet in front of where the water was hitting on the eastern side of the bridge, in just about the only place that wasn't getting hammered by rain or other water sources. But I quickly realized that I had another problem—I'd traded one potential death trap for another.

When they built the bridge, they'd actually narrowed the right shoulder. It was less than a car width wide between the right lane line and the solid, concrete abutment that held up the northern end of the bridge span. My bike, being about three feet wide, took up half of the available width, and my body, standing to the right of it, consumed another two feet. I could easily reach out and touch the solid surface of the abutment. If a car or truck lost sight of the right lane line (as I had earlier) and drifted over, it would crush me against a concrete wall and take my bike along with it. Sensing the danger, I walked forward to the western edge of the bridge—a distance of maybe ten yards—and quickly realized that my new position was even worse. If anything hit my bike, it would be thrown directly towards me in a shower of disintegrating metal parts. Thinking that maybe I was a little paranoid, I walked back towards my bike and watched the passing line of traffic. A large rig was barreling ahead in the left lane, generating massive waves of spray. Seconds later it approached the bridge with a thunderous, gear whining roar, and I noticed that something seemed strange. I could clearly see every bolt on the hub of the right front wheel as well as the semi-elliptical cutouts within the wheel itself. It wasn't moving. Further back, on the trailer, some of the wheels actually looked to be turning slowly backward. The truck was dangerously hydroplaning; the driver could have quickly lost control. I had to find a safer place to wait out the remainder of the storm.

Walking forward, towards the traffic flow, I slipped my legs over the guard rail that tapered into the bridge abutment and landed on the other side. My plan was to position myself outside of the bridge abutment but still under the span so that I'd be protected from both the weather and anything that might hit my bike. It was a reasonably good plan, but as with just about everything on the trip so far, I quickly discovered there was a catch. The space to the outside of the bridge abutment was a concrete lined V-shaped drainage gulley that started from the wall, ran downward, and then back up towards the ground. The only way I could stand was to straddle the gulley with a boot planted on each side cocked at about a thirty-degree angle. With seemingly no other choice, I tried several times to hold the position but my boots kept slipping into the water, and it soon became deep enough that I couldn't straddle it anymore. Great, I thought, now you're going to be carried away by a flash flood. Determined not to be beaten. I moved both of my feet to the side of the gulley closest to the abutment. Away from the growing river of water, I carefully planted my lower foot at an outward angle with my other foot slightly above it and leaned back against the wall, facing the flow of traffic. It wasn't comfortable, but it worked.

For the next fifteen minutes or so I watched the storm and the flow of traffic. Though raindrops were still sneaking under the bridge, pelting my helmet and occasionally slipping down my neck, I felt strangely contented. I'd made it through the abyss. It couldn't get any worse.

To reinforce the feeling, I pulled out my iPhone, punched the Radar US application and watched, with each successive radar image update, as the storm front tracked slowly to the east. While there was still a lot of rain out ahead of me, it looked like the worst was over. Still, I almost didn't want to get going again. It was oddly peaceful. I decided to wait for a sign: a break in the clouds, a few soft rays of the sun, a lightening of the sky, or a prolonged softening in the rain to motivate me back onto my bike.

The sign turned out to be two Harley Electra Glide motorcycles that rolled past in the left lane, their riders confidently staring straight ahead, backs upright, seemingly unconcerned about the rain. If they could do it, I could do it. Quickly snapping out of my serene state, I crawled back towards the guard rail, hopped over, and strutted back to my bike. After a quick final wipe of my glasses with the tail end of my t-shirt, I swung my right leg over, snapped the engine cutoff switch to run, turned off the hazard flashers, and hit the starter. It was still raining with the storm intensity meter set at mid-level, maybe a "5," but the thunder and lightning had passed, at least for now. After pacing the traffic flow, I quickly accelerated back onto the interstate.

With the rain coming at me moderately hard and visibility still limited, I didn't want to push it, so I settled into riding at a modest pace just over the transition speed into sixth gear, about 60 mph. It felt great to be moving again and my rain gear was holding up well. More importantly, the bike had performed admirably. It was the first time I'd ridden through such a deluge of water and it hadn't missed a beat. I'd put on the mesh rain sock that came with my cone style air cleaner before leaving home and it had prevented water from saturating the paper element of the filter, as designed. Everything associated with the electrical system also appeared to be working correctly, despite all of the water trying to defeat it from multiple entry points. These Harleys, I thought, really are tough.

Unfortunately, it wasn't over. In what seemed like an instant after complimenting my bike, Mother Nature decided to play with me again and turned the dial back up to level "8." This time, however, I was much less flustered. Having been through the drill before, I knew what to do. Grinning at the challenge, I downshifted into fifth, slowed a bit, pressed both turn signal switches inward to turn on my flashers, and glanced down at the row of indicator lights above the front fork lock, waiting for the small green turn signal arrows to start flashing together at their usual pace.

Instead, unexpectedly, they began flashing rapidly—the easily recognizable telltale sign that is built into modern Harley electrical systems that indicate that a light, or perhaps several lamps, are no longer working properly. I'd lost a bulb or maybe several of them, but didn't know where. If it was one of my rear lights or all of them, I was in danger. In heavy rain, nobody would be able to see me. I could easily get crushed from behind. I had to get off, again.

Scanning ahead, I spotted another bridge with a simple exit before it about a half a mile further down the road. Regardless of what was there, it would have to do. I rolled off and stopped at the end of the exit ramp. A single lane road stretched out in both directions between some large corn fields, gently sloping up towards either side of the horizon. To the right there was a single building, a meeting place of some kind with a narrow covered porch. It didn't look open, but at least I could pull up, check my lights, and then wait under the porch for the latest, unexpected storm cell to pass. A small access road led to the parking lot.

Shortly after turning onto the access road I realized that the building's parking lot, much larger than it had seemed from the stop sign at the end of the exit, wasn't paved. It was dirt and gravel and pockmarked with puddles, like a muddy moonscape that someone had tried to fill with water. There was no way I was going in there. Slowing to a crawl, I attempted to execute a U-turn before entering, but the road was too narrow and I had to stop with my front tire just over the crown. Turning the front fork all the way to the right, I heaved with my legs to try and push the bike back over the crown, but my boots, as usual, slipped on the wet asphalt surface. I was stuck. Trying again and losing traction once more, I managed to make the situation only worse, rolling slightly forward so that my front tire was now at the entrance to the lot. It was drawing me in like quicksand.

Beyond frustrated, I belted out a string of cuss words that would have made a sailor proud, gunned the engine more than I needed to, feathered the clutch, and slowly, reluctantly, entered the parking lot. I turned in a large circle in a way that weaved around the edges of the larger potholes, knowing that if I stopped I'd more than likely dump my bike. I threaded the obstacle course and emerged back on the access road. A few seconds later I was back on the farm road, wondering what to do next. The only place to pull over that looked reasonably safe was the interstate access ramp on the opposite side, so I stopped on a full concrete section of it and shut down again.

Leaving my ignition on, I dismounted and quickly walked around the bike to see if the main running lights (headlight, passing lamps and rear taillight) were on. They were. Then I tapped the rear brake lever with my foot to see if my taillights were working correctly, and tested each turn signal. Sure enough, a bulb was out, but it was probably the one I needed the least, the right front turn signal. Relieved, I sat back down on the bike and did nothing for a few minutes but listen to the rain hitting my helmet, study the sky, and gaze at the Missouri cornfields. The sky was confused with a mixture of dark, thick cloud bands that were close to the horizon, disorganized steel gray thunderheads, and lighter, wispy strands of water vapor that zipped along as if they were chasing each other. There were even a few additional clouds to ground lightning strikes, but they were off to the east in the direction I'd just come from. The worst of it was behind me.

A few minutes later, sensing that I was needlessly wasting time, I checked my watch and the bike's trip computer. It was already past one o'clock and I'd only traveled 310 miles. With all of the unplanned stops, I was averaging just 50 mph. At this rate, I wouldn't make it to Grand Island, Nebraska until after dark. It was time to get moving again, and this time, I had to keep going. Two things, however, were bothering me. My hands were soaking wet, a little cold, and cramping, particularly my left hand that worked the clutch. Remembering that I brought along additional pairs of gloves, I opened my left saddlebag, found the full-fingered Texport gloves I'd brought and switched them out with the waterlogged half-gloves I'd been wearing. The second issue was the blown turn signal bulb. I knew that it probably wouldn't matter, particularly with highway travel, but I just didn't like riding with any piece of safety equipment inoperable. It always came back to bite you, somehow. There was a chance, however, that I might be able to fix it.

One of the beautiful things about Harley-Davidson is they have an excellent dealer network. Every major city has one (or several) and they're usually located close to well-travelled interstates. Maybe, I thought, I just might get lucky and see one riding by Kansas City. If I did, I promised myself I'd stop in and buy a replacement bulb. Reenergized, I fired up my bike and accelerated rapidly down the access ramp back onto I-70, smiling at the sound of the pipes as I ran through the gears.

Over the next several miles, having some experience now with riding in the moderate rain, I tried several times to approach the speed limit (70 mph), but Mother Nature quickly unleashed another counterpunch that I hadn't anticipated. Behind the storm front, as the level moved east, the winds that were rotating counterclockwise around its center howled in from the north across the unbroken fields of the plains. Gusting at 25 to 35 mph, and sometimes more, they whipped the rain into horizontal sheets that pelted the right side of my bike, and, like dull needles, poked at my eyes. Instinctively, I tried turning my head into the path of the wind so my glasses would offer some protection, but at highway speed, surrounded by heavy trucks, I couldn't afford to keep looking away. Even more unnerving, with each gust the force of the wind would jerk the bike spasmodically to the left without warning. To counter the effect, I had to quickly add a little right lean. Then, a second or two later when the gust had expended its energy, the force would drop away and I'd have to bend back to the left again to stay riding in the center of the lane. Speed, I quickly figured out, mattered a lot. Every time I approached or exceeded the speed limit of 70 mph I felt like I was exponentially less in control. While at 60 mph, particularly during bursts of heavier rain and wind, I felt like I was riding on my ability. If these conditions continued, I wasn't going to be able to make much over 65 mph.

Other than prolonging my riding day more than I would have liked, this wouldn't have mattered much, but, yet again, it created another complication. Before the rain and wind, when I'd been happily rolling along at 72 mph or so, I'd been moving at a speed generally faster than most of the heavy rigs. This required me to continuously pass them, but other than enduring a lot of air turbulence during each passing cycle, the situation was manageable. Now, in the rain and crosswinds, the situation was reversed. The trucks, some eighty times heavier than my bike, were less affected by the wind and the rain wasn't heavy enough to cause hydroplaning. Trying to make up time, they rolled on at an average pace of about the speed limit (now 5 mph greater than my speed), continually passing me in the left lane like a slow moving train of evenly spaced but decoupled rail cars.

The net effect over the next hour was to generate the most miserable riding experience of my life. Every time a truck passed, about once a minute on average, a massive tornado-like vortex of rain and spray would swirl around me with tropical storm force winds. Lasting for roughly ten to fifteen seconds, each mini-tempest would try to temporarily blind me, penetrate every seam of my rain gear and further cripple my bike. A more rational person probably would have pulled off and waited for the rain to stop, but I was determined not to lose any more time. I was on a mission, and nothing short of the calamity was going to slow me down. Besides, the guys on the Electra Glides in front of me, I was sure, were still rolling. If they could take it, I could take it.

Undeterred, I amused myself by observing, as best I could, the nature of each truck-induced enema and how my bike and rain gear were handling it. The bike was comfortable. There was no further degradation in performance. My rain gear was also holding up well despite insidious attacks from every angle. Other than my face and hands, I still felt reasonably dry. If there was any major discomfort, it was mainly from inhaling large quantities of water vapor up my nose and the continued sting of the rain.

Finally, about an hour outside of Kansas City, conditions improved. The rain ended and the roads rapidly dried in the summer heat. I exhaled deeply, sped up a little, and studied the ribbons of light streaming down from the dissipating cloud banks. It looked as if the sun was overstretching its arms after a long summer's day nap. Within another half an hour, the sky cleared into a light blue haze. I had hoped that the storm front would bring in cooler air, as they often do, but the temperature and humidity rapidly climbed, even with the wind. Still in my rain gear with the sun out in full force and my sweat soaked clothes providing an additional source of moisture, I started to cook. Deciding to make any changes in gear as quickly as possible, I pulled over at a rest stop, promptly removed my rain jacket, and stuffed it into the space above my tour pack bag. The pants, I figured, could wait. I'd take those off during the next stop for gas and food.

A short time later, past the town of Oak Grove on the outskirts of Kansas City, I finally caught a break. Rolling along at close to 70 mph, still fighting the crosswinds, I spotted a large billboard with the familiar Harley-Davidson bar and shield logo. A dealership was located right off the interstate a few exits ahead. It was half past two on a Friday afternoon. They'd be open. As an added bonus, there were plenty of food and fuel choices at the stipulated exit. I could dash into the dealership, buy a replacement turn signal bulb, down a quick lunch and a cup of coffee at one of the fast-food joints, gas up, and hit the road again with minimal loss of time.

The dealership, Blue Springs Harley-Davidson, was located off a road that ran parallel to the interstate, a couple of hundred yards back in the opposite direction I'd been traveling. Within a minute or two of rolling off of I-70, I was in their parking lot passing a row of new, gleaming bikes. Luckily I found a space right in front of the main entrance. Hot, tired, and cramping, I shut down, dismounted, pulled my glasses off, released the clasp on my chin strap and removed my helmet, trying my best to look like an experienced rider. After a stretch or two, with a determined look, I walked smartly towards the building, helmet in hand. My goal was to be in and out within ten minutes.

As I approached the front door, I made eye contact with a middle-aged dealership employee who leaned against a front entrance pillar, enjoying a smoke. Tall with a lanky build, sandy blonde hair, and a pockmarked face, he gave me a prolonged, serious looking nod but said nothing else. I grabbed the front door handle to the building, pulled it carefully and entered, but something strange had just happened and I paused for a moment to reflect on it.

I'd visited a handful of Harley dealerships in my life and I'd always been greeted with a polite but somewhat distant acceptance. The people they hire are typically Harley enthusiasts from the ranks of real bikers. They're always courteous, but I often have the feeling they know I'm a fake and can spot others like me. We're all probably alike. Clean shaven and lacking any kind of road scars, we pull up on newer, perfectly clean bikes with unblemished riding gear wearing jeans, a t-shirt, and maybe a skull cap with a knot in the back to try to look cool. We walk in with our tattoo free bodies, clean fingernails, and expensive watches and try to look like we know what we're doing. The employees are always helpful because the owner wants our money and they want their jobs, but they instantly peg us for what we are: a bunch of corporate executives, lawyers, bankers, doctors, and small business owners with too much money and too little time on our hands who just want to look and act like bad boys for a few hours on a beautiful weekend day. Usually, they're right.

This time, however, the greeting was different because I was different. I was riding a bike that had obviously been on a long and challenging road trip. My rain pants were covered with grime and bug splat, and my t-shirt was stained with concentric sweat rings. My face was severely wind burned and my hair was a matted mess. He didn't say a word because he didn't have to—his nod had said it all. It was a sign of respect from one biker to another. I'd crossed a new threshold: somebody thought I was the real thing. Warmed by the thought, I started walking towards the parts department, which is always in the back.

The parts counter in a Harley dealership is usually where all of the action is because customizing a bike to suit your stylistic preferences and riding needs is a never-ending process. It's one of the major things that differentiate Harley from the other brands: there's almost an infinite number of ways to make one your own. The accessories catalog is thicker than a phone book and there are options for almost every parts category. You can increase engine power and torque, and change the pipes, paint, wheels, suspension, lighting, cargo carrying capacity, seats, hand grips, handlebars, footrests, badging, and chrome accessories in dozens of ways each (even including, believe it or not, the bolts that attach the chrome accessories). There are also scores of aftermarket sources for anything from pipes to GPS systems for every model. Given all of the potential choices, it takes a good deal of patience and time to figure out what you want, whether or not it will fit on your bike, and the other changes necessary to make everything work together properly. If you switch out the pipes, for instance, the backpressure in the cylinders could be different, necessitating a change in engine control unit mapping. If you raise the handlebars, you may need longer power cables. It never ends. What you tend to see, therefore, particularly on a busy weekend day, are two groups of people milling around the parts counter: a group that's asking questions regarding possible accessory purchases, and a group that's actually buying parts. The unwritten rule is that customers buying parts, particularly if they're for immediate repairs so they can get back on the road, take precedence. You always step aside for real bikers doing real riding. Fakes trying to figure things out should let them pass. Until that moment, I'd always been one of the latter.

Since it was a Friday afternoon, the parts counter wasn't exactly swarmed. Besides me, there was only one other potential customer. Catalog in hand, he was chatting with the lone parts salesman in a lighthearted way, probably discussing some possible upgrades to his bike. Walking with a gait that signaled fierce determination, I approached the counter. The salesman saw me first and snapped to attention. Reading the change in his demeanor, the potential customer turned and gave me a quick scan. Startled and probably a little annoyed at having his conversation truncated, he nonetheless quickly surmised what he had to do.

Taking a step backward, he waved his hand and said, "Please, go ahead."

I hadn't even said a word and I made it across another threshold: I took precedence.

Stepping up to the counter, I opened up with, "Hi, I need a front turn signal bulb for an oh-eight Screaming Eagle Road King."

The salesman, now focused exclusively on me, replied enthusiastically, "I think I can help you with that!"

After a few more questions, he marched off to search the parts bins in the storage area. Within a minute, he was back with a small white box in his hand.

Smiling for the first time, I said, "Thanks, how much do I owe you?"

"It's four-sixty-two with tax. Is there anything else you need?"

Laser-focused on making a proper repair, I asked, "Do you have any of the dielectric greases you're supposed to smear on the contacts?" They reduce the possibility of shorts caused by water intrusion, something I'd learned a long time ago working on old cars.

The potential customer, who'd pretty much been ignoring me until then, raised his eyebrows and nodded briefly. He thought I knew what I was doing. The salesman was caught a little off guard and scrambled to open the box.

"I'm sorry," he said, "it's not in here . . . but it *should* be in here . . ." and his voice died off.

A moment later he was noisily rummaging beneath the counter. After some hushed curses, he popped back up with a small plastic tube and handed it to me.

"This will fix you up."

"Thanks," I said. "Appreciate it."

Glad that I had everything I needed, I quickly turned and made for the exit. As I walked out, I realized this was the first time that I felt like I really belonged in a Harley dealership.

Back outside, I fished a penny out my right front pocket, walked up to my bike, inserted it in the small indentation under the right front turn signal lens and twisted. It popped right off. Then I reached into the light cavity, pushed the blown bulb in, turned it to the left and extracted it. After smearing grease on the contacts, I inserted the new bulb, pushed down, turned it to the right, and snapped the lens back on. My first road repair had taken less than thirty seconds. A quick press of the right front turn signal confirmed that it worked. After discarding my trash in a nearby can, I pulled my helmet down, snapped the chin strap buckle, slid my glasses back on, and restarted the engine. I glanced at my watch and noted the time. I'd been stopped for a total of fewer than ten minutes. Proud of myself, I pulled out of the parking lot and back onto the access road faster than necessary, showing off a little. I chuckled afterward at the realization that I'd only replaced a stupid light bulb. It wasn't exactly something to brag about. At least I hadn't screwed it up.

When I stopped at a McDonald's across the road for lunch, I made sure to park on the back side of the restaurant. With thoughts of the rain pants dressing disaster still fresh in my mind, I wanted to take them off away from any potential witnesses. Sitting on a curb, I removed my boots and pulled the pants off smoothly, wondering how I'd made such a mess of putting them on in the first place. Twenty minutes later, after polishing off the cup of coffee with my meal, refilling the bike, smearing on some suntan lotion, and changing back to my half-gloves, I was back on I-70 West again. It was hot, almost stifling, but in what seemed like no time I rolled onto the I-435 Kansas City Beltway, heading north.

It was just after three o'clock and I wanted to make Grand Island before dusk.

A half an hour later, I was on my way to St. Joseph, Missouri, riding north on I-29. I had hoped that riding into the wind, which was still gusting from the north, would help to stabilize the bike, and it did, but as usual I wound up trading one problem for another. My bike had one major weakness and I knew it. It was the windshield. Harley makes two basic kinds: short, smoked units that are made to look cool but offer no real protection; and larger, lightly smoked or clear polycarbonate ones that are meant to deflect the wind, rain, and debris. They come in different heights to account for differences in riders, helmet types, and stylistic preferences. The stock windshield on my bike was a heavily smoked, fourteen-inch high version that looked racy but was otherwise useless. Beyond 40 mph or so it offered little protection, and below that speed you really don't need one. As soon as I got the bike home I decided to change it but didn't know which of the larger sizes to buy. Overthinking things as usual, I bought an eighteen-inch unit figuring that it would be okay for someone of average height. For a while it worked well, so I thought I'd made the right choice.

What I didn't anticipate was that I would change helmets. After Chris's accident I switched to a full-faced type that was about two inches taller when resting on my head than my previous half-helmet, so my windshield was, in effect, lowered. I noticed immediately that something was different the first time I approached highway speed: the airstream was now clipping the top of the helmet. It shook my head in a rapid jiggling motion as if someone had placed it in a paint can shaker that was set to oscillate a quarter inch to either side. On short trips, it had proved to be only a minor annoyance, but on this trip the constant shaking, intensified by riding into a stiff headwind, was starting to have pernicious effects. The first was that it was making it a lot harder for me to read road signs. The second was that it was rapidly increasing my state of mental exhaustion. Basically, I was slowly scrambling my brains. The only way to reduce the effect, since I couldn't control the wind, was to slow down or dip my head slightly to get my helmet out of the slipstream. The former was a non-starter—I had to make time. So I rolled on, ducking a little lower every now and then to give myself a break.

North of St. Joseph, the landscape turned back into some of the most beautiful farmland I'd ever seen. The fields had a gentle, lazy roll to them with an occasional small hill, and the predominant crop was soybeans instead of corn. Laid out in soft, s-curve like waves, the rows of lush, dark green plants were correctly spaced and looked to be almost professionally manicured. Every now and then a barn or a field house would add some color, its red or white paint offering a perfect accent to what was now a brilliantly blue sky. I never had, in all my life, seen a juxtaposition of deep colors like this on such a large scale. Despite the wind, I was starting to really enjoy myself again.

Still marveling at the countryside, something in the distance, on my left near the edge of the horizon, caught my eye. The fields in that direction were flatter and some of them were reflecting like mirrors. At first I thought it was a type of mirage-like the wavy shimmering effect that roads make during the summer when hot air hovering over them refracts light. But this was different. The air over the fields wasn't moving and everything was still. A short time later, I saw a barn standing in the center of one of the fields that also seemed strange. Its proportions were all wrong. The walls were too short and the roof was too close to the ground. Finally, it dawned on me. The fields were flooded. I almost couldn't believe it. It was August. How could this be?

The first seeds of the floods of 2011 were planted the preceding fall in the Pacific Ocean, when sea surface temperatures around the equator cooled to lower temperatures than normal, creating a La Niña event. Directed by winds aloft, cool, wetter than usual air poured across the upper Rocky Mountains, triggering record snowfall. By early spring, the snowpack in Montana and Wyoming was over two hundred percent above normal. Then, in the second two weeks of May, about the time of peak snowmelt (delayed because of the cold spring), the same region received almost a year's worth of rain. To further complicate things, in late June, rainfall in the Upper Midwest surged to six hundred percent above normal. It was as if Mother Nature had studied a map of the Missouri River basin and its series of dams, cocked her left arm back, and swung with a powerful jab aimed at Eastern Montana. Then, when she knew the basin was reeling, she followed it with a right cross centered in Northern

Missouri. It was the perfect combination of punches at precisely the right times to precipitate massive flooding.

The Army Corps of Engineers, responsible for the Flood Control Act of 1944 for managing the dams, was handed a problem with no real solutions. No matter what they did people were going to lose, so they did what most rational planners would do: they tried to minimize potential damage to the primary population and commercial centers. Larger cities like Omaha, Kansas City, and St. Louis had to be protected. Smaller cities like Bismarck, North Dakota, Yankton, South Dakota, Sioux City, Iowa, and St. Joseph, Missouri were more expendable. The rural, flat farmland surrounding the river in Iowa, Nebraska, and Missouri was a particularly inviting place to bleed off the flow. The water could spread out over hundreds of thousands of acres. Given the enormous volume of water they were dealing with, they set the flow rates at each of the dams to an average of 2.3 times above previous peak records, making the flood of 2011 over twice as bad as any previous flood since the dams were built. That's not a little worse, it's a *lot* worse, and most of the water wound up in the small cities and farmland surrounding the river.

The great Missouri River flood of 2011 never dominated the 24-7 national news cycle. It wasn't that type of story. It didn't happen quickly and without warning. Scores of people weren't killed and there was no catastrophic property damage like the EF-5 tornado that had destroyed Joplin, Missouri months earlier. Local television affiliates and newspapers kept the story alive for the region's residents. In large part, because it severely disrupted road and rail transportation, but for most people outside of the area it probably barely registered or was quickly forgotten. To an East Coast resident like me, Midwestern flooding is something that happens in the spring almost every year. Small towns and farms get flooded, people get displaced, and politicians ask for federal help. It's an unfortunate annual cycle. A voracious reader of national news, I might have scanned a few stories about it, but by early August they were long forgotten.

Having completely missed the story, my first reaction to viewing some of the hardest hit areas of the flooding was to ponder how it had happened. How people affected by it were coping, and how much longer it would last. Obviously, it wasn't going away quickly. In fact, with every mile it seemed to be getting worse. Flooded fields filled most of the left side of my view, to the west, and I even passed several smaller fields and ditches that were flooded to my right. The water must have crossed the road at some point, how I didn't know.

A short time later I passed a portable road sign, the kind that has a large reconfigurable digital screen that's powered by a small generator. It read "I-29N Closed at Exit 110." I wasn't sure where exit 110 was located, as I'd lost track of the mile markers along the highway, and in any event, my experience with portable road signs was that they were almost always wrong. Usually the accident, road construction, or another impediment to travel they warned about had long since been removed before they got back to updating the sign. I was used to ignoring them, so I quickly dismissed it. It never occurred to me that the flooding could have been the reason. Enjoying the late afternoon sun, still ducking behind the windshield every now and then as a respite from the wind, I rode on, eagerly anticipating crossing the Iowa border.

Unfortunately, just as the previous portable road sign had indicated, right at Exit 110, around Rock Port Missouri, the interstate ended. Large wood and metal barriers blocked each lane with "Road Closed" signs and another portable road sign said only, "All Traffic Must Exit Now." Even though I'd been warned, it still struck me as abrupt. Traveling in the left lane at close to 70 mph, having just passed a truck, I leaned to the right, released the throttle, downshifted, and aimed for the exit. Though curious, I was mostly agitated. It could only mean additional delay.

As I approached the stop sign at the end of the exit, I saw a small orange detour sign with an arrow to the left. On the other side of the crossroad, to the right, a multi-wheeled Army truck with a rigid canvas canopy was parked in a manner meant to block the northbound entrance to the interstate. A National Guard soldier sat on the top of the truck with a rifle in his hands. I'd never seen a road guarded by soldiers before, at least in the United States, so obviously they were serious. Slowly, I made the left turn as the sign indicated, watching in my mirrors as the truck behind me did the same thing. A moment later I saw another set of roadblocks just like the ones on I-29. The crossroad I was on that headed back towards the river was also closed, guarded by another Army truck with more soldiers. It didn't make sense. The detour sign had said to turn left. Why would they make us turn into yet another roadblock?

Thinking that maybe I'd read the sign in error, I made a left turn into what looked like an abandoned truck stop and shut down. The tractor-trailer behind me did the same thing, pulling up next to me with a loud "peh-pssst" of its air brakes. The driver glanced over at me, shrugged his shoulders, and turned his hands upward. He was as baffled as I was.

With nowhere else to go, I restarted my bike. Inched back to the crossroad and made a slow right turn back towards the first Army truck, thinking, for a tantalizing moment, that I could easily get it and dash back to the highway. By the time I swerved around, gunned the engine and tore down the northbound on-ramp, the soldier would still be aiming his rifle. He probably wouldn't shoot anyway. Instead, he'd call ahead on his radio and within minutes I'd hear a cacophony of sirens and see dozens of blue flashing lights in my mirrors, slowly growing in size. A short time later, as the cruisers approached, I'd hear the "whup-whup" sound and feel the downward air wash associated with an overhead helicopter. A breaking news flash would interrupt local television broadcasts with a grainy live video of the scene. The breathless announcers would say that a crazed biker was leading police on a deadly high-speed chase on the closed portion of I-29 North. Trying to fill in the air time, they'd speculate as to my motivations. Maybe I'd lost my job or was enduring a terrible divorce, or maybe I was drunk or high on PCP. People would stop and gather around available television monitors to watch the live feed, waiting to witness the mistake that would get me caught or killed. They'd never suspect that I was just a boring suburban dad trying to make seven hundred miles in a single day on his motorcycle who'd run into one too many obstacles and snapped.

Amused by the thought, but knowing that I never would do it, I saw another detour sign with an arrow pointing straight ahead. Confused again, I decided to stop at a gas station a hundred yards up the road on the left. I could refuel and check for alternate routes at the same time. Seeing that the pump islands and the store were located on the crest of a small hill, I turned into the parking lot and pulled up to the island that offered the best view of the flooding. An older style Harley Electra Glide was parked at a pump in front of me. As soon as I shut down the rider looked back at me, smiled and raised his hands with a kind of resigned exasperation. He'd been surprised by the detour as well. Waiting for him to refuel first, I walked over towards the edge of the lot and studied the countryside. Water covered the landscape to the north and west almost to the horizon with only the tops of trees, roofs, and telephone poles visibly rising from its glassy surface. I'd never seen such extensive, yet calm, floodwaters.

When he was finished, we had a brief conversation. His name was Mike. Older than me with deeply weathered, baggy skin and a mostly gray ponytail, he was also on his way to Sturgis, and, like me, hadn't anticipated the road block. As we chatted about possible alternate routes, a younger man with puffy black hair walked up to us. He'd just pulled up in a new Dodge pickup truck with Missouri tags.

Seeing me studying my iPhone and correctly surmising that we were confused about the detours, he pointed at the adjacent road and said, "If I were you, I'd ignore the detour signs and follow this path to State Route 59, turn left, and take it all the way to Interstate 80."

Trying to clarify, pointing in the same direction, I asked, "The road we were just on? That one?"

"Yeah, it's the best way to reach Omaha and points north."

He stated it with such confidence that Mike and I simultaneously looked at each other, nodded, and holstered our phones. It was all the advice on directions that two guys needed. Not knowing the area very well, I guessed the new route would be roughly a ten to twenty-mile ride.

After buying and downing a Gatorade in the store, I started up again, pulled back onto the crossroad heading east, and found 59 North at a town called Tarkio. The road was an older, two-lane divided asphalt highway with narrow gravel shoulders, thousands of meandering black streaks from previous crack repairs, and a 60 mph speed limit. Almost entirely straight, it cut between the soybean and corn fields north of town with long, steep changes in grade that matched the rise and fall of the surrounding hills. Still trying my best to make time, I set the cruise control at 65 mph and watched the fields pass by. The air had cooled, probably down into the eighties and the sun was still warming me to the west. The headwinds also seemed to have died down a bit, so I bumped up my speed an additional few notches. Soon, however, I ran into another unexpected challenge.

To avoid Omaha city traffic and the closed portions of I-29. A good part of the truckers hauling goods southbound from the Dakotas to Kansas City were diverting east onto I-80 and then heading south on Route 59 to Rock Port where the interstate was open. With good weather and dry road conditions. They were moving along at an average pace that was above the speed limit, often times going faster even more down the long hills to avoid slowing too much on the inclines. Riding northbound in the opposite direction, I watched them close in on me at relative speeds approaching 140 mph. Then, with only a half a lane separating me from their forty-ton hulks. They'd pass with an earsplitting roar and a quick, hurricane force blast of the wind that would simultaneously shove my bike into a right lean, snap my head back, and twist my left shoulder.

Trying to manage the situation without having to slow, I quickly developed and experimented with a method to minimize the effects. First, well before the pass, I tried to position myself as far over in my lane as possible, somewhere between the center and the right shoulder line. Next, I switched off the cruise control to momentarily reduce speed. Then, right before the pass, I leaned forward, cocked my head a little to the right and ducked behind the windshield. It worked, at least well enough to allow me keep rolling at the same speed, but like the previous ride on I-70, I didn't exactly enjoy it. The only good news was that the trucks were spread out more and it wasn't raining. At least it won't last long, I thought; I should be in Iowa soon and the interstate's probably no more than twenty miles after the state line.

After about twenty minutes, I slowed for the approach to the first town. Not sure if I was still in Missouri (with all the concentration that I had to put on the trucks passing me I could have easily missed signs for the Iowa state line), I searched for clues. The sign for the town said only "Shenandoah" and the plates of most of the parked cars were a mixture of Missouri and Iowa. It could have been in either state. With a growing concern that I could be lost, that maybe the guy with the Ray Milano pompadour at the gas station didn't know what he was talking about, I rolled out of town and accelerated back to highway speed.

For the next forty-five minutes, the cycle kept repeating itself. I'd slow and move into a small town with a solid, American name like Emerson, Carson, Oakland, or Hancock, search for clues that I had crossed into Iowa and was nearing I-80, discover nothing that would help to solve the mystery, then sprint back to highway speed so I could be whiplashed by more trucks. Something else was going on, however, that surprised me. I'd never seen farm towns like these before. While not possessing the architectural charm of the typical New England hamlet, they weren't the dying basket cases we've all driven through either—the ones with sagging houses, unkempt yards, bar covered store windows, and abandoned, rusting industrial facilities. The houses were well maintained with freshly cut lawns and attractive flower beds. The vehicles in the driveways, mostly American minivans and pickups, were clean. The stores were bright and inviting, their curbs and lots free of weeds, trash, and debris. The equipment in all of the industrial centers was arranged in neat rows. One town even had what looked to be a new community center, with a large outdoor pool and a colorful assortment of playground equipment arranged on nicely landscaped grounds. Though quiet, the small towns in this part of the country exuded pride. People liked living here.

By the time I reached a town called Avoca, however, I was almost panicked. Though fairly sure by now that I was in Iowa, I'd been riding for well over an hour and I still hadn't seen any signs for I-80. Unable to bear the tension any longer of not knowing where I was, I begrudgingly pulled over, hit the engine stop switch, pulled out my phone, and tapped the icon for Google Maps. Luckily, the cellular service was good, and within a few seconds the familiar blue dot appeared on the map. I was in fact well into Iowa and only a few miles south of I-80. The bad news, which took me a while to absorb, was that I was much further north than I had anticipated. To reach Grand Island, assuming I could get across the Missouri River—which was by no means guaranteed—I'd have to travel a considerable distance back to the southwest. That meant that my objective for the day, the one I'd fought so hard to reach, my singular focus through so many obstacles, no longer made sense. It would be much faster and probably less risky to take I-80 to I-29, turn north, and ride all the way into South Dakota. The only question in my mind was where to stop for the evening. I'd already been riding for almost twelve hours, my rear end was aching, and I was having difficulty concentrating. Though I had plenty of fuel, the trip odometer already registered 615 miles. It was past six o'clock and the sun was steadily lowering in the cloudless western sky. Considering my options for a moment longer, I decided, as usual, to just take it a mile at a time. After a few quick sitting stretches, I fired up my bike, quickly rolled through Avoca, found I-80 and headed west.

What I saw over the next half an hour made me think that I was being rewarded somehow for making it through the trials of the current day. It was as if someone had taken the best pieces of everything that I'd seen so far on the trip—the rolling hills of Kentucky, the neatly plowed soybeans fields of Missouri, the meticulously maintained farm buildings of Iowa, the big sky feel of the Great Plains, an advancing, gentle summer sunset—and wrapped it all into a gift that you couldn't look at without a total sense of wonderment. What struck me the most, aside from how it all seemed to go on forever in every direction, was the intensity of the green colors. It reminded me of Ireland or places in the Northeast after a cold, wet spring. In the distance, I spotted a few roads higher up on the hills with some light traffic, but nothing could mar the landscape in a way that did anything but add to its beauty. I actually had the thought that if the roads were made of yellow bricks, it could have been the Land of Oz. I had no idea that western Iowa was this stunning. No wonder why the people who live here are so proud, I thought. They've got one of the best-kept secrets in America.

While the scenery heading west had generated some adrenaline, and the wind had subsided somewhat with the advancing afternoon, by the time I was rolling north on I-29 again, I was rapidly starting to fatigue. Things that normally would have piqued my curiosity, like portable levees that occasionally lined the shoulders on both sides of the road, were becoming irritants. I was especially annoyed by the groups of motorcycles that were sometimes passing me in the left lane. Probably heading to Sturgis, at any other time I might have tried to tag along, but I was so tired I couldn't imagine riding at the 80 mph or greater speed required to keep up with them. I was also starting to worry again. There didn't seem to be much infrastructure around. I wondered how long it would be until I saw signs of anything even resembling a regular hotel chain.

Finally, about an hour later, I saw a sign for an exit and a blue services billboard with a reasonable assortment of gas station and restaurant logos. There were also some hotels listed, but I didn't recognize any of them, so they had to be local one-offs. Other hastily constructed signs said "biker friendly" and "free water," which were welcome benefits, but for some reason, I hesitated. The town was off the road to the east and I wanted to be closer to the interstate. The food choices were also limited to the cheaper chains that didn't serve alcohol. I had to admit it, after nearly seven hundred miles, I needed a drink.

Some time later, I spotted a thin rectangular green sign. Sioux City was less than sixty miles ahead. If I could make it that far, there would certainly be a better hotel and food choices. But it wasn't going to be easy. By now it was past seven-thirty and the sun was occasionally dipping below the tree lines to the west, creating rapidly changing patterns of shadows and light that were causing my eyes to water. The air had turned cooler and I could feel the heat rapidly dissipating from my sunburned arms. I was getting cold. My rear end was also aching terribly, requiring me to lift off the saddle every minute or two, rock gently forward and back, and shift it from side to side. Willing myself to keep pressing forward, I stopped quickly at a rest area, put my jacket back on, took a few quick stretches, gulped some water, and rolled back onto the highway.

By the time I started seeing billboards for the attractions and amenities of Sioux City, I knew I was in trouble. I'd crossed another threshold, a place I'd never been before: a state beyond physical exhaustion. I could no longer think. It was as if after hours of constant head jiggling I'd damaged the circuitry in my brain so badly that my central processor, buckling under the strain of trying to reroute millions of incoming information signals and outgoing physical control responses, was crashing. I wasn't just falling asleep, I was *locking up*. About the only thing I could process was a growing internal voice shouting at me to stop. I'd reach the point where I couldn't ride another mile. If I did, I knew I was going to crash. Out of options, I slowed, downshifted, turned on my right turn signal and rolled off at the next exit. The only thing I could discern from the sign describing it was "downtown."

Unable to determine the best direction to head at the end of the off-ramp, I turned right and slowly rotated my head from side to side, scanning for hotels. In what seemed like an instant, I spotted a Holiday Inn to my left, but it came up so quickly that I rode right by the entrance. Dejected, I slowed to a crawl and momentarily considered trying to make a U-turn, but I didn't have the confidence. If I got stuck, as I had near the entrance to the muddy parking lot in Missouri, I wasn't sure if I'd have the leg strength to push myself back. Instead, with one last surge of energy, I rode down to the next traffic light, made a left onto a side street, and cut through a parking lot. I found the original road I'd been on, turned in the opposite direction, and then made a full right turn into the hotel parking lot. Slowly, with my boots dragging across the ground, I pulled up in front of the restaurant to the left of the main entrance and switched off the engine. After breathing a few times deeply, I looked down at the trip odometer and my watch. I'd clocked 765 miles in fourteen hours.

"They'd better have rooms," I said to myself.

As I walked to the hotel entrance, I noticed the parking lot was over half full and there were more bikes and trailers around. Several couples walked by me in the opposite direction as I approached the front door. Almost all of them were wearing some kind of riding gear, and others were slipping in ahead of me. No doubt with legs that had more spring. The place was busy. When I opened the door and walked into the lobby, my heart sank. There were two check-in lines, both with three groups of people in front of me. Worried that the hotel might be full, but at the same time relieved to be off my bike, my brain slowly rebooting from its near crash, I waited patiently for my turn.

I picked the line with the female clerk, who was cute with dark straight hair, and when I finally reached her, I opened up with an exaggerated, "*Please* tell me you have rooms."

Flashing a quick smile, she said, "Yes. We have a few left at ninety-nine dollars a night."

I immediately responded, "I'll take one."

After unpacking a few items, I took a long gaze at myself in the bathroom mirror. It looked as if I'd aged five years in a single day. My nose, cheeks, and the bottom part of my forehead were a reddish purple color, made all the more noticeable because the open portion of my helmet only covered the inner half of my cheeks. Outside of the helmet line, my skin was light brown. The skin around my eyes was even lighter—no doubt due to the sunglasses. And when I smiled, deep wrinkles formed that cut across the upper part of my cheekbones to my ears with noticeably contrasting flesh tones. My eyes seemed even lighter than normal and my hair, though almost entirely covered by the helmet, was even more salt and pepper gray. Even my goatee, typically mostly dark brown, seemed to have sprouted a few more white whiskers. I looked like a worn out, poorly painted clown.

After a quick wash-up and change of my t-shirt, I walked back outside and scanned the parking lot again. More pickups with bike trailers had arrived and it was already dark. Too tired to walk very far, I noticed immediately that there was a Chili's restaurant to my right and an I-Hop to the left. The decision didn't take long. Chili's would have a bar.

Still wearing my riding boots, I took a seat at the bar towards the far back exit overlooking one of the televisions. A baseball game was on, but I couldn't focus on it. Within a few minutes, I was enjoying a large, cold draft beer and flipping through one of those complicated chain restaurant menus that have too many choices. After the bartender had taken my food order, I asked him to snap a picture of me with my phone. When he handed it back to me, I compared the new picture with the one my waitress had taken the night before in Kentucky. I had at least twice as many wrinkles, my eyes were duller, the bags under my eyes were larger, my hair seemed lighter, and even my chest had slumped. If you keep deteriorating at this rate, I thought, you'll be dead within a week.

By the time my food arrived, the bar area was filling in, and a short time later, a couple walked up and took the two stools to my right. He was a little taller than me, maybe six feet, with a massive barrel chest, a thick neck, and paw-like hands. Wearing a tank top with a broad neckline that highlighted a beefy chain link necklace and a chest tattoo, it was obvious he was a real biker. His companion was more petite and probably fifteen years younger, with shoulder length black hair and a charming, innocent smile. She was wearing a Harley black leather jacket, jeans, and riding boots, but was far too gentle looking to be a hardcore biker chick. He has to be a decent guy, I figured.

When the bartender came back, he ordered a Jack Daniels and Coke. Even though I'd switched to wine, which would normally be the kiss of death to start a conversation with any sort of real biker, we immediately hit it off. His name was Daniel and he owned and operated some kind of machine shop that sounded like it was a pretty successful business. They were from a town in Northern Missouri and were riding to Sturgis, taking their time, making about three hundred miles a day. He'd recently been through a nasty divorce and Sissy, his girlfriend, had been his savior. I told him where I was from, and some of the stories from the ride I'd just completed, and he warmed up to me even more.

After several more glasses of wine and Jack and Cokes, we started talking about Harleys.

"I gotta tell ya, Daniel," I said, "I'm getting really beat up on my Road King on this trip."

"How come?"

"Crosswinds. They've been terrible all across the Plains."

"You need an Electra Glide."

"Do the fairings help?"

"Yeah, definitely. Particularly with headwinds and in truck passing situations."

"I suppose that's why they're so popular."

"You bet. But the most stable bike, the one that can take almost anything, is the Road Glide."

"How come?"

"The fairing's attached to the frame instead of the front fork. So when the wind hits it, the forces are better distributed."

"It's not affected at all?"

"Nope, barely moves."

"But I don't like the look of them. The dual headlights are too European for me."

"A lot of people feel that way. But if maximum stability is what you're looking for in a bike buddy, you can't beat a Road Glide."

"How are they with crosswinds?"

"Well, all bikes will struggle, particularly if you have a lot of side surface area from tour packs and gear."

"So what do you do then?"

"You just lean into it. And when it gets awful—when they're flat-out howling - you've got to *really* lean into it. It's all you can do."

After a final drink and a few more stories, we paid our bills, wished each other a safe ride and said we might see each other again. But I knew, and he probably knew, that with nearly half a million people converging on the rally the chances of that happening were minuscule. Pleased that I'd at least found someone interesting to talk to, I walked back to the hotel and up to my room thinking about his main piece of advice. It was like an advertising jingle that I couldn't get out of my head, and I kept repeating it as I drifted off to sleep.

"You've got to lean into it . . . *you've got to lean into it . . .*"

Day 3: On to the Promised Land

With only one relatively short leg of the trip remaining, I was planning to sleep in a little, but as usual, I woke up early and pulled the curtains open in my room. It was cloudy and humid outside with a flat, gray sky, and for a moment I thought about going back to bed. After a quick scan of the radar applications on my phone, however, I decided to get moving. Another smaller, more disorganized front had swept down from the Dakotas during the night and had already crossed I-90 to the northwest. It was heading to the southeast and the predictions showed that it would pass over the Sioux City area in about an hour and a half. The rain was generally light, showing up as mostly light and darker green on the map, but there were a few yellow spots that looked troublesome.

Packing up everything except my bathroom bag, I walked out and surveyed my bike. It was filthy. The pipes and chrome were coated with a thin layer of tan colored grime infused with specks of asphalt. The tires, normally a matte black, were brownish gray. The saddle bags and tour pack were covered with the same gritty aggregate as the pipes. My license plate was almost unreadable. The worst part, however, was the bugs. They must have been out in full force once the rain ended in Missouri because scores of them had managed to sacrifice themselves, like kamikazes, on just about every surface that faced the wind. A few exceptionally talented ones had even managed to hit the edges of my seat. After a deep sigh, thinking about how long it would take to get her back into perfectly detailed condition, I decided to gas up at the station next to the hotel, clean my windshield and light lenses as best I could, park, and then grab some breakfast at the IHOP.

When I walked in, the host escorted me to a booth in the back abutting a large window. Taking a seat facing forward so I could see the most of the other tables, I brought up the last email that Jim had sent me which included directions to the lodge. I entered the address and studied the route for a while. It was fairly simple, with only three turns and a total distance of 463 miles. If I were on the road by eight o'clock and averaged 60 mph with stops (good pace on a motorcycle), I'd be there by four in the afternoon, check-in time. Jim and Theresa were flying into Rapid City and would be arriving two hours earlier. Their bike had already been shipped and would be waiting for them. The email included a security code for the house so I wouldn't have to rely on them to gain access, but I wanted to get there after they did. For once, I wouldn't have to push it.

When my waitress arrived, I ordered a cup of coffee while reading the news on my phone. When she came back, coffee pot in hand, I lifted my head to say thanks and noticed, for the first time, her physique. She was tall for a woman, about my height, with neck length blonde hair and thick, sculpted arms. A cotton blouse was stretched tightly over her broad, square shoulders. In fact, her entire torso looked like a rectangular concrete block that was tapered down the sides of her waist. This was one powerful woman.

As she was filling my cup, she asked for my order. Her tone was professional but not overly friendly. Still scanning the menu, I ordered a standard American breakfast and finally glanced upward to make eye contact. Her makeup was thick, presumably meant to cover the dark shadows that were still visible on the lower half of her face. It was evident. She was a man.

Trying not to look surprised, I finished ordering and went back to reading the news on my phone, wondering what having a transvestite waitress might portend for the day. After what I'd been through already, I was starting to believe in signs, that amongst all of the chaos, things happen for a reason. Maybe it's why the Native Americans and the original settlers of the Great Plains were so spiritual, I thought. They lived day after day on the edge, exposed to the vicissitudes of nature, and just couldn't explain how they could see an indescribably beautiful sunset one day, and a twister carry off their family the next. To cope, they had to have faith that it wasn't all completely random. Otherwise, life would be that much more frightening. Wondering what was in store for me on my last leg, I polished off another cup of coffee and walked out.

After a final look at the weather radar images, I adjusted the loads on my bike, rolled out of the parking lot, and headed back onto I-29 North. The air was cooler than I had originally thought and the sky was darker, especially to the northwest. The road surface was damp, with wispy hints of summer fog swirling just above the pavement. Small puddles filled the wake-up ridges on the left shoulder. The road seemed as if it couldn't decide whether it was going to dry or not.

In what seemed like no time, I crossed into South Dakota and the speed limit changed to 75 mph. Being from the East, I'd never seen a 75 mph speed limit before. On any other day, particularly if I were driving a car, I probably would have greeted it with an enthusiastic "Wahoo!" and a further stab of the throttle. On this day, however, I was disappointed. I wanted a smooth ride, and with the wind already gusting from the east and the weather threatening, I wasn't going to be able to ride very fast. My rear end was also throbbing with pain after less than twenty minutes, which wasn't a good sign. Already cold, aching, and fighting the crosswinds, I wasn't even a half an hour into the day's ride and felt like quitting.

What kept me going was a change in the scenery and the sky. Around Sioux City, the land had been mostly flat soybean fields broken only by occasional businesses and housing complexes. But further north, it opened up into gently rolling, grassy farmland that was dotted with hay bales and small rock outcroppings. Occasionally, taller hills would line each side of the highway, and when I'd emerge from the valleys between them, the land seemed to stretch out even more. A few farm buildings and a line of telephone poles stood far off in the distance, looking utterly insignificant against the enormity of the view. To the northwest, the clouds were reaching the ground in places with dark perpendicular streaks, indicating rain. Above me, the cloud ceiling, now higher, had formed into a more tightly defined, convex shaped dome. On the lower surface of its gray bottom, spider lightning crackled with tentacles and sub-branches that stretched in all directions. Though I probably should have been scared, I felt strangely intrigued, discounting any potential danger. It couldn't possibly develop, I figured, into anything worse than yesterday.

As I was riding between an unusually tall set of hills, a gust of wind hit me from the northwest. The air, even cooler, was laced with water vapor that coated my windshield with a fine mist. Glancing over at the other side of the highway, I saw a car traveling with its windshield wipers on delayed swipe. There was rain ahead, but it wasn't heavy. With luck, it would remain light and I could keep rolling. From what I remembered of the radar images, I had to be on the east side of it, and since I was riding north and it was moving southeast, I'd be past it quickly.

Just as I was emerging from the valley, with my view of the countryside opening up again, a vicious blast of the wind, more powerful than anything I'd ever experienced, slammed into my right side from the east. Remembering what Daniel had told me the night before, I pushed down hard on my right handgrip to counter the effect, but I was still moving to the left. Determined to make him proud, I slowed and leaned into it even more, to the point where I felt like if the gust stopped I'd ride straight on the right shoulder and into a field. I was almost too scared to look down at the speedometer, but I did anyway. I was down to 55 mph, twenty miles per hour under the speed limit, and I was pushing against a force of wind that seemed to be almost ridiculous. But Daniel was right—if you really leaned into it, you could keep riding in a straight line. It was either that or stop, and there was no shelter.

For the next twenty miles or so I fought the gusts, leaning into them as much as possible and then correcting back to the left as they'd ease. With each successive blast, I learned to be especially wary when I emerged back into the open from between any hills. Rain also started to tease me, starting and stopping again, seemingly without reason or correlation with any of the cloud cover overhead. Occasionally the road would get wet enough for the few cars and trucks that were passing me to generate some spray, but just as quickly it would almost dry out. At one point when the rain restarted with moderate intensity, I considered pulling under a bridge ahead. But it was even smaller than the one I'd hid under the day before, almost a waste of time. Instead, I rolled on, watching the sky brighten to the north and east and become more disorganized. Over time, patches of blue appeared, the pavement started to dry, and the crosswinds, though they still gusted from time to time, abated. Although it had been pretty unsettling at times, for once I'd been right. It hadn't been worse than yesterday.

An hour later I was finally on I-90, the interstate that would lead me all the way to Sturgis. Traffic was moving at a pace of about the speed limit and I tried to keep up with it, but 70 to 72 mph was the best speed I could comfortably ride with the wind. Seemingly just to annoy me, it had shifted back to the north as soon as I had turned west and was pummeling me, once again, from the right. As a result, just about everyone was passing me, but unlike yesterday, the traffic stream was mostly motorcycles. I'd never seen so many heading in one direction: almost all Harleys, with probably half of them Electra Glides. I watched in amazement as they sped by with a kaleidoscope-like mix of changing colors, chrome accessories, and lights. The riders and their passengers (if they were riding "two-up") were just as diverse, sporting an assortment of leather jackets, vests, eye protection, t-shirts, tank tops, head gear, riding pants, boots, and jewelry that could have filled a department store. One woman, probably about thirty, was wearing only a bikini top, jeans, and riding boots. Another guy, riding a black Fat Boy, passed me doing close to 90 mph with nothing above his waist except a tank top and goggles. They must have been freezing. I was wearing jeans, chaps, a t-shirt, and a jacket along with gloves and a helmet, and I was cold. Maybe you're getting soft, I thought and bumped up my speed a bit.

The other major types of vehicles sharing the interstate that morning were pickup trucks and RVs of all varieties, pulling either open or enclosed motorcycle trailers. A growing proportion of bikes at the rally arrive this way and for good reasons: you can ride through almost any kind of weather unscathed; your bike can stay clean (if it's in an enclosed trailer); you can make better time; and, of course, it's safer. As might be expected, a lot of the open trailers were carrying the Harley models that aren't as comfortable for highway travel—Sportsters, Dynas, and Softails. The beautiful custom bikes with extended front forks, swept-back handlebars, sleek gas tanks, and super fat rear wheels were probably riding in the enclosed trailers, happily sheltered from the elements. In a way, I envied them.

A short time later, I saw what looked to be a Road King Classic ahead in my lane and realized that I was closing the distance to it. Somebody was actually riding slower than I was. Looking carefully in my left mirror I waited for the next group of bikes to ride by and slid over into the left lane behind them. Another group of bikes was running up behind me, so I didn't have much time, but it looked like I could pass without bothering anyone. When I was abreast of the straggler, I looked over out of curiosity to see what he was like. He was about my age, with mostly gray hair and an overdue shave. Wearing only a T-shirt and jeans, without a helmet, he was crouching slightly below the windshield with a death grip on each hand grip and a tired, dour looking expression on his face. He was miserable. Probably an inexperienced rider, he'd decided not to put on his jacket when he'd headed out after breakfast and was questioning his decision with every mile, wondering how much longer he could take it. While not usually taking pleasure in the suffering of others, I have to admit, I smiled as he faded in my mirrors. He was just like me.

After what seemed like an agonizingly long time, the sky finally cleared and the sun, now rising steadily behind me, was warming my back. Feeling better, I pulled into a rest area for a quick break.

Just inside the entrance, a short woman with graying hair, glasses, and a handful of pamphlets greeted me. Pointing to a row of tables, she asked if I wouldn't mind signing in at the appropriate place according to the state I was from. She was with the State of South Dakota and they were taking some kind of survey. There were about ten signs on the table with groups of two-letter state postal abbreviations, and it took me some time to find the one that included "SC" because none of the groupings made sense. They didn't appear to be in alphabetical order, organized by region, or arranged in any other logical configuration. Recalling that this was a government operation, I let out a half chuckle and picked up the pen lying on the correct clipboard. There were about a dozen signatures for my group of states. I was the first to sign in from South Carolina. A quick scan of the other boards indicated that most of the people were coming from the Midwest, but there were also a considerable number from Texas and Florida.

When I walked back outside, the air temperature seemed to be at least five degrees warmer and the sun was so bright I was squinting under my sunglasses. The sky was a deep, brilliant blue with just a few strands of thin, cirrostratus clouds left over from the earlier storm. Taking a cue from the hundreds of other bikers around, I removed my chaps and jacket, stored them in my saddlebags, applied some suntan lotion to my face and arms, and restarted my bike. I was going to be rewarded, I hoped, with a picture perfect riding day for the rest of the trip. Maybe even the wind would take a break.

As usual, it didn't last, and it would take me a while, another few days actually, to truly grasp the capricious nature of South Dakota weather. Being located nearly equidistant between the Gulf of Mexico and the Northwest Territories of Canada, the Mount Rushmore State lies in the perfect position to serve as a mixing bowl for a wide variety of air masses. It's far enough north to receive cool, dry Canadian air, and it's far enough south and not too far to the west to receive warm, moist air from the Gulf of Mexico. The Rocky Mountains provide another source feed—funneling Pacific air as it snakes through the canyons and valleys of Montana and Wyoming into great swirling eddies that spill out onto the plains—the jet stream. That river of fast moving air which causes almost all storm fronts to move eastward can flow right over the state during the summer, stirring the air like a giant spatula moving over a water surface, swirling the liquid beneath it. As a result, since all weather is a result of air mixing in one way or another, South Dakota has some of the most unpredictable weather in North America, with both the fastest temperature rise and drop ever recorded (-49°F in 2 minutes and +49°F in 15 minutes), and the largest diameter hailstone ever measured (8 inches).

Perhaps to hint at future surprises, within twenty minutes of exiting the rest stop the clouds returned, the crosswinds came back, and the temperature cooled by what seemed like ten degrees. Struggling to stay warm, with goose bumps spreading over the exposed portions of my arms, I pulled over on an extensive part of the shoulder behind a group of other bikes. Cursing at myself for packing so poorly, I pulled my jacket out of my saddlebag, donned it again, and started a mental list of the things I needed to acquire if and when I ever got to Sturgis. First on the list was a new pair of riding boots that could actually grip something. I'd also need a long sleeved t-shirt and a sweatshirt to round out the layers I should have brought in the first place. If there was a windshield swap of some sort I might trade mine in for a larger one, but I figured that would be a long shot. There were usually places to install LED light strips and louder pipes at rallies, but not much else unless you wanted to visit a dealership. A new windshield would cost $400 and I didn't wish to admit that I'd made such an expensive mistake.

Just as I was thinking that maybe I ought to quit being cheap and switch out the windshield, the landscape abruptly changed. Petite, perfectly shaped pine trees began appearing in lines that snaked gently along the ridges of higher, more jagged hills running perpendicular to the highway. To the north and south, the fields of short grasses folded into the ridges of the hills like a severely stretched outdoor carpet. I was also climbing slightly in elevation and lost sight of the interstate ahead, so I figured I had to be approaching a valley. Thinking about the crosswinds, I slowed a bit and waited for the crest to appear, wondering what was in store below.

The largest body of water that bisects I-90 in South Dakota is Lake Francis Case. Formed by the Fort Randall Dam in Pickstown, it meanders to the northwest for almost a hundred miles to the next upstream dam in the Missouri River system at Fort Thompson. The interstate crosses it about a quarter of the way down from Fort Thompson, just south of Chamberlain, on a southeast to northwest line. As I crested the final ridge, I couldn't help but marvel at the tranquil beauty of the lake and the surrounding small towns below. Though it was still mostly overcast, bands of sunlight were poking through gaps in the clouds and illuminating patches of water like pointed downward searchlights. Additional cone-shaped pine trees and small buildings dotted the steep green hills that led to the shores, reminding me of an alpine valley. Up ahead, a two-lane concrete bridge crossed the lake with relatively high concrete guard rails. Realizing that the wind would be blowing directly across it, I tried not to gain speed as I rolled down the last steep decline towards the bridge, sneaking some last glances as best I could, of the choppy bluish-gray water.

I should have known better, especially since I was anticipating an increase in wind strength as I crossed the bridge, but the first crosswind blast struck with such unexpected force that I momentarily froze with fear. As a result, it easily pushed my bike into a left lean and I zigged almost instantly into the left lane. Realizing that I was headed directly towards the concrete guard rail on the opposite side and possibly straight into the lake, I released the throttle, pushed down on the right handlebar, snapped into a good lean, and quickly crossed back into my original lane. A few seconds later, a couple of bikes rumbled by on my left and one of the riders, a forty-something hard-core type with a mustache and intricate arm tattoos, turned towards me briefly and grinned. He was trying not to laugh but rubbing it in a little just the same, probably remembering, like all experienced riders, the first time he got blown across a lane. It's not something you easily forget.

Further west the panorama changed in a way that I didn't expect. Especially to the north, the fields were overrun with summer wildflowers, particularly of the yellow variety, including black-eyed susans, sunflowers, and marigolds. Sometimes they appeared as if exclusively planted in fields of considerable acreage, while at other times they were mixed together between long, open patches of grasses, rippling in unison to the patterns of the wind. Every now and then, as if to further complement the view, clover, white asters, and milkweeds were mixed with lavender hyssop and blazing star, providing a contrasting palette of whites, blues, and purples amongst the yellows. It was one of the most attractive canvases of wildflowers I'd ever seen, on a scale that was almost surreal. Rolling along at 72 mph, with the sky clearing again, I started to imagine Lakota Indians sitting on their horses amongst the flowers, perhaps out to hunt, surveying the land. No wonder they had such a connection to this area, I thought. Even with the fickle weather, there was no way that anyone who lived off the land, as they did, couldn't fall in love with it.

Over the next hour, I started seeing billboards for an antique car museum and other attractions located in a town called Murdo. There were smart features on the signs designed to capture and heighten your interest as you approach, much like South of the Border advertising on I-95. It was clear by the time I reached the exit that it had all of the amenities that someone traveling through central South Dakota might want:

gas stations, restaurants, hotels, and interesting attractions all very close to the interstate. Hungry and knowing that I had time to explore, I rolled off, but with little expectations. All I really wanted was a decent lunch. If the car museum was close by and it didn't look too cheesy, I might give it a try.

A short distance down the crossroad, there were two gas stations, one on either side of the street. The larger one, though filled with bikes, had a gravel parking lot, so I chose the station on the left across the street mainly because the lot was paved. When I pulled in, I realized it also had a restaurant and the car museum was tacked onto its right side. The museum seemed smaller than I anticipated, at least initially, but the parking lot was nearly full and people were continually entering and exiting. Already tired and very saddle-sore, I sneaked into one of the few open spaces, shut down, and took my time dismounting.

The restaurant was built to resemble a 1950s era diner. With most of the tables already made, I sat down at the counter next to a harmless looking biker who had just been served some kind of pot roast. He was about my age, maybe a few years older, with mostly gray hair hidden by a skull cap and a pale, smooth face. His fingernails were perfectly manicured and he was wearing a decent watch. Even I could spot them now—without any windburn or other road scars, he had to be towing his bike; probably on a trip with a few friends. Wearing jeans, a T-shirt and riding boots, they'd probably been suckered in by the amusing road signs like me, but had slipped on their vests and skull caps before entering to try to fit in. After a while, we started to talk.

"That pot roast any good?" I asked.

"It's alright. Nothing is unusual. Where are you from?"

"South Carolina."

"Ah. I'm from Chicago. We're trailering."

He didn't need to say that, I'd already figured it out.

"What do you do there?"

"Bank executive."

Seeing that I was wearing chaps and that I probably looked a lot more road-worn than he did, he asked, "You riding the whole way?"

"Yeah, over eighteen hundred miles."

"I'd never have the time to do that," he said. "It's all I can do to slip away for a few hours on a weekend."

I thought about talking with him some more, maybe about my oldest son who was studying at the University of Chicago, but his body language wasn't friendly. He was inching his way away from me and furiously downing the last bits of his lunch. So I turned back to studying my menu and when my waitress came back, I quietly ordered a BLT.

He quickly finished his soda, paid his bill, and walked away without speaking another word. All in all, I thought he was a bit of a stuffy jerk. I wondered if that's how I'd have come across to somebody I thought was a "real biker" when I was an executive, not so long ago.

With the restaurant crowd slowly thinning, I spent the next half an hour enjoying my sandwich, sipping a cup of coffee, and reading a small brochure about the car museum. Increasingly curious, I queried my waitress about it when she came back to check on me.

"So what do you think? Is it worth it?"

"Absolutely honey," she replied. "Especially with this."

It was a coupon that would save a dollar off of the $10 admission price. She had a bunch of them on a pad. Trying her best to help—or maybe to earn a small kickback—she ripped one off and handed it to me.

"Thanks," I said. "Every bit helps."

Figuring that I had another hour to kill, I walked into the gift shop and bought a ticket. The entrance was through a doorway at the back of the store and when I walked through it into a small foyer, another gentleman greeted me. He was tall with a great mass of thick, white hair and a broad, genuinely friendly smile. Taking my ticket, he handed me a map of the museum and started to rattle off all of the things I should see in a naturally proud manner. Still not expecting much, I half listened to his advice, gave the map a quick glance, shoved it into my jacket pocket, and stepped into the first exhibit room.

The museum was much larger overall than I expected and it took me more than an hour just to wind through the main exhibits. Spread out over a campus of more than a dozen buildings and stuffed with items continually collected for over half a century, it was hard to take it all in. Not only were there over two hundred antique cars, spanning the early

1900s to the 1980s, but there were also antique tractors, farm equipment, motorcycles, bicycles, scooters, pedal cars, and an array of small appliances, household equipment, and memorabilia that were simply mind-boggling. Profits generated from the gas station and the restaurant over the decades of the museum's existence probably paid for the collection, with revenue collected from admissions, perhaps, going to maintenance. Still, I thought, it must have taken the full-time dedication of the family owners through two generations to acquire all of the items and make the museum work.

My favorite part was the pre-World War II vehicles, particularly from the period of 1910 to the early 1930s. What impressed me the most was the completeness of the collection, particularly the Ford Model T and Model A sections. Nearly every model year was represented along with most body styles, so you could see the progression of the design, slight as it was, until the significant change in the Model A in 1928. Along with the Fords, however, there were a host of other lesser known brands, including Ajax, Auburn, Beardsley Electric, Chalmers, Durant, Elgin, Franklin, Grant, Haynes, Maxwell, Overland, and Saxon. All part of the club of over eighteen hundred automobile companies that once operated in the United States but are now defunct. It's something that's always fascinated me about the auto industry: it was an enormous magnet for investment capital in the late nineteenth and early twentieth centuries. If you were a young person at that time and wanted to get in on the hottest new thing, you went into the car business. It was the place to be, the dot-com boom of its day. In 1920, there were over four hundred car companies operating in the Unites States alone.

I also liked some of the later model cars, particularly the 1971 Pontiac Ventura once owned by Senator Tom Daschel. It's the type of car you don't see in most collections because it's not sexy, fast, or rare, but precisely the kind you can appreciate because it's what most of us actually drove. Exotic muscle cars of the era like Boss Mustangs, Corvettes, Hemi Cudas, and tri-power GTOs were beautiful, but nobody I knew could afford one. Mostly, every family seemed to have at least one "plain Jane" people hauler like a Ford Fairlane, a Chevy Nova, or a Plymouth Valiant, with a straight six or a small block V8, AM radio, crank windows, and a heater. We beat the hell out of them generally, but they got us to where we needed to go cheaply and without a lot of fuss. I smiled thinking about what it must have been like for the young Mr. Daschel to canvas the state in his Ventura, visiting small towns, farms, and Indian reservations along state highways and back roads that probably wore his tires bald many times over. It was even an ugly green color, probably someone else's discard he bought used because it was a great deal. My brother had a Chevy Nova like that.

By the time I reached the last building with the "premier" muscle cars, it was past three o'clock, my target time for getting back on the road. After a perfunctory look at the collection, I walked out and scanned the sky. It was still in the process of clearing. Small white clouds with light purple edges were lingering towards the lower part of the horizon. It was also hotter by a good ten degrees, so I decided to ride the final leg without my jacket. Wondering exactly how far that would be, I pulled out my phone, punched in the address of the lodge again and analyzed the route. It was 170 miles away with just two turns: a left onto Boulder Canyon Road from the interstate and then a right onto the road to the lodge. The first turn was the most important one, and I repeated the name of the road to myself several times to make sure I wouldn't forget it.

After murmuring "boulder canyon" a few more times under my breath, I took a final few stretches, stowed my jacket in my saddlebag, snapped the lid down, restarted, and pulled up to the gas station to top off. Within minutes, I was back on I-90 West studying, yet again, the scenery. The seas of wildflowers were gone, replaced instead with fields of brownish-green grasses dotted with an occasional bush or short broadleaf tree to add some distance perspective. It wasn't quite as beautiful, but the scale of the view was even larger, and the interstate, particularly when it dipped in elevation and ran flat again towards the horizon, looked like a stretched out ribbon of thin gray tape. I was crossing the Buffalo Gap National Grassland.

A half an hour later the sky cleared into a perfect dome of progressively shaded blues, with lighter shades at the horizon and a deeper, more electric blue at the apex. I could also see the outlines of some flat, rocky outcroppings in the distance to the south, which had to be the start of the Badlands. The main change, however, which made me realize that I was getting closer to Rapid City, was the steadily increasing bike traffic. With the sun blazing against a picture perfect blue sky and the air temperature around eighty-five degrees, many of the people pulling trailers were stopping at gas stations, rest stops, or even on the shoulder to unload one or more of their bikes and allow a portion of their party to ride the last distance to Sturgis. A lot of the new riders were females straddling smaller Harleys and customized choppers; probably itching to get away from their increasingly cranky husbands or boyfriends, they may have argued that they weren't as qualified to drive the bike hauler. The groups that were all guys had probably drawn straws to choose who got to ride and who had to keep driving the pickup truck or the RV. I wondered how many fights it was all causing.

Another interesting side effect of the increase in motorcycle traffic, particularly as I entered the outskirts of Rapid City, was that I started to pass more. With the surrounding hills and city infrastructure blocking the crosswinds, I was able to ride faster. At the same time, a lot of the new riders were poking along at well under the 75 mph speed limit to stay within their abilities, as they should have. Moving at relative speeds of 15 to 20 mph or more, I'd blow by them on my disheveled Road King, feeling somewhat superior. They may have been riding the last hundred miles, but I'd clocked over eighteen hundred and fifty in three days. This time I had the experience. To reinforce that perspective, whenever the road widened I'd pass whole groups of them by rapidly moving to the left across two or three lanes and then smartly swerve back, watching as they quickly receded in my mirrors.

My feeling of smug superiority, however, didn't last long. I'd been concentrating so hard on passing all of the new bike traffic safely that I forgot the name of the road for my first turn. I knew it was canyon-something, but none of the exit signs listed anything that remotely resembled that word. Figuring that I must have missed it, I veered off at an exit north of town, stopped at a crossroad and fumbled for my phone. The road I was looking for was about five miles back and it became apparent why I'd missed it. Boulder Canyon Road, to the east of I-90 in Sturgis, is called Lazelle Street, which is also State Route 14. I'd been looking for the wrong name. "Serves you right," I said to myself and rolled back onto I-90 heading in the opposite direction.

It seemed to take forever to ride the last few miles back to Route

14, even though I was moving at the fastest pace of the trip. Knowing that there were no speed traps since I'd covered the same portion of the interstate minutes earlier, I rolled on enough throttle to briefly reach 90 mph figuring that I deserved, by now, at least one unsafe indulgence. But it didn't last long. Slowing well before the exit, I rolled off and merged into an extensive line of bike traffic waiting to make a right. One by one, we all turned west toward Deadwood.

After three full days of almost exclusive solo riding, I wasn't prepared for the shock of suddenly being thrust into the largest unorganized "group ride" of my life. Aside from the thunderous cadence of thousands of V-twin cylinders firing indiscriminately, what struck me the most was the heterogeneity of the rider congregation heading in both directions. It was as if someone had assembled just about every type of Harley-Davidson motorcycle and custom chopper available onto a pallet with hundreds of possible paint jobs and fifty thousand accessories, put it all in a giant Powerball hopper, and then, with considerable effort, turned an enormous crank to create two thousand bikes in whatever mix of models, colors, and accessories that had stuck together (with some quality control afterward to reject ugly or taboo combinations, like a windshield on a chopper). At the same time, someone else used a second hopper filled with three thousand riders varying in age, sex, and physical description, plus fifteen thousand pieces of riding equipment and clothing, to create a mix of different rider combinations. Next, a giant claw pulled bike combinations from the first hopper, extracted rider combinations from the second, mounted one or two riders on each bike, and gently placed them on the road until they hit a complete set of two thousand units. There was absolutely no discernible pattern.

The second thing that struck me, somewhat surprisingly, was that everyone was more or less behaving. When we'd slow for a light or a stop sign, the group would compress into a line of two to three abreast with enough distance between each bike and no haphazard zigging. When inching along in traffic, everyone would gun their engines a bit to show off the sound of their pipes (as is proper), but when it was time to accelerate again, we'd move out smartly with no burnouts or racing, even for short sprints. Once the speed of traffic increased, the group would naturally thin out into a staggered single file configuration, the textbook technique. My first experience with a casual group riding, even with scores of bikers who didn't know each other, wasn't that taxing. In fact, it was really fun.

The real shock was the realization that I was actually *there* and right in the middle of it. Three days earlier I'd been in shorts and tennis shoes walking our dogs through a flat, palm tree lined neighborhood two miles from the Atlantic Ocean. Now I was in the Black Hills of South Dakota, the promised land of bike rallies, riding my motorcycle amongst thousands of other bikers I didn't know. The two worlds couldn't have been more different. At the same time, it was odd how quickly and effortlessly I'd blended into this new one. My Harley looked like any other bike, there were other people wearing full-faced helmets (though not many), and plenty of middle-aged men with goatees wearing jeans, boots, and a t-shirt. I supposed that a lot of us were probably alike, mostly ordinary people who only days ago had very different lives. Maybe, I thought, that's why rallies are so popular. It's a second, whole other reality you can slip into and out of in more or less an instant. You can't do that during a typical vacation. The venue may change, from snow to a tropical sun or from the city to mountains, but nothing else changes that radically. You don't enter another dimension, a parallel universe, complete with its own set of landscapes, material assets, meeting places, dress, and culture. After pondering the thought for a while longer, I fell into a line of other touring bikes heading west and glanced at my watch. It was just past five o'clock.

Route 14 is a two-lane, winding thoroughfare that carves through the steep, rocky hills and pine forests located east of Deadwood. It's a dangerous road for motorcycles. Knowing this, probably through years of experience cleaning up accidents during rally week, the local authorities use portable road signs to highlight the maximum safe entry speed for the curves, and fixed radar devices to display your speed before you reach them. Concentrating on staying in the correct position within my lane and moving at a safe but respectable speed (no one was slowing to precisely the speed limit), I missed the small street sign for the road that led to the lodge. Realizing my mistake, I made a U-turn and called Jim to let him know that I was close. He confirmed what I thought—the access road was a few miles back along a steeply downhill graded portion of Route 14. Five minutes later I found it and turned left, being careful to avoid the large patch of fine gravel along the edge closest to the highway. Someone's going to hit that and wipe out, I thought.

The access road to the lodge wound steeply upward through three or four hairpin turns into the bluffs overlooking the highway. On one of the final straight legs before the last turn, climbing steadily, I looked to my left and spotted what looked to be a large two-story ski lodge with a spacious outdoor deck protected by a railing. Two people, a tall man, and a woman were leaning against it and waving wildly. The man was wearing a riding club vest and the woman a bright orange long-sleeved shirt. It was Jim and Theresa. I tapped the air horn twice to signal hello, turned left onto the lodge road, saw that there were two driveway entrances, and abruptly stopped. Both of the driveways, which connected together just short of a small, concrete landing in front of the garage, were soft gravel. To make matters worse, the one that would have been safer, the one that had only a mild slope and was relatively straight, was blocked by a large pickup truck with an attached motorcycle trailer. The other driveway, located further down the lodge road, connected to the first one at a right angle very close to the steeply upward-sloped last portion before the landing. If I used this driveway to reach the garage, which was the only option because of the way the truck was parked, I'd have to make a very tight right turn on a steep upward slope—on soft gravel. It was more challenging than the potential turn from the access road back onto Route 14 toward Deadwood.

Not wanting to give up but deciding to minimize the risk, I turned left from the lodge road onto the second driveway, rode straight up it at a reasonable speed to the intersection with the first one, stopped, and shut down. It was good enough. I could unload the bike from this spot and move it into the garage later. After a deep breath, I slapped the side of the gas tank in a gesture of thanks and looked upward to offer another round.

I'd made it.

Jim and Theresa were beside me before I even had my helmet chin strap unbuckled.

Jim was grinning broadly, and after a quick man-hug he cupped his right hand, slapped it into mine, leaned towards me and said softly, "Man, am I glad you're here."

Theresa flashed her white teeth, gave me an additional hug, and said in her thick Long Island accent, "You must be exhausted."

Relieved just to be off my bike, I told Jim why I'd parked it in its current spot and he immediately understood. It wasn't worth trying to ride it into the garage given the load. Within a few minutes, with my tour pack and large travel bags in hand, we walked through the two car garage and into the house, passing Jim's bike and several others along the way. The only other bike I recognized was Larry's electric-blue Road King, looking perfect as usual.

After dropping my bags off into his bedroom, Jim took me on a quick tour of the lodge. It was about what I expected, with a large living area, kitchen and dining room on the main floor arranged in an open floor plan. A small hallway between the living room and the kitchen led to the front door. Two bedrooms were accessible from the hallway. Downstairs there were three more bedrooms, another living area with a game room, and a small laundry. A spacious wood deck built on pilings was accessible from the main floor through sliding glass doors. Another concrete patio was laid out below it on the ground floor. A hot tub sat on the patio, protected by the wood deck above. I lifted the cover and peeked inside. The water was a pale shade of green and smelled like mold. Jim looked over my shoulder and said quietly, "Yeah, I have to call them about that." Otherwise, the place was clean and in surprisingly good shape.

After being introduced to an enormous cooler in the garage that was already iced with what looked to be at least three cases of beer. I twisted the top off of an exceptionally cold one, walked out onto the deck, and met some of the other members of our party. Including me, ten had made it to the lodge so far. The wives of two of the guys would be flying in on Monday, bringing us at that point to an even "dirty dozen."

The first to approach was Larry. Recognizing me almost immediately, he looked up with a crooked smile, gripped my hand, and said, "You were the guy we rode with in Gettysburg with your son!"

"Yes, that was me, and it's good to see you again."

He asked about Chris and I told him that he'd made a remarkable recovery. After a few remarks about my long ride and knowing how fastidious he was about bike cleanliness, I asked him if there was any way we could wash our bikes at the lodge. Thankfully the answer was yes. He'd already checked it out. There was a hose on the downstairs patio that could be rigged to reach the garage landing and I was welcome to use any of the cleaning supplies he'd brought along. With most of a beer already in me and the knowledge that I could bring my bike back to life, the stress of the trip rapidly started to fade. This might just be more fun than I'd initially thought.

Hector introduced himself next. He looked like a Latin American diplomat with gray hair, dazzling brown eyes, and a small, perfectly groomed goatee. His wife, Cindy, was about two inches taller. Slender and fit like Hector with short blonde hair, blue eyes, and soft, fair skin, I guessed she was of German or Scandinavian descent. They'd brought along some snacks and wine and said that I was welcome to any of it. Even more importantly, they'd rented a car (their bike, which was being separately shipped, was delayed on route), so we had another way to get into town if we chose not to ride. Sensing that he was a decent guy and wanting to offer something of my own, I mentioned that I'd brought along a good bottle of scotch.

Leaning in so that no one else could hear us, he gripped my arm and said with an aristocratic sounding Spanish accent, "Well, my friend, then I can supply the cigars."

This was definitely looking up.

The only other member of our gang actually at the lodge at that point (the others had already run into town) was Tom. The youngest of our group, he was an auto body repair technician who worked at a Mercedes-Benz dealership across the Delaware River in New Jersey. His wife had elected to stay home with their toddler-aged children, so like me and Larry, he was a geographic bachelor for the trip. A little taller than me, with brown hair and an even darker thin mustache and goatee, he had a gentleness about him that made him come off as exactly what he was: a really nice, responsible young father who just liked riding. An anti-fake, a guy who wouldn't try to be something he wasn't and didn't care. I liked him immediately.

After some more small talk, I settled into finishing my beer and studying the surrounding area, as I was still getting used to it. Overall, it reminded me of the White Mountains in Northern New Hampshire. The steep hills in the distance were mostly covered with pine trees, but with enough fir, birch, maple, and other deciduous varieties to mix it up. Breaks in the tree line would occasionally reveal whitish-gray rocky crags. To the west, where our yard met the deck, the forest was semi-cleared with a bed of pine straw serving as a kind of mulch. Smaller, young broadleaf saplings swayed gently in the breeze, their green leaves already starting to turn. Autumn would come quickly in just a few more weeks. Remembering how cold even summer mornings could be in New Hampshire, I pulled out my phone, checked the signal, tapped on the weather icon, and brought up Sturgis. Partly cloudy symbols filled the ten-day forecast, with highs in the mid-seventies to low eighties, and lows in the low to high fifties. A few of the middle days next week would be the coolest. No single day listed a probability of rain greater than 30%. The first time we ride into town, I thought, I'll buy the extra clothing and the new pair of boots on my shopping list.

With renewed energy from the fresh air, I decided to wash my bike before going out for dinner. With no real food, we'd probably be heading into town, and since no one seemed to be in any particular hurry about anything, I'd have time. Jim decided to join me and we walked back to my bike, stopped and stared at it, mentally sizing up the magnitude of the required cleaning job.

"Wow," he said, "This is the first time I've ever seen this bike with actual dirt on it," and added with a wink, "I kind of like it."

Not looking back at him, I said under my breath, "Well, I don't," and reached for the levers that removed the tour pack. The first step was to take it off.

Washing and detailing a bike is a ritual that most Harley owners take seriously and is correctly done only by the motorcycle's owner. It's not something you outsource to someone else, and, of course, there's no such thing as an automated bike wash. Bikers do occasionally bring their bikes to free or low-cost services like "bikini bike washes," but that's mainly for the eye candy. No one seriously thinks they're going to get a proper cleaning out of such a session. And most bikers I know who care about their rides would never let another person, even an attractive woman showing off a salacious figure, touch it.

Having removed the tour pack, I started up, turned the front fork slightly, pulled smartly up onto the concrete garage landing and shut down. Jim walked into the garage, mounted his bike, and rolled it backward to a position exactly adjacent to mine. Before he was off his bike, I was back in the garage foraging for what we needed. Larry had brought a wash bucket, soap, sponge, and an additional box filled with polish, wax, bug remover, windshield cleaner, detailing spray, and rags. After removing our watches, wedding rings, and belts to avoid inadvertently scratching the paint or chrome, we pulled the hose over, removed our saddlebags, and went straight to work. Alternately trading the wash sponge and the hose, we labored in silence, thoroughly enjoying the process. It's something that a lot of people don't understand. They think we enjoy washing and detailing our prized toys so they stand out more and so, by association, we look better, but I've always thought the motivation to keep them in like-new condition runs a lot deeper than vanity.

Detailing is an art that requires the dexterous use of your hands, like painting, sculpting, or carpentry, but with one critical difference. It doesn't need you to create anything. Instead, using a few carefully selected products, some simple tools, and proper technique, you renew something that's already been established. Once you're good at it, with sustained effort, you can keep a machine looking like the day it rolled off the showroom floor for decades. Unfortunately, we can't do that with our own bodies.

After a final rinse and some careful drying (always using two towels, one for the big water that you periodically wring out and another one for the fine residue), we stepped back and studied our work. With a little more effort, our bikes would be perfect again. Celebrating with a high five, we each opened another beer, took a few long gulps, and walked back into the lodge. It was time to start organizing for dinner.

The decision to head into Deadwood was an easy one. Closer to our lodge than Sturgis, it offered at least as many dining and entertainment options and probably wouldn't be as crowded. Jim and Theresa were going to ride into town, like most of the others, but after three days of averaging over six hundred miles a day, I decided to travel in the car (or, in biker jargon, a "cage") with Hector and Cindy. I just didn't have the energy, at least at that point, to worry about dodging thousands of other bikers again. Particularly at night, or finding a parking space, or carefully monitoring how much I was drinking. I needed to relax. Jim, as the official ride leader of the trip, had already selected a preferred bar and restaurant. We'd be following him in, which was fine with me.

Located at the bottom of a narrow gulch and covering only four and a half square miles of land, Deadwood, South Dakota was founded in 1876 during the Black Hills Gold Rush. By 1878, after the opening of the Homestead Gold Mine in nearby Lead, the population had swelled to over five thousand. Known for its brothels, saloons, opium dens, fires, murders, and general lawlessness, the city itself was judged to be illegal since it was built on land granted by treaty to the Lakota Indians. Deadwood quickly became an important wholesale supply center for the mining industry in Lawrence County and much of the Upper West. As was typical of western boom towns in the late nineteenth century, after a few generations of relative prosperity, the city began to steadily atrophy. By the early 1960s, despite the entire town being named a National Historic Landmark, Deadwood was on life support. The final kiss of death was being bypassed by the I-90 interstate. Within a few years of its completion, even the prostitutes had cleared out. The last brothel was closed during a raid in 1980.

Recognizing that it was about to be lost forever, a group of citizens in the mid-1980s decided to take a chance and see if legalized gambling could revitalize the city. At that time, only one state (Nevada) and one city (Atlantic City, New Jersey) permitted it. But casino gambling, particularly if they maintained the original look of the town, would fit well with its character. It wouldn't be easy. The Constitution of the State of South Dakota would have to be amended, the State Legislature would have to approve it, and town residents would have to vote for it by at least a sixty percent majority. But they pulled it off. On November 1, 1989, legalized gambling began in Deadwood.

The effects on the town were immediate, sustained, and profound. Taxes from gambling revenue, over seventy times what were projected in just the first year, flooded the city's coffers. Within a few years, the cobblestone streets were restored, new street lamps were installed, and the aging, crumbling sewer system was replaced. Several years later, additional parking structures were built to accommodate the steadily increasing tourist traffic.

Of course, it wasn't all roses. Many of the remaining retail establishments in the town were lost to competition from the casinos, restaurants, and bars that consumed two-thirds of the real estate on Main Street, and parking, to this day, remains a problem. But the town was saved. Today, it hosts an estimated one to two million visitors a year with a population of only 1,270 permanent residents[1], a ratio of more than a thousand to one. Few small towns in America, by this measure, come close to Deadwood's popularity as a tourist destination. Ocracoke Island, North Carolina, for example, with a population similar to Deadwood's, hosts about 80,000 visitors a year (a ratio of only 80:1). Paducah, Kentucky has a population of roughly 25,000. If it were as popular as Deadwood, it would have to host over twenty-five million visitors a year or 68,500 per day. When I'd rolled into Paducah forty-eight hours earlier, I'd struggled to count ten.

The scene in Deadwood on the first Saturday night of the rally was markedly different. As we approached the town, following Jim and Theresa on their bike, the motorcycle traffic thickened into a dense, rumbling horde. Bikes were everywhere. Parked facing outward and nearly touching one another, they lined every square foot of curb space along Main Street. The parking lots of all of the hotels, restaurants, and stores were similarly stuffed to capacity, hosting more than their owners had probably ever envisioned. The city parking garage and the lot next to it were also busy but had some spaces left for a fee of $5. Being in the cage, we chose the city parking garage while Jim and Theresa turned into a lot which was mostly bikes. Within about five minutes, we joined up again on the side street that led into town. The others would meet up with us separately at our first destination, a famous bar called Saloon #10.

When we turned onto the sidewalk on Lower Main Street, we quickly blended into a crowd of thousands of other bikers walking in both directions. Moving along in a kind of dazed shuffle, we studied our

---

1 Per 2010 Census

new world. The town itself was appealing in a way that went beyond the competent preservation of its late nineteenth-century Victorian architecture. The rough and tumble biker crowd; the absence of any recognizable retail, restaurant, or hotel chains; the bike traffic (you could almost imagine them as horses); the roughed up wood of the store fronts; and the dusty cobblestone streets gave it a genuine feel. It wasn't a Disney theme park attraction, a storybook version of a western town where everything was too perfect. You could imagine it as it was in 1876 with horses and wagons filling the streets, unwashed miners in tattered clothing spilling out of the saloons, and real gunfights.

At the same time, we marveled at the display of beautifully customized, modern day Harleys parked along the street. The sights and sounds of the passing bike parade, and, of course, the bikers themselves. Surging forward in a sea of denim, boots, and black leather, they wandered into and out of the Main Street establishments trying, like us, to satiate their needs. The people that had it the best, we quickly surmised, were the ones who'd arrived early and staked out a position on the balcony or by the open window of one of the restaurants or saloons. If you had a group large enough to hold the spot while people alternately brought back food and drinks, you could keep yourself acceptably fed, liquored up, and entertained for hours. Police presence appeared to be minimal, which was at first surprising, but we quickly figured out their strategy. They intended to rapidly contain any trouble. With officers on foot patrol and police duty bikes parked at each intersection, they could quickly swarm any troublemakers and close off a block in less than a minute.

After crossing back over Main Street, we finally arrived at the Old Style Saloon #10. Part museum and part bar, it's an icon in Deadwood because Wild Bill Hickok was shot there during a poker game in 1876. As with many legends, it's not all entirely true (he was killed in a bar known as Saloon #10, but the original building was in a different location on Main Street). But everything else about the place, like the town itself, was entirely believable. The chair he was shot in was prominently displayed, and the walls were covered with interesting photographs, paintings, and period correct artifacts. The owners had also scattered sawdust on the floor, which, though probably meant to absorb beer spills, added to the ambiance. Soon, we found a table in the back with tall stools and settled in. The plan was to have a drink and then send a runner over to make a dinner reservation at our target restaurant which was located in a nearby casino. After a quick beer, I volunteered. Jim offered to go with me since he knew the location.

Within a few minutes, we were inside. Given the size of our group (ten) they wouldn't be able to seat us until ten o'clock, but we didn't mind. We wanted to spend more time at the bar anyway. Making a fast exit, we were back at our table at Saloon #10 before the next round had even been ordered. Even better, the others in our group had arrived.

Aside from the two wives who'd be flying in on Monday, there were three other guys I hadn't met, and we introduced ourselves in rapid succession. Alan, the oldest of our group, might have been a bantamweight fighter when he was young. Barely five feet tall with white, wavy hair, a thin mustache, and a dark tan, he'd managed to maintain his athletic physique well into his sixties. Energetic and confident while still self-deprecating, he'd wind up being a never ending source of hilarious "little guy" jokes. He was also a wine drinker. Discovering that I was too, he offered to buy a round and walked off to the bar.

Before he was back, I met Paul and Bill. The only one of us with a full beard, Paul was a facilities manager for a company in the Philadelphia area. Of average height but with short, stubby legs, he'd turn out to be the moodiest of the group—at times offering intensely funny, sarcastic comments, but at other times acting introverted in a way that made him more intimidating than shy. Bill, Alan's stepson, owned a landscaping business and carried himself with the confidence of a successful small businessman. Tall, with a sonorous, easily recognizable laugh, he had an opinion about everything and turned out to be the hardest partier, with his wife Carrie (when she arrived), Larry, and Paul close behind.

Thoroughly enjoying our conversations, we almost didn't want to leave. But by the time we were close to our dinner reservation, our collective hunger pulled us back to the casino. As might be expected, it was even more crowded, with people standing behind each of the gaming tables, every slot machine in full use, and plenty of other bikers either gawking or passing through. After nearly having to scream at the hostess over the noise of the crowd, she finally found our reservation and allowed us to pass.

The restaurant was in the basement, down a staircase with two ninety-degree turns. Within minutes, we found a couple of tables and were off to the buffet. Knowing that there was no food at the lodge and with no plans that I could discern to obtain any, at least anytime soon, I decided, like most of us, to eat as much as possible. The spread was bountiful and pretty good, maybe on par with a discount cruise ship, and we ate more than our money's worth. Within a half an hour, we were all sitting like stuffed, contented cats, quietly contemplating our next move.

Recognizing the lull, Jim pulled out a map of the area and described what he wanted to do for our first "ride around" day. Tomorrow, starting around ten o'clock in the morning, we'd head back to Deadwood, gas up, and then ride north into a town called Spearfish. Then we'd turn southwest into the Black Hills and ride back to Sturgis. After a late lunch or early dinner, we'd head back to the lodge and decide what to do next. I added that I'd like to find a place to grab some breakfast before heading out, but the "hard party" clique demurred. They knew, even then, they'd never get up for it. The only decision left was what to do for the remainder of the evening.

Surprisingly, we all decided to head back to the lodge. I probably had the best excuse for being fatigued but the others had traveled long distances as well, and the food, beer, wine, and mental strain associated with acclimating to our new surroundings were rapidly sapping our energy. After a quick discussion regarding the dangers of the gravel on the access road, we paid our bills and worked our way through the crowds on Main Street to our respective parking places.

On the way back, riding in the rental Monte Carlo, Hector and Cindy discussed their plans for the day since they were still without their bike. As they debated their options, I trailed off into a half sleep, barely realizing after we'd stopped that we were back at the house.

After a final drink and some small talk, half of us headed to our respective rooms. Bill, Larry, Paul, Alan, and Tom found new energy and decided to head into Sturgis for some additional merriment. They were going to be smart, however, and take the truck. Driving in, as opposed to riding, would require finding and paying for only one parking space and, while the rest of them could responsibly imbibe, an unlucky one would be selected as the designated driver. By the time they headed back out, I was fast asleep.

A few hours later, I woke up to the sound of a deep pounding on what seemed like the inside garage wall. Recognizing my mistake immediately, I sprang up from the bed, pulled on some gym shorts and sprinted into the living room. Being wife-trained for nearly twenty-five years, as a last step before retiring, I'd walked around and locked all of the doors, including the two that led to the garage. It was a stupid mistake, borne of habit, but having been locked out of my own house more times than I could count, I knew how irritating it could be.

Shouting, "Hang on," I opened the mudroom door, leaped across to the inside garage door and slid back the deadbolt.

Before I could reach the lock on the door knob, the pounding started again, accompanied this time by someone roaring, "Who the fuck locked the *FUCKING* door?!"

It was Larry, and he was hot. Something was wrong. Apologizing as they stumbled in, I asked, "Is everything OK?" It wasn't. There had been an arrest and someone was in jail.

Hearing the commotion, Jim and Hector walked out of their bedrooms and we all assembled in the kitchen, eager to hear the story. It was a good one. As they'd planned, they drove the truck into Sturgis, parked it in one of the temporary lots close to the main drag and entered a bar. Paul, as the designated driver, abstained from alcohol, but Larry and Bill consumed what they wanted and became recognizably, though not obnoxiously, intoxicated. After leaving, they walked back to the truck, a Ford F-250 with a crew cab and an eight-foot bed, and found it nearly boxed in by two other vehicles that had arrived while they were at the bar. Given his relative inexperience with driving large vehicles in very close quarters, Paul told Bill, who owned the truck, that he wasn't comfortable moving it. Bill offered to back it out but Paul wasn't sure. He knew that Bill had been drinking, and while the truck only had to be moved a distance a little more than its own length backward, he wasn't comfortable handing him the keys.

As they debated whether or not to do it, three undercover police officers who'd followed them out of the bar were crouched below a row of nearby bushes, out of sight, listening to their conversation. One had a video camera. Tired and not wanting to wait it out, Paul gave in and tossed Bill the keys. With Paul and the others watching, Bill slid between his truck and the car parked beside it, cracked the driver's side door open, slipped inside and placed the keys in the ignition. Before he could even start the engine, the cops swooped in, turned on a portable spotlight, hit record on their camera, and asked him to step out and take a breathalyzer test. After he failed (he was just over), they informed him that they were placing him under arrest. Paul and Bill did their best to explain the situation without getting overly heated, but the cops wouldn't listen to any of their pleadings. Bill had been behind the wheel with the keys in the ignition and he was over the legal limit. That was all they needed.

As they recounted the story, we offered some man-support, a few well-placed "that's bullshit"'s, and "you gotta' be shittin' me"'s, but it sounded to us like Bill was screwed. It was certainly a cheap arrest, but legally the cops were probably right. After seventy years of experience with the Sturgis rally, with an average of over four hundred DUI arrests per year in the last five years alone, they had to know where the lines were. I also had the thought that as much as Paul's explanation sounded rational, they'd probably heard thousands of similar ones before. A lot of people probably said something like, "I was just moving the car." Or, "I'm only a mile from home," or, "I wasn't even doing anything." I doubt many of them said. "Yes Sir, you're right: I had ten beers in the last two hours, I fully intended to move my vehicle, and thank you for stopping me." But it wasn't time to say stuff like that, given the emotions. The last thing a guy needs in a situation like this is an armchair lawyer, particularly one playing the part of a prosecutor. So I listened along with Jim and Hector but didn't say much. In any event, we all agreed, when we finally broke up, that Bill would probably get it reduced. It was just a matter of how long it would take and how much it would cost.

As I tried to fall asleep again, I wondered what the next day would bring. Saturday had started with a transvestite waitress serving me breakfast and ended with a member of our group being railroaded into a local jail. Not much, it seemed, was turning out like I expected. The last three days had been exciting at times, fun, and incredibly interesting, but I had a growing sense of foreboding. I'd already had way too many close calls and the sneaky hand of misfortune had just reached out and snatched a member of our own group. I was playing a dangerous game.

And, as a Marine Gunnery Sergeant who once trained me liked to say, "If you keep rollin' the dice boy . . . they're gonna come up snake eyes."

Part III: Riding Around
Day 4: Hard Lessons

My first "ride around" day began with severe calf cramps. During an initial stretch in bed, they both twisted into knots. Trying not to wake anyone, I let out a muffled grunt, leaped out of bed, and hobbled into the living room, wondering why they were punishing me. It had to be the backrest. Like a lot of Harley touring motorcycles, my bike has a small rider's backrest that sticks up from the rear of the main saddle. And when I'm riding, to ease the strain on my back, I push against it using subtle pressure from my feet.

To simulate the difference, sit as you normally would in a chair with both feet comfortably on the ground about shoulder width apart. Now lean back into the chair, press the small of your back against it, and move your feet outward about a foot. Be sure to keep them parallel to your body and pointing straight ahead. That's the riding position on a touring bike. What you'll notice is that your calves as well as your inner thighs move slightly into tension, which, for a few minutes, probably wouldn't matter much. But if you hold them this way for twelve hours a day for three straight days, no matter what kind of physical condition you're in, they'll find a way to retaliate. I'd been up less than five minutes and I was already being taught another unexpected lesson about riding a motorcycle.

Once the cramps subsided, my thoughts turned to coffee. Thankfully, the surprises this time were more pleasant. There were two machines, plenty of filters, and someone had left an enormous tub of Folgers in the refrigerator that was still about half full. Knowing we had a group of ten, I made two pots, poured myself a cup, and walked out onto the deck. The air was moist, fresh, and chilly, but the sky was clear and the sun had already moved around to the east side of the house. It was going to be a perfect summer day.

After downing a cup and grabbing a refill, I pulled out my phone and hit the speed-dial for my wife. It was still early and since it was Sunday, she'd probably still be in bed, but we only had a few minutes to chat the day before.

After a few rings, she picked up and said in an obviously groggy voice, "Good morning."

Prattling on like a teenager, I told her about the events of the previous evening and our plans for the day, but she didn't say much. About all I could get out of her was that the pool company would be coming in a few days to fix the pump I'd blown up, and my mother had called wondering if I was still alive. But right at the end, just before we hung up with our final "love you," she said something unexpected.

Almost deadpan, in a voice an octave lower, she said, "Wear your helmet."

Shaking my head, I shoved my phone into my pocket and stared out at the morning sky, wondering how she could have known. The truth was, ever since my spontaneous group ride of the day before, I'd been contemplating riding without my helmet. It's another thing that all riders struggle with because like so many other aspects of riding, the decision isn't as easy as you might think. On the plus side, there's no doubt that wearing a helmet reduces a rider's chances of being injured or killed in an accident. Helmets also offer protection against wind, rain, rocks, road debris, and other hazards. Wearing one, as every rider course teaches, is the responsible thing to do. It's also often required by law.

The problem is, helmets suck. They significantly reduce your total field of vision, increase wind resistance, and muffle incoming sounds. They're also uncomfortable, expensive, and surprisingly fragile (if you drop one hard it has to be replaced.) Storing a helmet on a bike is also tricky, given their bulk. The worst part, however, is how much they reduce the physical and spiritual pleasures of riding. You don't feel the wind rippling through your hair or get the same sense of freedom. It's like the difference between driving a convertible with the top up versus down, or like wearing a condom or not during intercourse. And most guys can relate to that difference. If you can manage the risks, it's a lot better without one.

Peer pressure can also come into play. It's a reasonable human desire to want to fit in, and it was clear to me, particularly after the trip to Deadwood the night before, that most of my fellow rally attendees were riding "unadorned." It's probably another reason, I thought, why the three largest motorcycle rallies in the country are held in South Dakota (Sturgis), New Hampshire (Laconia), and Florida (Daytona). All three states don't require adult riders to wear helmets.

So I struggled with the decision. Riding without a helmet for the next few "ride around" days would certainly be more enjoyable. The risks, I figured, were also manageable. The routes were safer (slower speeds with fewer cars and trucks) and I had more experience. On the other hand, I'd ignored my wife's prescience before, prior to the trip with Chris, and he'd nearly been killed. I'd also learned the hard way, through that accident, that helmets work. And I'd made Chris a promise. But the day was too beautiful, the air too scented with pine pitch, and I needed to maximize my fun. Walking out to my bike, I lifted my helmet off the saddle and placed it on the shelf in the mudroom. For one day, just one day, I'd take the chance.

When I came back, the kitchen was filled with other members of the group, including Jim and Theresa, and we chatted for a while over more coffee. The story from the previous evening was retold for the benefit of the girls, but there was no new information other than what they planned to do. They were all going to spend the day springing Bill from jail. Hector and Cindy said they planned to visit a museum outside of Sturgis. This meant that Jim and Theresa and I would have the day to ourselves. I felt sorry for Bill and looked forward to riding with the group, but I also thought that it would be good to have a day with just family.

The subject then turned to food. I was starving, but no one else except Jim and Theresa wanted to find a restaurant for breakfast. Recognizing the implications, Jim turned towards me and said in a whisper, "I guess we're on our own for that one too."

But I didn't mind. Jim had spotted a place on the way to Deadwood the night before and we both wanted to try it. We could start our day ride from there.

After showers and some final unpacking, Jim and I walked out to our bikes. It was something else we had in common other than being related: we both had Road Kings. Black with matching hard saddlebags and skinny whitewalls, Jim's was mostly stock with just a few added safety and comfort-related accessories. Before he left Pennsylvania, however, he'd splurged and changed out the pipes, and I reminded him that he owed me a proper demonstration. Nodding with a smile, he opened the garage door, twisted the ignition switch, and hit the starter. They were louder than mine at idle and made a rapid fire, raspy, popping noise when he blipped the throttle. Not over the top, but distinctive. A good choice. After a quick thumbs-up, he shut down. When Theresa came out, we put on our jackets and slipped on our gloves. And then he did it.

Noticing that my helmet wasn't anywhere in sight, he said in a somewhat surprised way, "Dude, you're not wearing one today?"

Blushing with guilt, I stared back without responding and the battle in my mind quickly restarted. Moving more rapidly now, like a DVD that's set to play at 4x speed, the arguments for and against silently raged, and after a few seconds, with growing anger, I took a few steps towards the mudroom. I was going to wear it. But I couldn't let it go. Stopping one last time to look at Jim, hoping to pick up a sign, anything that would cause me to change my mind again, I noticed that he was mounting his bike. He was moving on.

"No," I finally replied, "I'm not wearing it. I deserve a day off."

There was no reaction. Relieved, I walked up to my bike, threw my leg over and started it up. Moments later our two Road Kings were burbling down the driveway. The die had been cast.

When we turned onto Route 14 towards Deadwood, I was nearly overwhelmed. The air was even sweeter as it whipped through my hair, the sun was warming my neck, and the magical beauty of the Black Hills was further revealing itself with every twist of the road. The sights and sounds of the hundreds of fellow motorcyclists riding by were an additional adrenaline pumper, infusing me with a sense of excitement and energy that was acting like a supercharger to my emotions. Even if,

I thought, something else goes wrong on this trip, this one ride, this one glorious indulgence, will have been worth it.

After stopping to refuel at a station just inside the town limits, we rolled into the center of Deadwood. The restaurant that Jim was thinking about was located on the back side of a casino and it took a while for us to find it. It was small, with a tiny kitchen and only a few tables, so we decided to eat outside. After we had ordered, I pulled out my phone and checked the weather forecast again, more out of boredom than any concern. The prediction was still for partly cloudy skies with a high of 82°F, but there'd been a subtle change. For the first time, it said there was a slight chance of thunderstorms and that some of them could contain hail. The probability of rain had also increased slightly from the typical humid air summertime forecast of 30% to 40%. I knew from experience that 40% was the threshold that usually meant that something bad might just happen, so I mentioned the change to Jim. He dismissed it. It was so beautiful outside he couldn't imagine we'd run into any trouble. I had to agree.

When the food arrived any further thoughts about the weather quickly vanished. The breakfasts were excellent and the fresh squeezed orange juice was to die for. Theresa gave it a five-star rating. We'd be back.

After a final cup of coffee, we slowly walked back to our bikes. The air had already warmed considerably and a few birds had landed in a nearby tree, chirping in the way they do on beautiful mornings to make sure that you recognize, and appreciate, the blessing. A light breeze had also sprung up from the southwest, the summer wind that usually signals calm. It seemed almost impossible, but the day was getting even better. Feeling the warmth on our backs, we all took off our jackets and quietly stowed them in our saddlebags. Once he'd buckled his helmet chin strap, Jim finally looked at me and softly cleared his throat. He was gearing up to say something. I figured it would be some kind of a "pre-operational" briefing filled with details of what we were going to do, including the roads we'd be taking, where we'd turn, safety tips, and backup plans—but that wasn't his style. Instead, after opening his mouth and pausing slightly in a way that was meant to build up my anticipation, he just said, "Follow me."

I smiled and mounted my bike, thinking that of all the pre-operational briefings I'd listened to in my life, including the ones in the Navy, Jim's had been the best. He got it done in two words.

The first leg was riding north to Spearfish along Route 85 on the northern edge of the Black Hills National Forest. It was the perfect road to complement a perfect morning: a winding, single lane highway divided by a double yellow line the whole way (reducing the chances of being greeted by an oncoming car or truck trying to pass), and shoulders that widened at points so you could stop and take in the scenery. Jim rode near the left side of the northbound lane and I followed behind and to the right, towards the shoulder line. Staggering like this is safer because oncoming traffic sees more lights spread across the road, making the cycles seem larger, and if a rider has to stop quickly and the cycle behind can't slow fast enough, there's room to run up beside the other bike. I don't know who figured this out or when, and nobody ever actually told me this, but it's something that just intuitively makes sense and you pick it up over time. Doing it well, however, in an enormous group, at high speed, and with tight tolerances, is a lot more difficult. But I didn't have to worry about that, at least for now.

Somewhere on the very northern edge of the forest, the sound of Jim's pipes trailed off, his brake lights came on, and he started drifting to the right. I didn't understand why at first, but when we rounded the next curve I saw what he was aiming for. A small brown sign listed the name of a local waterfall. Naturally, they wanted to see it.

The pull off, large enough for about a dozen cars or fifty bikes, was busy, but we found two parking spaces at the southern edge, backed in, and shut down. The sun had risen over the rock peak on the other side of the road at an angle such that its rays were only illuminating the pavement and the rock face behind us, leaving the road and the waterfall in shadows. Dismounting without saying anything, we all instinctively walked towards the road to get a better look at the waterfall, and as soon as we stepped into the shadows, the air seemed to cool by fifteen degrees. It had to be from the mist.

As soon as I stepped back into the sun, an older woman wearing khaki shorts and a white blouse started walking towards me. When we were within speaking distance, she stopped and pulled out a coupon book and a pen. Trying to act professional but with an undertone of playfulness, she made a few check marks on the first ticket and handed it to me. It was a ticket. I was being cited for riding without a helmet, "girl-watching," and being handsome. The fine was $10 and if I paid it immediately, I'd get a Sturgis rally hat. The rest of the proceeds would go to a local charity. Always a sucker for smart marketing, I laughed and pulled out my wallet. As I was handing her the money, I pointed to Jim and said she ought to cite him too. She'd have to come up with something different because he had a helmet, his girl was with him, and he wasn't as handsome, but I knew he was good for it. She blurted out a laugh and enthusiastically made a few more checks on the next coupon. When Jim walked up, looking baffled, I told him to break out a ten dollar bill. The hats turned out to be pretty nice.

After stowing our new hats and snapping a few pictures, we decided to move on. The next stop was Spearfish. Somewhere on the outskirts of town, Jim pulled into a large hotel and restaurant complex that resembled a mountaintop ski lodge. The parking lot this time was larger and filled with bikes, and we had to split up to find two spaces. There were also temporary tents set up that were selling various kinds of merchandise, presumably catering to the rally crowd. When we finally found each other, I asked him why he'd stopped. The restaurant was apparently highly rated and he wanted to check it out. We might want to have dinner there one night. There was also a walking path that led to a gorge that was a recommended scenic attraction. Theresa wanted to try it. He didn't have to explain why. Fifteen years ago one of her legs had been nearly crushed in a freak parking lot accident and it had never fully recovered. She couldn't go more than a couple of hours without exercise.

The restaurant seemed like a solid bet but every minute we were inside felt like torture. It was simply too nice out. Increasingly impatient, I walked out before they did, escaping back into the fresh air. Rock music was blaring from a portable system under one of the tents. The party, whatever it was, had already started. For a moment, we considered staying for lunch, but I could tell Jim wanted to keep moving.

Twenty minutes later, after a quick walk into the gorge to stretch Theresa's legs, we were back in the Black Hills National Forest, riding southwest on Route 14. It was a good ride, with a lot of turns, changing road conditions (single lane to double and back again), and interesting changes in scenery. At times, we'd be snaking up between sharply defined ridges, at times riding between lower hills with more grasses, and at other times rolling through valleys dotted with small ranches. I couldn't keep track of it all. Finally, somewhere deep in the forest, we started up a long, steep incline, and when we reached the crest, I noticed that the sky had changed. Some large gray thunderclouds were building to my right and portions of them were breaking off and occasionally blocking out the sun. The horizon to the east was also dotted with low, puffy lighter gray and white clouds, but they didn't appear to be moving.

The descent from the crest seemed to take forever, and I was so focused on managing my speed correctly through the tightly coiled turns, I barely looked at anything but the lane lines on the road. But finally, the road flattened out and the tree cover on either side of it abruptly ended, exposing a large field with gently swaying tall grass. A small road to the right cut across the field and led to some dark brown log cabin style buildings. It looked like some kind of a park or picnic area. Cramping and increasingly cold, I was relieved to see Jim's brake lights illuminate again. A few seconds later his right turn signal started flashing. He was turning onto the field road. It was a good call.

A hundred yards or so after the turn, Jim stopped and pulled over. There was no shoulder, but the road was wide enough so we wouldn't bother anyone. They apparently just wanted to stretch and maybe put on their jackets.

Dismounting carefully to avoid inducing any cramps, I walked over and said, "Wow, that was great."

Jim and Theresa were in the process of taking off their helmets and we broke into a relaxed conversation. Theresa was mad at herself for not having her camera accessible. Jim loved the last pass through the hills. We all wondered what people did around here for a living and for fun.

As we put our jackets back on, the gray thundercloud that had previously been to our right passed overhead, blocking out the sun, cooling the air, and, it seemed, muffling the remaining ambient sound. The surroundings now eerily quiet, we looked back at each other with curious expressions and noticed something else. Two deer had wandered into the field, a young buck and a doe, and they were moving, ever so slowly, back towards the road. In the distance, we heard the distinct burbling of a Harley V-twin decelerating against the backpressure of its engine. A rider was winding down the road and would cross over the open field in just a few moments. Looking back at each other again, this time more sternly, I could tell we had the same thought. The deer were too close; the rider was in danger. As we wondered what to do about it, the buck broke into a run and dashed towards the road at the point where the tree line ended. The doe was right behind him. If they emerged from there, the rider wouldn't have time to do anything. A second later, just as we were about to start running and flailing our arms wildly, which is about the only thing I thought we could do, they made a hard left turn and scampered into the trees. The rider rumbled by, completely unaware. He probably never knew how close he'd come.

Relaxing again beside Jim's bike in the cool, still air; we noticed another sound, slowly growing in amplitude. It was a very soft "tink tink tink" and we both looked at each other and said, almost simultaneously, "Now what?"

Rapidly trying to solve the mystery, I started to assess available clues. My hair felt like it was being compressed at points and there were sharp, quick sensations of cold. When I looked down at the ground, bb-sized ice pellets were alternately spreading across the pavement and melting. Thinking at first that it might be sleet, I quickly remembered that it was summer. It had to be hail. The confirmation came when I looked over at my bike and saw tiny ice balls dancing off the gas tank and other exposed metal parts. With each collision, they were emitting a small "tink."

Having figured it out more or less at the same time, we stood by our bikes, listening to the sound, still somewhat in disbelief. There'd been no rain, thunder, or warning of any kind. But it didn't last long. Before Jim and Theresa could even put their helmets back on, it was gone.

Looking up at the sky, Jim walked over to me and said, "What do you think we should do? Should we wait a while?"

I was way ahead of him, having already scanned the sky, and noted that the thundercloud had crossed the road.

"We should be OK—as long as the road doesn't turn towards the east. If that happens, we'll be under it again."

Jim wasn't sure about the road, but as we stood there and discussed it, the menacing "black cloud" drifted further away from us.

"I think we'll be okay," Jim said. "Let's get going."

Almost immediately after turning back onto the main road, I noticed that the black cloud wasn't moving away anymore. It was lingering to my left as if it was trying to make up its mind. We were moving to the south at a pretty good pace, about 55 mph, and climbing slightly between two hills, but on the down-slope the road started to twist. Focusing on following Jim, I lost track of what direction we were traveling in, and as we were reaching the bottom of a small valley, the black cloud started to rapidly overspread us again from above. We must have turned to the east.

Just as we were rolling on some throttle and starting to climb again, I was thoroughly startled by a loud, abrupt, *"THWACK!"* Thinking at first that I'd been hit by a rock, I looked down and saw something clinging to the lower portion of my windshield just below the stability crossbar. It was a large frozen blob of ice that had deformed on impact and was slowly melting in the seventy-degree heat, waiting, it seemed, for me to notice it. Instinctively releasing the throttle, I said out loud, as if speaking to my wife again, "Ma, this can't be good."

A moment later the heavens opened up with sheets of falling ping pong balls. When the first wave hit the pavement most of them bounced upward into the air, some as high as fifteen feet, but when the subsequent sheets fell we were riding through a popcorn popper of hailstones. They were hitting my jacket with "whupps" and bouncing up through the engine guards on my bike, pelting my thighs. They were hitting the tops of my legs, my knees, and even my groin. And then, an instant later, the first one hit exposed skin. It landed on the knuckle of my right index finger with a sharp, intense pain that rapidly spread throughout the rest of my hand, and, just as quickly, numbed the point of impact. It hurt, and I mean it *really hurt*. The scariest part, however, was when the balls started to hit my head. At first I tried to maintain a sense of humor, letting out a long, exaggerated "Oooooowwwwww!" with each collision, but when a ball cracked into my right eye socket bone just below my eyebrow and fell on my glasses, it wasn't funny anymore. I could lose an eye or worse.

Still, I couldn't believe it was happening. Usually, hail falls as part of a severe thunderstorm. It's formed when water droplets in a thunderhead get caught in its updraft and rise into a part of the cloud that's cold enough for them to start freezing. As they freeze and grow in size by combining with other water droplets around them, their mass increases. When the force of the updraft can't hold the weight of the stone anymore, it falls. Thus, in general, the stronger the updraft of the thunderstorm, the more potential there is for large stones or severe hail. But severe thunderstorms with strong updrafts are usually accompanied by high winds, thunder, lightning, and torrential rains. This storm was strangely reserved. The sky overhead was dark, but there was no sound. The wind was calm and I didn't feel as much as a sprinkle. So when the hail started falling, it seemed to just come out of nowhere.

Thinking for a moment that it was an aberration, that maybe we could ride on, I leaned as far forward towards the windshield as I could, trying to protect my eyes. But I didn't have a helmet and my hands were occupied steering the bike. There was no way to cover my head. So the hailstones just kept smacking it and bouncing off, wearing me down. Stability was also becoming a problem because the asphalt had disappeared. It was like riding a bicycle across a driving range carpeted with ice balls while hundreds of golfers were taking swings at you. About all we could do was slow further and search for shelter. But we couldn't find any. The tree line to the right was about a hundred yards away and to reach it we'd have to stop, dismount, run down a steep drainage ditch and scale back up the other side. To the left was an open pasture. Finally, about the time when I was seriously considering just stopping, lying flat on the ground, and cupping my hands over my head, Jim took off again. He'd spotted a large storage shed at the end of a short gravel driveway on the left side of the road and one of its sliding doors was partially open.

When we hit the driveway, I knew we'd only have one chance. Luckily, as we approached, now moving at about 25 mph, I saw a couple of people standing inside. They were almost hidden in the shadows, but they were frantically waving us in. There was room. Jim slipped through the partially opened door so quickly I wondered if he'd be able to stop before crashing into the other side. But an instant later his brake lights illuminated and his bike skidded to a stop. The problem was his rear fender was only an inch inside the door. There was no room for me.

With no other options, I stopped as quickly as I dared, hit the engine kill switch, threw down the kickstand with a single thrust of my boot heel, and dismounted so fast I wasn't sure if the bike would topple when it fell on the stand. Thinking at first that I'd make for a nearby tree, I heard people inside the shed shouting, "Come on! Come on!" So I broke into a run with my hands over my head straight towards the doors. When I bolted through I was moving so fast, I nearly tackled Jim.

After a few deep inhales to catch my breath, I looked at Jim and Theresa and the two other bikers who were inside and we all broke into laughter. Jim was especially jubilant, but my mood quickly soured again when I looked back at my bike. The balls were hitting it with loud metallic "thacks!" and "dungs!" instead of "tinks." It was getting hammered. But there was nothing I could do, so I just shrugged my shoulders. Jim's smile quickly faded when he saw it too. No biker likes to watch a beautiful Harley getting beat up. Theresa, meanwhile, was standing behind me and parting my hair, scanning for injuries. I had a headache and most of my scalp was still numb, but I was unharmed.

After one last distinctive "pang!" on the engine air intake, the sound of the hail rapidly faded. In the distance, towards the horizon, rays of sunshine were breaking through the clouds and quickly warming the air. Not wanting to venture back outside, at least not yet, we poked our heads out of the shed doors like scared turtles and studied the area. The ground was mostly covered with hailstones, but they were rapidly melting. Everything else was still.

"Maybe we can leave now," I asked.

Nobody backed me up. The biker standing next to Jim just kept shaking his head and muttering, "Damn'dest thing."

When the sun hit the shed doors, we knew it was time to leave, and one by one, without saying anything, we cautiously crept out. My first concern was my bike, so I walked over to it, switched off the ignition, and started a rapid scan for damage. Miraculously, it didn't have a scratch. Laughing anew, I picked up some ice balls from the ground, threw them at Jim like a ten-year-old boy, and walked back to the shed. Theresa was relieved to hear that my bike was fine but thought we should inspect Jim's. So he backed it out onto the driveway and we started another walk-around. About halfway through he suddenly stiffened and pointed accusingly at the left side. I saw it too. The gas tank had a slight dent, about the size of a car door ding, and the black paint on the battery cover was scratched, probably from a glancing blow by a more irregular hailstone. It was a strange irony: the bike that had been sheltered for at least a portion of the storm—his bike—was the one that had sustained damage.

Seeing that Jim was upset, Theresa tried to change the subject. She started by saying that she was glad that I was OK and that we'd all been pretty fortunate. But she quickly reverted into a scolding about riding without my helmet. I tried to show some repentance by mentioning that her sister-in-law had reminded me to wear it before we left for breakfast—and I should have listened to her—but that only added fuel to the fire.

Raising her tone a final time with a kind of mock indignation, she said, "Ah ha! You see! You didn't listen to your wife and she found a way to punish you!"

Jim and I looked at each other and rolled our eyes. He'd been married even longer than me, so we both knew the same thing. There was no winning this one. She was right.

The two other bikers with us in the shed, a middle-aged couple from Colorado, were the first to leave. As they pulled out, almost as an afterthought, I said to Jim that we ought to record the size of the hailstones. Walking around like beachcombers looking for attractive shells, we gathered up a few and snapped a round of photos with our respective phone cameras. They'd all melted to various degrees, so they were smaller than what actually hit us during the storm, but some of them were still the size of a half dollar. Nobody in our group was going to believe it.

Having survived the hail ordeal, our next objective was Sturgis. Jim pulled out the paper map he had of the area and spread it out on his saddle. We were close to a little town called Nemo that was roughly twenty miles to the south. As long as there were no weather surprises, we could roll through Nemo and arrive in Sturgis in about forty minutes. We were both looking forward to finally reaching the "mecca" of bike rally towns, though we didn't know what to expect. I'd researched it briefly on the internet before I left South Carolina. About all I could remember was there was a Harley dealership somewhere, a lot of bars, and an assortment of temporary stores that sold merchandise.

Jim was able to lift my spirits with a single question. After stowing his jacket and grabbing a water bottle, he walked over and asked, "You want to get your new boots?"

It was a thoughtful thing to suggest since there were about a hundred other more exciting things we could have started with. But it was exactly what I needed. A way to begin our Sturgis adventure by fulfilling a practical need so I could eliminate a worry, relax, and start to enjoy myself again. It was the kind of thing that only a superb friend does for you. So I smiled and said, "Thanks, I needed that."

He looked back with a quizzical expression, probably wondering why I'd responded that way, but chose not to ask about it. Instead, we gulped some more water and walked across the street. Theresa was right behind us. She wanted to do some shopping too.

As we'd anticipated, the dealership lot was completely stuffed with bikes and the entrance was blocked off with a large, V-shaped "LOT FULL" sign. Being careful not to touch anybody else's ride, we snaked our way between the rows and finally made it to the entrance. We figured it would be crowded, judging from the number of people that were flowing in and out, but when we stepped inside, it looked like a Walmart store on Black Friday. There were people swarming every department, especially clothing. What really struck me, however, was the number of store employees. The owners, through experience, must have known that rally week was everything—probably an enormous proportion of their annual profits—and maximizing the flow of shoppers through the store was the key. So whatever it took, they were going to find what you wanted and get you through the registers as quickly as possible with no wait time. As a result, it was teeming with employees. There were people in every aisle of every department. Each check-out counter had no less than four people working the sale: one preparing the items for scanning, one working the monetary transaction, one preparing them for packaging, and one assisting in placing them into the bags. Store employees were even easy to spot. They were all wearing bright yellow shirts, something entirely different than what any rider would wear.

After admiring the operation for a while, I wandered into the footwear department. A sweet older woman wearing the unmistakable store uniform greeted me.

Lifting my right leg a little and cocking it so she could see the underside of one of my boots, I said, "I think I need a new pair of riding boots."

Seeing that the orange skid pad, the part that's supposed to grip, was nearly smooth with wear, she responded, "Yes, sir. It sure looks like you do."

When I sat down, she started her sales pitch.

"We have all kinds of boots here," she said, "from cowboy boots to lace-up style military boots, to things that look like high-top basketball sneakers."

What I really wanted was exactly the same thing, a direct replacement. So I slid off one of my boots, handed it to her, and said, "Well, what I'd really like is something just like this, but new."

It's something that I suspect that everybody who wears cowboy boots feels at some point. It's hard enough to find the perfect pair, ones that look good with anything and feel acceptably comfortable when they're new. But over time, after they wear into a soft, perfectly conforming glove, you can't imagine life without them. So your first desire is always to find the same thing you've been wearing and don't want to part with in the first place. But I could see from the look in her eyes that I was in for a disappointment.

Trying to break it to me gently, she said, "Well . . . they haven't made these for about ten years now, but I do have something similar."

It figures, I thought. I'm out of date again. My kids regularly dig me about this; parents always seem to be at least a decade behind in everything.

My oldest son was loading some songs into my iPod once and felt compelled to razz me over one of my playlist titles. Under "Recent" I'd parked some of the songs I'd picked up from college and he thought this was somehow hilarious. "Dad," he said, "some of these are from the *nineties*."

Like that was ancient.

When she came back with a few boxes, I quickly cycled through the selections but none of them were even close. Knowing that I had a pair of combat style riding boots at home, I focused on the high-top sneaker choices. After trying on a half a dozen more, I found a pair that was reasonably nondescript looking, waterproof, and very comfortable. Even better, they had a very aggressive tread pattern across the entire heel and sole. They'd stick like tar paper.

When we reached the check-out counter, I let Jim and Theresa go first because I needed time to think about what to do with my old boots. It's something you never have to worry about with a car. The average trunk has about fifteen cubic feet of storage space and the back seats offer even more. On a bike, however, storage space is always an issue, and I had even less than the day before. I'd taken off the tour pack and replaced it with the small, passenger backrest the previous afternoon when we were detailing our bikes. All I had were the saddlebags and they were already stuffed with gear and supplies. The saddlebags on Jim's bike were even worse. He had to stow both his gear and Theresa's. So when the nice young man helping the cashier asked me what I wanted to do with them, I was torn. They still had life left in them, at least for walking, but I had no room.

After mentioning my predicament, he said, "Maybe we could ship them wherever you want."

But I figured that wasn't practical. Knowing my luck, if the store remembered to do it at all, they'd wind up somewhere in Africa and I'd have to spend weeks tracking them down.

"I guess they're yours," I said. "Do what you want, I have no room."

I still feel guilty about it.

Back out on the street, we debated for a moment and decided to take a slow tour of the area. Jim wanted to stop at a biker bar called The Broken Spoke, but we were in no rush. It was time to see what Sturgis was really like.

We started by wandering into a few of the temporary stores lining Junction Avenue, slowly absorbing what they had to offer. The first store turned out to be the most interesting. It sold T-shirts, patches, pins, bandanas, skull caps, jewelry, and souvenirs, and the variety was fantastic. Some of the patches were particularly irreverent in the way that biker humor tends to be, and I had to chuckle at them. I could just see my wife,

I thought, attending one of her tennis socials wearing her Harley leather jacket (which she's only worn once) with a patch that read, "My Sexual Preference is OFTEN," or, "LOOKING FOR A FEW GOOD RIDES." More likely, if she ever did buy a patch, it would be like the one that read, "Will Trade Husband for CUPCAKE." That was definitely more her speed.

Mostly, as I continued to browse, I realized that I was missing something that would convert me, at least in terms of dress, into more of a real biker. I didn't have a vest. Most bikers, at least those that are more into the culture, have a denim or leather jacket that goes everywhere they do and over time they place carefully chosen patches and pins onto it. Things like the club they ride with, the places they've been, and the rallies they've attended. A vest also has to convey a sense of their personality. So over time they pick up more patches, like the ones I was looking at, that give away a little bit about who they are, what they believe in, and how they think. A great vest is like a book. It tells a story. So I thought, for a moment, that maybe it was time to tell my story, that maybe I should at least take the first step and buy one. But I decided not to. It was too hard, and if I were anywhere near honest, I'd be a magnet for ridicule. Nobody walks around wearing a vest with no riding club affiliation and only a single rally patch. I'd just be advertising that I was a hopeless fake. Perhaps they should make patches for guys like me, I thought. Something like: "Yeah, I Just Started, SO WHAT," or, "You May Have Cooler Patches, but I CAN STILL KICK YOUR ASS." That one might just get me stabbed.

When we turned the corner onto Main Street, the first thing that struck us was the bikes. There was curb street parking for distance and then a single, gigantic center parking area that was created by diverting vehicle traffic onto adjacent side streets. If you put the curbside and center parking areas together, there were probably over twenty thousand bikes available for view. They even had a fifteen-foot viewing platform set up in the middle of the street. For a $5 fee, you could climb up and observe the entire spectacle and snap a few pictures.

The best bikes were usually parked along the curb. Almost all of them were heavily customized choppers, and the variety and craftsmanship were truly amazing. One bike had a serrated gas tank that looked like a lightning bolt. It must have taken a hundred man-hours of labor just to fabricate it. Others had swooping, custom-designed instrument clusters that were as intricate as jewelry. I always checked the license plates because I was curious to see where people came from. Most of them were from the Midwest, but there were also plenty from the East Coast and the Interior South, except, of course, from South Carolina. Nobody, it seemed, was interested in attending the rally from the Palmetto State.

We also engaged in some people watching, and occasionally, amongst all of the black leather jackets, pony-tails, and tattoos, we spotted some real stand-outs. My favorite was a shirtless guy standing just outside of one of the bars who looked like a character out of a *Mad Max* movie. He was huge, well over six feet, with a scarred face and the steroid enhanced musculature of a professional body builder. Wearing black leather pants and a fur-lined, leather football helmet that had two inverted steer horns sticking out of the top, he just stood there, expressionless, flexing his muscles. It was all meant to be intimidating, and it was, but my first thought was that he could have done better. A battle ax would have been an excellent complement or maybe one of those huge, spiked clubs. But I was wrong. He had another prop that I didn't see at first. It was his girl. She was standing beside him, wearing a black leather miniskirt, a bikini top, and a studded, leather dog collar. A chain was attached to the collar and he was holding it. She was on a leash.

It was hard not to stare at them, but we tried not to judge. Bikers are like that. As long as you don't look like a complete nerd and don't bother anyone, it doesn't matter how much you're into the culture or how far you take it. If you choose to go all out, that's fine. If not, that's OK too. We all know, of course, that a lot of the outrageousness is for show. The guy holding the leash probably had a job and kids and paid taxes like all of us. And he probably didn't show up for work or "parents' night" looking like that. But some people do take the outlaw culture more seriously than others and it would be rude—and potentially dangerous—to presume they're fakes. A bike rally isn't like a themed costume party where you might walk up to someone you don't know, point at something they're wearing, and say, "Hey where'd you get that? It's great!" I doubt anyone, for instance, passing "The Humungous" and his girlfriend that day said,

"Wow! Excellent hat dude! And where'd you get that dog collar? My wife's always wanted one!" Instead, out of respect for wherever anyone might fall on the biker cultural spectrum, you don't say anything. So about the only thing we did do as we walked by, like everyone else, was give him a full birth.

After a while, the basic layout of the rally started to make sense. The most important thing to the organizers, we supposed, was to keep everyone happy. The best way to do that was to provide easy access at any given point on the street to the four essential biker needs: food, booze, restrooms, and stuff. So the downtown area was essentially nothing but restaurants, food pavilions, bars, and temporary merchandise tents spaced alternately along both sides of the street. This allowed the bikers to gain access to anything they might need without having to walk very far or wait in any lines. As a result, though the crowd density was as bad as a Disney theme park during Easter week, people weren't rushing around and acting stressed out. There were no "star attractions" that you had to queue up for and wait an hour to see. Instead, people just ambled along, like us, poking their heads into various saloons, browsing through merchandise shops, scanning the bikes, and watching the people walk by. Aside from the rock music blaring from different places and the constant rumbling of the motorcycle traffic, it was actually all pretty tame.

After about an hour, our thoughts turned to food. The Broken Spoke Saloon was in the other direction, so we turned around, crossed back over Junction Avenue and found it. As soon as we stepped inside, I could see why it was so popular. Of all the places we'd visit during our time in Sturgis, it felt the most like a real biker bar. The floor was packed dirt. The seating was limited to simple, long picnic tables. A square wood-planked platform covered with skid marks served as the dance floor. The décor was also exactly what a bunch of bikers would want to see: bikes. The walls were decorated with vintage Harley-Davidson motorcycles including old Touring, Softail, and Sportster models with kick starters, manual chokes, and wire spoke wheels. The kind of bikes we all secretly admire because we know they were more persnickety and painful to ride. So the bikers back then, we also know, had to be tougher. The place wasn't very busy, probably because it was mid-afternoon, but some hardcore types were already there. About a dozen members of a gang with a bright red crest on their jackets sat at two of the picnic tables, quietly socializing and drinking.

Not sure if they served food, we decided to start with a round and found three stools at the bar. With Bill's arrest saga still fresh in our minds, we really didn't want to start drinking, but it wasn't the kind of place where you ordered a coke.

Otherwise occupied scanning the bikes on the wall, I barely noticed when the bartender delivered our drinks. After she walked away, however, when I finally got a good look at her, my eyebrows furled. Jim was similarly captivated. She was young, no more than twenty-five, with shoulder length, silky blonde hair and a body so perfectly formed you couldn't help but gawk. It wasn't fashion model thin, buxom, or particularly athletic, just balanced in a way that all significant figures tend to be. Of course, the fact that she was wearing a bikini top and lacy underwear made it easy to show off, but the way she handled herself was equally intriguing. Her movements around the bar were determined but graceful. Her small talk was engaging and mature, while her mannerisms were college girl cute. After checking her out a while longer, Jim and I turned towards each other and mouthed the word, "Wow."

My next thought came out audibly, and when he heard it, Jim silently nodded in agreement. After taking another sip of my beer, I said, "There's no way she's a local."

We never did find out where she came from, but as we'd find out later from a cab driver, my hunch was correct. A lot of the "talent" that works at the casinos, saloons, restaurants, and temporary vendor pavilions during rally week is imported. It has to be. The town issues over seven hundred temporary vendor licenses, and established businesses can see crowds that are a hundred times greater than normal. Though nearby Rapid City is relatively large, there's not enough people in the western South Dakota area to meet all of the labor requirements. Given this, advertising for temporary help goes on all year, but by early summer, employment websites bristle with opportunities. The highest demand, as might be expected, is for young, attractive females who are willing to dress in a way that bikers would appreciate. If you fall into that category, there are plenty of opportunities to make a lot of cash. The best jobs, the ones where you can make serious money, require experience. So professional dancers, bartenders, and working girls from Las Vegas, Phoenix, Denver, and other major cities flood the area during rally week and work the most famous casinos and bars, like the Broken Spoke. They can make over two thousand dollars a day just bartending. If they're willing to engage in after-hours partying with bikers who are prepared to pay for some "escort," they can make even more. A real pro can easily rake in over ten thousand dollars cash in a week.

As we wondered where she might be from, another biker called her over. He was Native American, about six foot four, and had the deeply pockmarked face of a guy who'd suffered from some pretty severe acne. Soon, he pulled out a $5 bill and we saw her nod and slip it into the top of her underwear. A moment later, she hopped up on the bar, kneeled close to him, and put her arms around his shoulders. His friend pulled out his cell phone and snapped a picture of the two of them as she smiled and stroked his chest. The fact that she was accepting tips for pictures was no big surprise to us. It was just another way of harmlessly making money. But the way she moved and handled the guy was impressive. She wasn't scared or intimidated in the least. You could tell that she knew, with complete confidence, that despite his size and badass biker appearance, she could control him like a lamb.

Looking at Jim again, I said, "She has to be a professional."

By this time Theresa had noticed her, and, unfortunately, the two of us seeing her.

"I think she's on to us," he whispered.

"Yep. We're nailed," I said.

But we weren't. Instead, with genuine enthusiasm, Theresa said, "Jim, you guys ought to take a picture with her!" Just to show that she was a good sport, she added, "And I'll even pay for it!"

Looking back at Theresa with a mixture of confusion and delight—probably because, like me, he couldn't believe it—Jim responded, "OK, I'll take that deal."

When we finally got the bartender's attention again, she glided over and asked what we needed.

Pointing at me, Jim said, "A picture with this guy if you don't mind."

After responding, "Sure!" she jumped up on the bar again, kneeled between us and threw her hair back.

Blushing and somewhat embarrassed, Jim and I looked at Theresa for any last instructions. She wanted us to move in a little closer and lean forward a bit, and the girl to lower herself a bit further. As Theresa was making her final camera adjustments, the girl, with one arm behind me and the other in front of Jim, started rubbing my back and Jim's chest. A second later Theresa snapped a photo of the three of us. It was the first, and probably the last time, I figured, that a wife would take a picture of me and her husband while a beautiful young woman fondled both of us. Only in Sturgis.

When Theresa handed her the $5 bill, I leaned in and asked, "What's your name?"

With the edge of her tongue running over her lips, she responded, "Luscious."

Jim almost spit his beer out, but after wiping his mouth, he said what was by now obvious to all of us, "Yep, she's a professional."

For the rest of the trip, whenever we engaged in girl-watching (I'd already gotten a ticket for it so I figured I might as well do some more) she was always the standard for comparison. Few others even came close.

By four o'clock in the afternoon, we were absolutely starving. Lacking the energy to try and wade through the crowd again, we walked through the parking lot of an adjacent restaurant and grabbed some grilled food from one of the temporary vendors. It wasn't great, but it was calories. Later, we wandered back to some of the clothing pavilions and I picked up the few remaining items on my shopping list. Jim also convinced me to buy an "I Rode Mine" t-shirt. Since most of the bikes at the rally are trailered or shipped, it's a point of pride these days if you actually ride there and back. I did find one but was disappointed to see that there was no way to indicate how far you'd come. It almost didn't seem fair; 1,865 miles had to be up there.

When we finally made it back to our bikes it was even hotter out, particularly at the level of the street. The afternoon sun had baked the asphalt to the point where it was radiating heat like a stove. We'd dispense with the jackets. The other part of the plan, discussed in only a few words, was to take a back road out of town. It wasn't wise, given the heat, to battle the long line of traffic now heading out of Sturgis. Interestingly enough, the traffic heading in was just as bad. A lot of people were riding in early for the evening festivities, I figured, probably trying to find better parking spaces.

Unfortunately, by the time we reached Lazelle Street again heading west back to the lodge, traffic was back to a near standstill. And like most of the riders around us at that point, we started to worry. The biggest weakness of any air-cooled Harley, all riders know, is heat. Without pressurized coolant, a radiator, and a fan, Harley engines have to rely on the air rushing over the fins of their cylinders to dissipate heat. If the bike isn't moving, the excess heat transfers to the oil circulating through the engine. Standard operating temperature for engine oil in a modern Harley V-twin on a hot day is about 235°F. But when it gets above 250°F, which is entirely possible in bumper-to-bumper (or fender-to-fender) traffic, bad things start to happen. The oil begins to rapidly oxidize, reducing its life. Oil pressure also begins to drop because, as oil heats, it thins. At 325°F, oil pressure at idle is almost zero, so the motor isn't being cooled or lubricated. It's a double whammy. Modern Harleys use synthetic oil and have engine management software that shuts down a cylinder at idle when the oil reaches a certain temperature. These features help to prolong the inevitable, but if you're stuck in traffic on a hot day on an air-cooled Harley and you don't shut down or get moving again, it will eventually self-destruct.

Bikes with fairings (Electra Glides and Street Glides of various sorts) have an oil temperature gauge built into the instrument cluster. Knowing how hot it is in any other type of bike requires the separate purchase of an oil tank thermometer. My bike has a digital one, but to read it you have to reach down with a finger and push a button. Since that requires a free hand, you can't do it while the bike is moving. So, like a lot of guys not riding fairing bikes that day, I kept periodically pushing the little button when we were stopped. At the peak, the oil temperature hit 275°F. Fortunately, when we reached the outskirts of Sturgis, traffic started to move again. By the time we were back at the lodge the oil had dropped back to 245°F. We'd dodged another bullet.

When we finally pulled into the garage and killed the engines, Jim took off his helmet and shouted, "What a day!"

Remembering that this was their first day of riding, I said. "Yeah, well, I've already had three others like this."

His response was to smile and open the top of the cooler in the garage.

The next sound we heard was the familiar "pa-pstt" of excess carbonation escaping from opening beer tops. Theresa chose to ruin the moment by asking me if I was ever going to ride without my helmet again. She didn't need to do that. I'd already made up my mind. The answer was no.

When we walked in everyone was there, including Bill. Eager to hear how their day went, we walked out onto the deck, found chairs, and settled in. Within minutes, we were all convulsing with laughter. It wasn't, as it turned out, so bad. The jail was crowded, but the guards were courteous and the other "guests" respectful. Everyone kept to themselves. The cell also had bunks, so he was able to sleep for a while. His jailers even brought them room service. For a late dinner, they offered him a bowl of Cocoa Puffs. Breakfast was Fruit Loops. None of this, he assured us, was made up.

When they finally got him out, there were plenty of advertisements for local lawyers working DUI cases. Figuring that it would be better to at least explore what they might be able to do, he called one. For a fee of $800 they could work the system, and, given the particulars of his case, probably get the citation reduced to reckless driving. The fine would still be stiff, usually at least $500, but after paying that and court costs, he could walk away. As an added bonus, the conviction would only be recorded in Meade County. It wouldn't transfer back to Pennsylvania. The courts were even respectful of the time of bikers. They didn't want them to have to travel back for a court date beyond rally week. So they staffed up and set the docket schedule to make sure they could hear all the cases before people had to leave. His case could be heard Tuesday morning. It was a no-brainer. He was going to suck it up, pay the lawyer, and get the hell out of Dodge.

When he was through with his story, we told ours. The hail saga was particularly entertaining. As we suspected, when they saw the pictures of the ice balls on our phones, no one believed it. Jim had to walk into the garage and show them the damage to his bike before they were convinced that we weren't exaggerating.

When we walked back inside the mood became more introspective. It seemed, we all agreed, that within twenty-four hours of arriving we'd all been taught some hard lessons about the Sturgis rally and riding around in the Black Hills. We needed to be completely sober before riding or driving, keep an eye on the weather, and always wear—or at least bring along—our helmets. And for the rest of the trip, we did.

Not wanting to tempt fate again, we spent the rest of the evening at the lodge. The hard party clique took the game room downstairs and drained a good case of beer. The girls camped out in the living room and chatted like sorority pledges. I broke out the scotch and joined Jim and Hector on the deck while later he brought out the cigars. They were the small cigarette type, imported from the Dominican Republic, and he assured me they were better than the fatter ones I was used to. You could smoke a bunch of these and not hate yourself for it in the morning.

He was right.

Day 5: Black Cloud Returns

Almost all motorcyclists, once they arrive at a rally, venture out at some point for day rides. You get to experience the joy of riding, see new things, and socialize with friends. A good route for a day trip combines scenic roads, unusual attractions, and reasonable distances. If the average traveling distance on an open highway for a motorcycle is about 450 miles a day, a reasonable distance for a day ride is about half of that. Any attraction that's less than about 225 miles away round trip, therefore (or 110 miles one way), is acceptable. A rider can wake up at a reasonable hour, have an excellent breakfast, ride out to the attraction and take some time to explore it, enjoy a long relaxing lunch, and arrive back at wherever they're staying by late afternoon or early evening. There's usually also plenty of time for breaks, refueling, or waiting out any weather events. The real trick is not to get too far from base camp.

One of the reasons why the Sturgis rally is so popular is there are dozens of scenic and historic attractions in South Dakota and Wyoming that are within 110 miles of the town. Popular day ride destinations include Mount Rushmore (62 miles), the Crazy Horse Memorial (67 miles), Devil's Tower, Wyoming (79 miles), Badlands National Park (110 miles), Custer State Park (75 miles), Spearfish Canyon (20 miles), and Deadwood (13 miles). More than fifty thousand motorcycles visit Mount Rushmore during rally week alone.

Since we'd all been to Deadwood, and Jim and I had already visited Spearfish, the plan for Monday was to ride into Wyoming for a short while, then cross back into South Dakota and stop at the Crazy Horse Memorial and Mount Rushmore. Then we'd ride back into Sturgis, have another later lunch or early dinner, and decide on the evening activities. Since Bill's wife, Carrie, and Alan's wife, Nancy, would be arriving by plane in the afternoon, Bill and Alan would stay behind. They also needed to work with the lawyer to prepare for Bill's court appearance the following day. Hector and Cindy would also be on their own again since their bike still hadn't arrived. This meant that Monday's day ride (Day 5 for me) would involve six riders on five bikes: Jim (with Theresa), Larry, Paul, Tom, and me. It would be the first time we'd ride together as a larger group.

Jim would be the "Road Captain," or the leader of the trip. It's a significant responsibility and harder than you would think because not only do you have to plan and organize the journey, but you also have to worry about everyone behind you. A good Road Captain selects roads and speeds that the most inexperienced rider in the group can handle. He has backup plans for all kinds of contingencies, including weather, lost riders (it's very easy to get separated, especially in traffic), fuel stops (different models have many different ranges), and breakdowns. The safety of the entire group is his or her responsibility. The Road Captain always leads and rides to the left of the center of the lane with the next rider behind and to the right, with others back in a staggered formation. Another experienced rider, the "Sweeper" usually takes the rear. The most inexperienced rider is usually right behind the Road Captain, to the right, like a sheltered duckling. I didn't know where Jim wanted me to ride, at least not yet, but I suspected he would want to keep me close. Theresa's job would be to point out road hazards with visual hand signals. She was experienced with this, as we'd find out.

The day started, as we expected, a little later than the previous one. The beer drinkers flopped out of bed at about eight thirty after we made enough noise to wake them up, and we weren't much ahead of them. It took me about ten minutes of constant teeth brushing and gargling to rid myself of the aftereffects of Hector's cigars, plus two water bottles to rehydrate. As the coffee was brewing, I vowed to take it a little easier. Most of the other guys made similar promises. When Larry came up, his generally deeply tanned face was slightly green.

His greeting was to clear his throat of phlegm and bark, "Whose fucking laundry is in the washer?"

Jim, Theresa, and the others flashed looks at each other that telegraphed a common thought: What's his problem?

I chose to reply with exaggerated cheerfulness, "Good morning, Larry!"

It had no effect.

Once we started to think more clearly, our thoughts turned to breakfast. Jim and I suggested that we stop at the same restaurant we'd been to the day before. Theresa's description of their orange juice clinched the deal. We'd leave in about an hour.

When everyone was more or less ready, we quietly filed out into the garage. It was the first time I'd actually studied Tom and Paul's bikes. Tom rode a blue Softail with an extended front fork and ape hangar handlebars—a real chopper—and when he hit the starter, we all momentarily jumped. It was so loud his mufflers must have had baffles the size of gauze pads. The windows in the garage actually shook. Paul also rode a Softail, a black Fat Boy with a stubby passenger backrest and straight pipes. What really set him apart, however, was his German pith helmet. Together with his black framed sunglasses, black leather jacket, and beard, he looked pretty fearsome. Though they didn't look it, both were actually more inexperienced riders than I was. It's often tough to tell, at least initially.

When Jim came out, he conferred with Larry and called us around. He'd take the lead, as we expected. I would stay directly behind him and to the right (he probably wanted to keep me close, knowing that his sister—my wife—would shoot him if anything happened to me). Larry would be the sweeper. But Tom objected. He was the most inexperienced rider and knew it, and because of this, he didn't like to ride very fast. He wanted to be able to trail off quickly if he had to. Larry looked at Jim and shrugged his shoulders. He didn't mind. I could tell that Jim didn't like it, but the assignments were changed. Larry would ride behind me, on my left, then Paul to the right. Tom would be the sweeper. Still hungover and groggy, about the other only thing we discussed was the weather. The forecast was about the same as yesterday's: partly cloudy with the possibility of afternoon thunderstorms accompanied by hail. If we had to stop, we would, but it wasn't going to change our plans. At least we'd all be riding with helmets.

For some reasons, the trip back into Deadwood wasn't as pleasant as the day before. I was wearing my helmet—which always reduces the pleasure—and my head was still aching from the previous night's liquor. I also had to concentrate more to stay in proper riding formation, which hurt my head even more. Although I was pretty good at staying to the right of Jim when the road was straight, it was difficult to remain in position when entering left turns because I naturally wanted to cut further into the lane. As a result, I'd drift to the left. Seeing this, Larry would fall back, as he should have, and when I'd drift back to the right again after the turn, he'd close the gap a little. Paul and Tom followed behind, a bit more spread out than was probably optimal, but not so much that we got split up by other bikes or cars. Considering that three of the five of us were fairly new to this, it actually wasn't half bad.

Breakfast turned out to be a big morale booster. By the time we were finished—and Theresa had passed out enough Advil—everyone was smiling again. After a final round of coffees, Jim went over a few more details. Instead of riding north to Spearfish, our first leg would be to the southwest, through the town of Lead on Route 85. This would take us all the way to Wyoming. To get to 85 South, we only needed to make two turns, a left out of the restaurant parking lot and then another left at the first light. As was typical of Jim, he didn't want to overload us with information. It was about all we could remember anyway.

To punctuate that point, I said, "Two lefts. Got it."

Everyone nodded. The other only tip from Jim was to wear our jackets. It was a little cooler out than yesterday and we'd be riding faster. No one objected. Within a minute, our five Harleys roared back to life.

We had been not even out of Deadwood before we lost half the group. Instead of making a left at the first light, Larry, Paul, and Tom turned right. In hindsight, it was an easy mistake to make. There were actually three turns instead of two, but I sensed something was wrong when I lost sight of Larry's lights after the turn onto Route 85. But it was hard to tell. By that time, traffic was heavy with hundreds of bikes behind us, pulling into and out of parking lots and passing in the other direction. And, of course, they were mostly all Harleys with the same light combinations.

It was a lot easier to lose someone than I thought. Jim was also having trouble, I could tell, because he kept going. A good Road Captain would have pulled over immediately to let the others catch up, and I knew he was experienced.

By the time we approached the turnoff to Spearfish, it was obvious we'd lost them. Slowing to a near crawl, I saw Jim's hazard flashers come on and we stopped in a part of the road that had a full shoulder.

Raising his arms in exasperation, he walked back to me and asked, "How the hell could they have lost us?"

Rather than pile on, I said, "Let's just wait and see if they catch up."

Obviously irritated, Jim pulled out his cell phone and speed-dialed Larry. He didn't pick up.

Just as we were discussing if we should circle back, I saw the unmistakable shine of Larry's Road King. Paul and Tom were right behind him. When they caught up with us, Larry was actually pretty good about it, giving Jim a mostly good-natured ribbing about being a lousy Road Captain. In any event, it was quickly forgotten. Once we were on Route 85, we knew things would be a lot easier. It would be all highway with no stoplights. All we had to do was ride in formation. And as long as we stuck reasonably close together, no one would bother us. It's an unwritten rule of group riding that almost all bikers know and respect: you don't mess with anybody else's group. If they pass you, they pass as a group. If you pass, you pass a group. No cutting in and out. If you decide to tag along, you come in from the rear and wait for a signal from the sweeper to see if you can slide in somewhere. Usually, the answer is no.

The ride into Wyoming was by far the best leg of the day. The sun was rising behind us, warming our backs, and the road was a winding, single lane divided highway that would occasionally widen to two lanes during hill climbs. The scenery was also spectacular, even more open than before, with grass-covered hills, forests of aspen and ponderosa pine, and rocky bluffs. Occasionally we'd even cross flat fields of gently swaying summer wheat. Larger mountains could be seen on the western horizon in blue and gray shadows, beckoning us, it seemed, to ride further. Our formation riding also improved. I stuck to Jim's right as a fighter pilot, back a safe but respectable distance, and Larry rode on my left wing, dropping back a little in turns so I could take more of the lane.

Paul and Tom also followed as they should have, with Tom keeping up a bit better. Theresa was also a pro at pointing out road hazards and we all learned to take her hand signals seriously. If she looked to the right and down, you could bet there was something you wanted to avoid and we'd drift a little to the left. Or vice versa. The road surface was worn in sections with some old crack repairs and she saved us from every one of them. I was having so much fun I almost forgot where we were, but the "Caution: Big Horn Sheep Crossing" signs brought me back to reality. You don't see those in the East.

A while later we turned south towards Newcastle, and when the landscape opened up to our right revealing a broad, deep valley, the sound of Jim's pipes trailed off. Theresa made the slowing hand signal (both hands pointed down and back and waving slightly) so there was no need to interpret his brake lights. We were stopping. A moment later he pulled off into a scenic overlook called Salt Creek.

One by one, without saying much, we dismounted, stretched, and absorbed the scenery. It was so peaceful no one wanted to spoil anything. After a while, we broke into some small talk about the weather, which, while still acceptable, had noticeably deteriorated. The sky was now mostly occluded with low, gray clouds that seemed to be heading towards us and the air had cooled with just a hint of mist. But we were all still happy. Everyone had kept up, no one was cold (at least not yet), the rain had held off, and the ride had been exhilarating. To celebrate, Theresa snapped a picture of the "five guys" with the Red River Valley behind us. As we saddled up again, Jim reminded us of the next turns. We all ignored him. It wasn't necessary to know. He was a competent Road Captain; all we had to do was follow. We could afford to be lazy.

By the time we were back into the Black Hills of South Dakota again, the low gray clouds that were streaming to the East had caught up with us. They'd also formed into more organized thunderheads with lower, darker, bulbous bottoms. Jim kept our speed up to about 60 mph, but when we started to descend into the lower valleys, the road twisted so badly we were down, at times, to less than half of that. On some of the descents, I was so focused on staying in the right position and not gaining too much speed. Using a combination of engine braking and a light application of the front and rear brakes, I completely missed the scenery.

At one point, deep in a valley between two ridges, Jim pulled over and we took a break.

Theresa, clearly elated, pulled off her helmet and exclaimed, "Wasn't that awesome! I've never seen such beauty! Did you guys see it?"

The others quietly nodded, but Tom and I just looked at each other with guilty expressions. We were thinking the same thing. We'd been so focused on the road and negotiating the turns correctly we hadn't noticed anything around us.

When we told Jim, he laughed and said, "The time will come after you have enough experience when taking turns like that will come naturally."

Tom replied with a sarcastic chuckle, "Well, that's a long way off for me."

I was getting better but wondered when I'd get to the point of being that comfortable.

Jim grabbed my arm, as if reading my mind, and said, "It takes twenty thousand accumulated miles."

Damn, I thought, I'm less than halfway there.

The rain held off, with only a few teasing sprinkles, but by the time we turned onto the access road for the Crazy Horse Memorial, the "black cloud" had overspread the area. Wanting to beat the rain, we found some parking spaces as quickly as possible, shut down and scurried under the overhang of the welcome center building. Thunder was rumbling in the distance, but for now, at least, we were safe and dry. Our plan was to take our time seeing the attraction and wait for the storm to pass. Apparently a lot of other bikers had the same idea because the lines to the ticket counters were packed.

I'm not sure what I was expecting, but the next two hours, to say the least, were a very pleasant surprise. The tour starts with a film covering the history of the memorial, which was fascinating. As the story goes, in 1942, a Lakota Sioux Chief named Henry Standing Bear asked a Polish sculptor known for his work on Mount Rushmore to build a memorial for the great Oglala Lakota War Leader, Crazy Horse. The idea was to pick a mountain site in the Black Hills that had an enormous granite face and carve it, over time, into the most major rock sculpture in the world. The sculptor, Korczak Ziolkowski, built a scale model and the Lakota elders approved the project. The memorial would resemble the upper torso of Crazy Horse, sitting on his stallion, pointing out towards the Black Hills. It was a pose meant to depict what he might have looked like as he uttered one of his most remembered quotes. When asked by federal authorities once where he thought his lands were, Crazy Horse pointed to the Black Hills and said, "My lands are where my dead lie buried." Those lands were ceded to the Lakota and other tribes in the Treaty of Fort Laramie in 1868 but seized again by the U.S. Government in 1877. It's been a source of friction with the Lakota ever since.

The scale of the task was daunting. The basic footprint of the memorial would be 563 feet high, 641 feet long, and 175 feet wide, before carving. Assuming that almost two-thirds of the material would be blasted and chiseled away, that's still about 22,000,000 cubic feet of solid granite. To put that in perspective, the Washington Monument in Washington, DC is 555 feet high and its total volume is 22,000 cubic feet. So the Crazy Horse memorial, when finished, will be roughly a thousand times as large in size and actually a bit taller. It will also completely dwarf Mount Rushmore. The faces of the presidents there are 60 feet high while Crazy Horse's head is 87.5 feet high. All four of the presidents' faces on Mount Rushmore, in terms of volume, could fit inside of Crazy Horse's head alone.

Aside from the scale, the other significant challenge was that the Lakota elders and the sculptor wanted development of the memorial to be privately funded. They didn't trust the government. There would also be no general contractor. Korczak Ziolkowski would have to do the work himself with minimal assistance and no starting infrastructure. It would take a lifetime of singular dedication to the task, and, given the scale, it wouldn't be finished until well after he died. Still, he accepted the challenge.

After constructing an access road, building a log home for himself and his wife, Ruth, and erecting a stairway leading to the face with 741 steps (the Washington Monument has 897 steps), work began in 1948. The primary process was simple, and it's still followed today. Measurements from the scale model were transferred to the rock face using precision measuring equipment. The material was blasted away using explosives, the blasted material was removed, and the remaining surface was shaped and finished using air-driven jackhammers and hand chisels. In the early days, it was all done by Korczak, working alone, with rudimentary equipment that broke down regularly. His first air compressor, called "Buda," was especially troublesome. Several times a day, after he'd walk up a staircase equivalent to a fifty story building carrying forty pounds of tools, its motor would stall. Then he'd have to walk all the way back down, manually adjust whatever was ailing the machine, restart it, and walk back up. But little by little, day by day, work progressed.

Ruth's workload was equally as impressive. Over the years, she would bear and raise ten children, start and run a dairy and sawmill, and manage all of the financial aspects of the projects. Along the way, donations of all kinds continued to pour in, and over time, seven of their children joined the effort. They also built, more recently, a forty thousand square foot welcome center and a Museum of American Indian History that's one of the best in the country. Over one million visitors stroll through each year. But it's still only about fifty percent completed. The face is done (completed in 1998). Work is progressing faster now, mainly because it's better funded. The equipment today is more sophisticated, but it will likely take another twenty or thirty years—for a total of a full century—before it's finally finished.

The museum was also better than we expected, with impressive displays of artifacts, territorial maps, and paintings. My favorite part, however, was the actual photographs of tribal chiefs and elders taken in the early part of the twentieth century, the last generation that actually participated in a lot of the defining Indian War battles between 1860 and 1885. You could see in their leather-like, deeply wrinkled faces the hardship and sorrow of their long struggle. But they also looked proud, content, and dignified in a way, I suspected, that was meant to reassure future generations. We could take away their land and their way of life, but not their spirit. I wondered if we could ever be that gracious.

There's also a replica of the Ziolkowski's first log cabin house with some of their original furnishings. But by the time we'd seen that and browsed a while in the gift shop, our minds were totally saturated. It was time to check what the weather was like.

I was the first to break outdoors. Overall, it looked like it was clearing. The menacing thundercloud that had chased us into the compound in the first place had moved on and there were visible patches of blue sky between higher banks of broken gray clouds. Rays of the sun were poking through them and occasionally bathing the deck in the sunlight. Warming ourselves like reptiles, we lingered on benches for a while and then snapped a few pictures with the memorial in the background. But soon, we all knew it was time to leave.

By the time we were standing by our bikes again, the black cloud had returned. Coming in from the northeast, it soon blocked out the sun. Moments later, as we were using our feet to back out of our parking spaces, it started to rain. The bands were light and sporadic, but rumbles of thunder could be heard echoing through the hills to the south. Trusting Jim, we didn't say anything, and he didn't say much in terms of a pre-brief. We were to follow him to Mount Rushmore in the same formation. That was it. So immediately after firing up, we fell into a line on the access road, as directed. What we didn't realize was that his plan, upon reaching Route 385 again, was to turn south towards Custer City. If we did this, just like yesterday, we'd be riding right under the menacing cloud.

As soon as we turned south onto Route 385, the weather rapidly deteriorated. The rain started to intensify with large drops that were bouncing off of the pavement and the black cloud lowered further, touching the taller hills, it seemed, with bands of gray fog. Already thinking that this was a wrong idea, I was relieved to see Jim's brake lights come on and we followed him over to the shoulder, closing the distance between us as we stopped. He apparently wanted to talk about it. A few seconds later, with our bikes still idling, I heard the familiar "tink tink tink" sound, only louder. It was hailing again. While not as bad as yesterday, maybe pea to marble sized, it was still quickly overspreading the road. When Jim reached Larry, who was closest to him, they both shut down and I listened as they debated the options. Jim thought we should wait it out by the side of the road. Larry thought we should head back to the memorial. I wasn't sure and didn't really care. I was just happy to have my helmet on—but a second later a lightning bolt shot out of the thundercloud and struck the hill ahead of us. It was a terrifying flash, thick and crooked looking, and the booming thunderclap associated with it scared Theresa so badly she jumped out of her seat and screamed.

That was it for Larry. After shouting, "Fuck this!" the next thing I heard was the sound of his pipes crackling to life. Executing a U-turn so fast his footboards scraped the ground, he took off in the other direction—north—with the roar of his V-twin revving all the way to its first gear redline. I was actually amazed he hadn't slid out.

Jim, trying to manage a feeble smile, said to the rest of us, "I guess we're heading in the other direction."

And one by one, turning a lot more carefully, we did.

The only problem was Larry didn't know where he was going. He hadn't studied the maps and Jim hadn't said anything about the turns we'd take to get to Mount Rushmore. So he just kept barreling blindly north, trying to outrun the storm. Once we managed to get ahead of it, he slowed, Jim passed, and we fell back into our standard formation. But we were well north of where we needed to be, almost to the town of Hill City. Theresa got us back on track, tapping Jim on the shoulder and pointing out the turns necessary to wind our way to Mount Rushmore. Mostly, we wound up making a slow clockwise loop around the storm. It wasn't pretty, but we'd survived.

When we finally stopped in the Mount Rushmore parking garage, I could tell that Jim was agitated. And I knew why. Larry had usurped his authority as Road Captain, and even though he'd probably be right (we needed to get away from the storm), he should have let Jim take the lead again sooner. I tried to smooth things over, but as we walked past the entrance to the memorial, Jim was still stewing. "It's not easy, you know," he grumbled, "I don't need to do this; let him map out all of the rides and watch everyone."

Trying to lighten the mood, I started pointing out irrelevant facts regarding the state flags that were hanging along the walkway to the viewing platform. Stuff like North Dakota and South Dakota became states in 1889 while Oklahoma, which was settled earlier, didn't join until 1907. And Hawaii's State Flag is the only one that incorporates the British Union Jack. A little girl also watching helped. I could see his eyeballs moving under his sunglasses as some of the sexier biker chicks walked by, and so were mine. I wondered if the presidents up on the rock face were also spying them. Jefferson, in particular, was no priest.

In any event, it worked. By the time we arrived on the viewing platform, Jim was smiling again. After we had swapped phone cameras a few times to take pictures of ourselves in front of the monument, we discussed our impressions. The best part, we agreed, was the platform. Situated less than a hundred yards away from the bottom of the mountain face, it was close enough so you could actually see the detail of the finished sixty-foot faces. It was also easily accessible. To see Crazy Horse up close, you had to take a small bus down an access road (something we never did). The viewing platform at Mount Rushmore, on the other hand, was within a walkable distance from the entrance. But it went downhill from there. The faces, at least from the platform, still looked surprisingly small. And there wasn't much else to see. There was a gift shop filled with cheap souvenirs and other trinkets, an overpriced cafeteria, and a bookstore, but no museum. Given this, we all agreed that it was a "once-and-doner", something you have to see before you die, but once you've checked it off your bucket list there's no need to go back. So by the time we linked up with the others and found our respective bikes in the garage again, we couldn't wait to get back on the road.

Jim, still brooding a little, kept his brief short, saying only, "Follow me. Same formation. Route 16 to Rapid City then I-90 to Sturgis. We get off at Junction Avenue."

Sensing the tension, Larry did his best to acknowledge Jim's role as the Road Captain, saying, "OK boss, we've got your wing."

I wondered how long their new peace would last.

The ride into Sturgis was uneventful except an encounter with a reckless rider, or, in biker jargon, a SQUID (Stupidly Quick, Underdressed and Imminently Dead). It happened on the last leg of the ride on Interstate 90 about ten miles outside of Sturgis. We were traveling in relatively tight formation at about 70 mph in the right lane with another small group ahead of us. A larger group was also approaching to pass us on the left. Watching the approaching group in my left side mirror, I saw a lone bike rapidly approaching Tom (still in last position) from behind at a speed that had to be at least 90 mph. Just at the point when I thought the maniac was going to have to commit to slam on his brakes. He swerved around Tom into the left lane just ahead of the group that was about to pass, narrowly missing both Tom and their Road Captain in the process. He wanted to pass the group ahead of us too, but they were

Day 1
South Carolina to Kentucky
685 Miles

Day 2
Kentucky to Iowa
765 Miles

Day 3
Iowa to South Dakota
460 Miles

Day 4
South Dakota

Day 4
Hail Storm from Hell

Day 4
Jim and Theresa

Day 4
Sturgis

Day 5
Wyoming

Day 5
Crazy Horse

Day 5
Crazy Horse Unfinished

Day 6
Mount Rushmore

Day 6
*Full Throttle Saloon
(burnt down 2015)*

Ann Marie
"Ringing of the Bell"

*Last Chemotherapy
Treatment*

November 2012

drifting to the left. His decision was to cut right, straight towards Larry, rapidly slow and wait a second or two.

To his credit, Larry didn't panic. He just calmly drifted over towards me. As I fell back, I was able to get a better look at the intruder. He was about thirty-five, with a colored neck tattoo and swept back sunglasses. He didn't seem all that crazy, except for the fact that he wasn't wearing any protective equipment, but it was tough to tell. His bike was a Harley, of course, but highly customized. A lowered Street Glide with sparkled magenta paint, purple flames and one of those short, highly smoked and useless windshields. The engine air intake was forward-pointed chrome and a black lance that was meant to look mean, and it did. Just when I'd finished studying his bike, he took off again. And since it still wasn't clear which way the group ahead of us was moving, he chose to downshift, floor it and split them right down the middle.

I don't know about the others, but for a moment I stopped breathing, waiting for the melee to begin. Bike accidents in a situation like this usually start with someone touching somebody else and one of the riders panicking. The overreaction then leads to a rear tire skid that snakes increasingly wildly from side to side, then a lay down accompanied by the sound of screeching metal and helmets (or heads) cracking against the pavement. Occasionally, if the physics are right, there can even be a side over side bike flip with the sound of crunching metal and breaking plastic that degenerates, as the bike dies, into a tumble of half-connected parts. And that's just one bike. When you put a half dozen together, all snaking, laying down, flipping, and crashing into each other, with a whole other group behind ready to join in (which would have been us), it can become quite a spectacle.

But it didn't happen. The riders in the group turned out to be experienced and they did exactly what they should have done: nothing. They all held station, without slowing, weaving, or trying any evasive maneuvers and the SQUID threaded through them as if they were stationary cones on a track. When he was ahead of them—and I was breathing again—he slowed for a moment, lifted his rear end out of his saddle, and cocked his head as far backward as he could, looking at all of us. Jim shook his head and Larry flipped him the bird, but no one else did anything. The SQUID, probably feeling a little bit guilty, gave us a half salute downward with a free hand, but his self-reflection didn't last long. A second later he downshifted again and roared off. We could still hear his pipes long after we'd lost sight of him. He was *moving*.

When we rolled into town, we found the same parking lot next to the Harley dealership and shut down. Since it was already close to five o'clock, food was the first subject of discussion, and Jim suggested that we try the Broken Spoke. By now everyone had heard the story about Luscious. But the other guys wanted to try something different, a place in the other direction down Main Street. It wasn't a hard sell since we never did eat at the Spoke, so Jim quickly agreed. After moving in a slow, disorganized wander, we found it.

It was a more typical restaurant and biker bar combination, with a linoleum tiled floor, a large gathering area in front of the bar, tables in the back, and a small dance floor that was surrounded by various game machines. The walls were decorated with all kinds of disorganized paraphernalia, from bike parts to ranch gear to nostalgic posters. We didn't say much before our waitress arrived, but once the food orders were in the conversation picked up. Larry mentioned the SQUID and we all wondered if he was still living. We'd heard sirens wailing to the west when we'd turned off onto Junction Avenue. They could have been for him. Paul, like me and Jim, was very impressed with Crazy Horse but underwhelmed by Mount Rushmore. Tom was just happy to be with us. He never got to ride like this back home.

With lunch—and what also turned out to be dinner—behind us, the guys wanted to pick up a few merchandise items, so we decided to split up and meet back at the bikes. Jim asked me what I wanted to do, and the only thing I could think of was something that had been nagging at me for some time. I thought it would go away after I arrived at the lodge and we started the shorter day rides. But it was getting progressively worse. The day before, I hadn't noticed it until we were nearly to Sturgis. Today, it had started right after we left the overlook in Wyoming. I was embarrassed to admit it because you never want to admit a physical weakness. The truth was my rear end was absolutely aching, from my sit bones straight through the flesh in my hind quarters and all the way to my hips. If it continued to worsen, I wasn't going to be able to complete the rest of the day rides, much less get back home.

When I told Jim about my "problem", he laughed and said, "That's nothing new. It's the reason why bikers who can ride a thousand miles in a single day are called 'iron butts.'"

Physically, it's tough to get around. When you sit in a saddle, the weight of your body puts enormous pressure on your sit bones and the surrounding tissue, reducing blood flow and ventilation, and over time the area begins to ache. The best way to alleviate this on a bike is to stop, get off, and rest, but picking the right saddle can undoubtedly help.

The first consideration is the type of riding you do. In general, wider softer saddles are better for shorter rides and firmer, narrower saddles are more appropriate for longer trips. The fit is even more critical. The proper width of a saddle should be slightly larger than the distance between your sit bones, and that varies for everyone. Women, in general, given their pelvic structures, require wider saddles than men. The type of bike also matters because there are constraints associated with each design. Touring bikes like mine have a full frame so the saddles tend to be wider. A saddle on the average Electra Glide wouldn't fit on a Sportster. It would hang over the frame of the bike like a muffin top.

Given all of the variables and constraints, it's virtually impossible to design a saddle for a particular model of bike that will fit everyone perfectly for every riding situation. In fact, you can almost guarantee the opposite. The odds for my particular Road King, for instance, were definitely stacked against me when I bought it. I have a relatively small waist and a compact rear end for a middle-aged man. The average male Road King rider, at least from my observation, is usually heftier, and the average woman, while smaller, has wider hips. So my seat, if the designers tailored it for the "average" rider (which they do for each model), was in all likelihood too broad. Great for short trips, but lousy for long trips.

"The natural solution," Jim said as we walked along, "is to buy a gel pad. The material on the pad relieves some of the pressure and they're easy to fit. Most just lay right on top of the saddle and attach with a little Velcro or straps. Sometimes you don't even need that. As long as you're sitting on it, it won't move."

Listening to our conversation while studying her rally guide, Theresa jumped in with an idea. "There's an advertisement in here for a

Pavilion on Main Street that sells them. If my map is right, it's about a ten-minute walk to the west."

"OK," I responded, "then that's where we're headed."

Jim was all for it too. Although he'd changed his saddle out a few years ago, including Theresa's passenger seat, they still weren't satisfied. Maybe we'd get lucky and find something for all of us.

The pavilion was right where Theresa thought it would be and we walked up to the counter, eager to see their products. A tall woman with shoulder-length blonde hair greeted us.

"Hi," I said, "do you have any gel pads that would fit on top of a Road King seat?"

"Ya," she replied in a Scandinavian accent, "we have something even better!"

After turning around, she walked to the back of the pavilion and started rifling through some boxes. As she was trying to find what she was looking for, we were able to get a better look at her. She was dressed, like a lot of the woman at the rally, in a provocative short black leather miniskirt with a similarly revealing open belly tank top. Jim and I tried to guess her age, but it was difficult. Her skin was smooth and she was reasonably fit, but the wrinkles around her eyes and lips suggested mid-forties. When she finally made it back to the counter holding a fur covered gel pad, I expected her to dive straight into her sales pitch. Instead, she stepped up on a small stool, bent over, and pulled me closer.

"You have to feel this," she said, stroking the fur, "its sheepskin. It will keep your butt warm in the winter and cool in the summer. Go ahead, stroke it."

I was trying to concentrate, but it wasn't easy. She was slightly above me and leaning over in a way that was meant for me to look directly at her cleavage, and since she wasn't wearing a bra, I didn't have much of a choice. If she bent over another eighth of an inch, I figured, I'd get the whole picture. Jim was trying to suppress a smile by holding a hand partially over his mouth, and Theresa was looking away, but mostly, I was embarrassed. It really wasn't necessary to get the sale. I was going to buy a damn gel pad, no matter how it was covered. My ass hurt so much, I would have bought a whoopee cushion. She had me.

But since she seemed to be genuinely more interested in having me look at her chest than the sale, I obliged and gave it a good stare. They were relatively large (C-cup), nicely rounded, and perky, but something wasn't right. There were ridges of tougher, raised skin on the edges of each breast as they tapered into her chest. Noticing that I was now checking her out, she smiled and kept going with her sales pitch, but I stopped listening. A conversation I'd had with an old friend about six months ago drifted into my mind and I replayed it because it offered clues. He'd recently been through a divorce and was describing what it was like to date again, in his forties, relative to when we first started in high school.

"It's so much better," he began. "You're a ton more confident, you don't have to play games, and you usually know, within an hour of the first date, if you're compatible. If you are, it's great because things move quickly. If not, you walk away and move on. And," he added, "I've learned a lot about boob jobs. I can tell a good one from a bad one now."

I didn't ask because I didn't want to seem like a sexual neophyte, but I wondered how he could tell. None of the girls I'd dated in high school or college, I was pretty sure, had been cosmetically altered. And my wife was still natural.

As she continued to drone on about the benefits of viscoelasticity and the breathing characteristics of sheepskin, I realized that what I was probably looking at was a bad boob job. It had to be. They looked like they'd been shot in her chest from a cannon. But it didn't matter. She appeared to be happy, even proud, and all I wanted was a gel pad. So after listening to the rest of her spiel, I forked over $125 for the sheepskin version. In the days ahead, I'd be glad I did. It was everything she said it would be.

On the way back to meet the others, we stopped at a large outdoor pavilion that displayed new Harleys. Since it's the one dominant motorcycle brand at the rally, everyone's always interested in seeing the latest technology enhancements and styling trends, particularly as embodied in their Customs Vehicle Operations (CVO) offerings. CVO bikes are Harley-Davidson models that are heavily customized right from the factory. With different and usually more elaborate paint jobs, engine power enhancements, and dozens of popular accessories that are blended into a distinctive, "themed" arrangement. Although expensive, they're very popular because they hold their value better than if you bought a stock bike and customized it yourself, and they also limit the production, making them somewhat rare. Every year they change the CVO mix, sometimes tailoring the same models while at other times dropping or adding new ones. The first CVO Road King, for instance, came out in 2001. They didn't get back to that model again until 2007, and then they customized it again (though differently) in 2008. The 2012 CVO offerings include a Softail "Convertible" (both touring and cruising capabilities), a Street Glide (a fairing bike, like an Electra Glide, but sexier), a Road Glide (fairing attached to the frame), and an Ultra Classic Electra Glide (the "Big Mama" of Harleys).

There were several new bikes on display and they drew a lot of gawkers, but the largest crowd was gathered around the 2012 CVO Road Glide. It even had its own viewing platform that held it upright on both sides so you could mount the saddle without having to worry about dropping it. Every Harley sales manager has their own stories of customers dropping bikes within the dealership and of the resulting damage (sometimes rows of bikes fall like dominos), which is why they generally always want a salesperson to be with you, especially if you wish to sit on one. It makes sense. They're expensive machines. Today, most of them cost as much as a car.

CVO models are usually offered with two different paint schemes, and the Road Glide on display that day was an off white, matte black combination. It was an excellent machine, a lot of the parts that would have been chrome ten years ago were blacked out. And it had all the latest doodads, but what I really wanted to see was how it felt. So when it was my turn, I mounted the saddle and grabbed the handlebars. Jim and Theresa were watching me like doting parents, waiting for a signal as to whether or not I liked it.

I didn't. It was racy, classy, and very well balanced, but it just didn't feel right. The handlebar and grips were thinner and everything about it felt lighter and less substantial. It's one of Harley's largest and heaviest bikes, so engineering-wise they did a marvelous job, but I'd grown accustomed to the feel of my Road King. And I realized, at that moment, that I'd crossed another threshold. My bike had become like a favorite pair of cowboy boots or jeans. We'd worn into each other.

It starts with the fit. Despite the fact that motorcycle seats don't have many adjustments, there are dozens of other minor changes and modifications that most riders make to their bike so it physically fits them better. I'd forgotten, for instance, that I'd already adjusted the shifter, the highway pegs, the angle of the handlebar, and the rider backrest on my bike. Another thing that all riders learn, over time, is how their bike runs. Not just how everything works, but how it *feels* when it's running because the sounds and vibrations of the motor and drive-train are transmitted right through your body. My Road King, for instance, runs and rides noticeably differently a hundred miles before and after a major service. Before the maintenance, the shifts feel sloppier, the motor runs with a little bit of "thrash," and it trembles a little when braking. Afterward, it just seems tighter in all respects.

The final piece of the puzzle is handling, and processing on a two-wheeler is all about balance. And the balance depends on weight distribution. Given how much Harleys are typically accessorized, the weight of the bike and how the weight is distributed can change considerably. When you add it all up, it means that no two bikes, even if they're the same model, will fit, run, and handle—to the same rider—exactly the same. It's almost impossible.

As you wear into each other, the rider and the bike also become more of a team. Like a good horse, you learn its personality, what it likes and doesn't like, and how it responds to various commands and your movements. And, over time, you begin to work together more effortlessly. I could tell, for instance, if my Road King was heating up by how much heat was radiating up through the seat, and by how the air felt hitting my legs as it rushed over the cylinder cooling fins. The oil tank thermometer was nice, but I didn't really need it anymore. I was also starting to handle the wind better. I knew about how far it would lean for a particular force of a gust, so I was instinctively countering the effect more accurately. I also knew, by sound and feel, when to shift. How fast it would slow with engine braking. How many times the starter would turn over the engine before it would catch, and a hundred other idiosyncrasies that made riding it easier, safer, and more enjoyable. I wasn't about to trade all of that—and start all over again—for better wind stability and a stereo.

Jim saw it in my eyes and gave me a reassuring nod. He wasn't going to trade either. But something else was gnawing at me. I'd decided to keep my bike for the foreseeable future, but it was time, I thought, to formally recognize our relationship. I wasn't getting sappy; it was, after all, only a machine. Yet in many ways it was like a boat. It operated in a hostile environment, it was significantly affected by weather, it required deft handling, and I depended on it for survival. And all good boats have a name. I also knew, as an ex-Navy guy, something else, a tradition that's been in place for thousands of years, at least in Europe and the West. In a time when most sea captains were men and were married, they named their boats after women. So, I reasoned, my bike should have a name, and it should be female. It would be bad luck to keep riding it without one.

On the way back to the lodge, sitting on my new sheepskin gel pad. I kept trying to think of a proper name, rattling through dozens of female names like you do when you're expecting a child, but nothing seemed to fit. She wasn't one of those older lady names like Gertrude, Agnes, Maude, or Dorothy, and she wasn't a more famous modern name like Kim or Emily. And she certainly wasn't a cutie pie like an Amber, Chastity, or Cinnamon. If I ever referred to my bike with a name like that, I wouldn't live long.

After we pulled into the garage and shut down, Jim and Larry said they wanted to wash their bikes. We'd ridden through plenty of rain around Mount Rushmore and a few light bands on the way into Sturgis, so they were all pretty grimy again. It was also a way, I figured, for them to bury the hatchet and bond again. A good bike washing, working side by side, and the Road Captain spat would be forgotten. Guys are like that. We don't hold grudges.

With not much else to do, I said I'd join them. A few minutes later, our three Road Kings were backed onto the concrete landing. Larry grabbed the wash materials and I brought up the hose. Jim passed out beers. This was going to be fun.

As I was washing and rinsing her off, I thought about how we'd come together. She was my second bike. My first was a 2001 Softail that I bought new from a dealer in Manchester, New Hampshire. The owner was a neighbor and his salespeople did a nice job, allowing me to sit on just about every bike they had before deciding which one was the best "starter" bike for me. The Heritage Classic model was configured like a touring bike but had a slightly narrower frame and lower seat height. It was also the first year they added the balance shaft to the twin-cam 88s in Softails. Since the engine is frame mounted in a Softail without rubber engine mounts, it greatly reduced vibration at idle. So compared to a touring bike, it was a little easier to handle and a lot smoother. The color was a stock two-tone green and black and I liked it because it was very close to the color of a great car I'd once owned. My wife loved the studded leather saddlebags.

Over the next few years, however, I couldn't leave it alone. I souped up the engine. Switched out the pipes, changed the saddlebags to the hard lockable type (my wife never forgave me), and started chroming everything—right down to the bolts that held the transmission and timing chain covers. I was experimenting and learning, but it was getting expensive. My wife also started to get resentful. She wanted to do some significant improvements to the house, and the truth was I was hardly riding it. With our kids in their most active school years and my job consuming more and more time, I was stealing away for an hour ride to our house maybe once a month. In 2005, I didn't even clock a thousand miles.

By that time, something else was grating on me as well. I'd gone too far with it. I was a typical executive rider with more money than time and I'd added so much chrome to it that it became garish. I'd turned it into a piece of bling, an overdone toy, a chrome candy bar. And I started liking it less and less. So when we were deep into the middle of a home improvement project that was way over budget, as they always tend to be, I agreed to let it go. Someday, I thought, I'll get back into it, maybe when the kids are off to college. A lot of riders go into and out of the sport, that's nothing new.

What I didn't expect was that I'd miss riding so much. Within a few years, I was quietly slinking into dealerships on the way home from work, checking out the latest machines. Maybe I could talk her into getting another bike, I told myself. Use your charm. You can work this.

The negotiation went surprisingly well. The new kitchen helped. The only real concession I had to make was to agree to buy one used. Overflowing with excitement, the next step was to figure out what I wanted. This time, since I was more experienced, I was going to move up a notch in size to a touring bike. But I still didn't think I was ready for the fairing type. So I settled on a Road King. I also liked a lot of power and the look of a customized bike (as long as it's not overdone). But I didn't want to go through the hassle of doing it myself or take an enormous financial hit if I ever sold it. That left only one viable option, a CVO Road King, and, as of 2009, they'd only made them in four years: 2001, 2002, 2007, and 2008.

One of the things I was never "into" as a kid was flames. I loved muscle cars like most of the guys I grew up with, but I never liked the kind with fat rear tires, mag wheels, hood scoops, and flames. It was all too in-your-face. My favorite cars were always "sleepers." Stock looking models with whitewall tires and vinyl roofs with only an engine badge. Dual exhausts and a rear sway bar that indicated that there was something more serious lurking under the hood (my Mom's Delta '88 was a classic sleeper). Chrome was always welcome because it added a touch of class, but that's all that was otherwise needed. Some guys liked Boss Mustangs and tricked out looking Camaros. I was always drawn to cars like the Chevy Monte Carlo or Pontiac Grand Prix and some of the sportier versions of the larger cars, like the Chevy Impala SS and the Ford Galaxy 500 XL. Because of this, all of my cars through the years have been sleepers of one kind or another, and none of them have had flames.

2001, 2002, and 2007 CVO Road King models had flame paint jobs, and on the 2007 model they even etched flames into the leather of the seats and the saddlebags. The guy who designed it must have been some kind of a pyromaniac. In 2008, however, they went in another direction, with more elegant two-tone paint jobs that allowed the colors, rather than the flames, to convey the sportiness. One of the color schemes, in particular, caught my eye. It was called "Smokey Gold and Black," but the gold portion—which was really a metallic burnt orange—was very close to the color of my first car. It was a Canyon Copper 1971 Pontiac LeMans two-door hardtop with a dark brown vinyl top. And like all of my cars, it was a sleeper. The 2008 Screamin' Eagle Road King was a two-wheeled reincarnation of it. I had to have one.

They'd already been out a year, but that was perfect. I'd have to buy it used. My wife hadn't said, after all, *how* used. So over the next few months, I scoured eBay and other used bike websites looking for one. One day, I got lucky. A dealer in Annapolis, Maryland had just taken one into inventory. It was Smokey Gold and Black. The previous owner had already changed out the pipes (stock Harley pipes, because of federal emissions regulations, are always very tame sounding, so most riders change them out very quickly) and added a few other enhancements. It was expensive, but it was located only an hour from where I lived at the time. Two days later, I took the afternoon off and drove out to see it.

As soon as I saw it, I knew. We haggled a bit, and I even walked out at one point, but a couple of hours later I signed the paperwork. Not wanting to overdo things again, the only thing I wanted to change, at least at that point, was the lighting. While almost all stock Road Kings come with passing lamps (the small lamps on either side of the main headlight), the factory removes them for CVO versions, presumably because it makes them look sportier. I wanted them back; they're a mandatory safety item, at least for me. The look to oncoming cars of the Harley triple light combination is unmistakable. I wanted to convert the rear turn signals into additional taillights. We worked all of that into the deal.

As I was walking out, I realized that I hadn't even started it and listened to the pipes, so I had them roll the bike into the service bay and hit the starter. They weren't quite as loud as I would have liked, but they were good enough and I liked the styling. The previous owner had also modified the right side exhaust to add a small loop around the transmission area so it would be as long as the left side pipe and equalize the back pressure. He'd added a cone-shaped, low restriction air cleaner. Both of these enhancements would give it even more power.

The following week, my wife drove me over and I picked it up. I was so excited I left my regular glasses dangling from the "V" in my t-shirt and as soon as I hit highway speed, they flew off. Minutes later I circled back and found them right in the middle of the freeway, undamaged. It was a good sign. She'd be lucky. I also discovered another thing on the way home. For a big bike, she *moved*. I had to be especially careful in first gear because once I cracked the throttle, even a little, she was instantly doing 25 mph. If I ever have to ride this thing slowly, I thought, it's not going to be easy. Everything else was great.

Two years later, having already changed out the windshield, the only thing she was missing was a name. So as I finished washing her, I kept thinking of candidates. Finally, it came to me.

It had happened only about a month ago, but as the event started to replay in my mind, I realized its meaning. A neighbor of mine who rides had asked me if I wanted to take a short day ride with him to the nearby town of Beaufort, South Carolina. It was a perfect Low Country summer day. Warm and humid but not too sunny, and all we were going to do was ride there, find a restaurant by the Broad River, have a relaxing lunch, and ride home. He rode a blacked out, souped-up Harley V-Rod, which is about as far from a Road King within the Harley model lineup as you can get. They're small, water-cooled bikes and they look like they can do a hundred miles an hour in first gear. He'd taken him even further. The pipes had bypasses that kicked in at higher rpms that made it sound like a dive-bombing fighter plane.

Somewhere on South Carolina Route 170, we both stopped at a light. Smiling at each other as the light aged, we started to blip our throttles, listening to our pipes pop. We both knew, of course, what that meant. With no one behind us and the road ahead clear, there was no way we were going to start moving out again like responsible adults. My strategy, given the weight of my bike, was to try and lure him into a rolling start. It works for heavy cars that have a lot of torques too. I used to race lighter muscle cars in my LeMans and as long as we started at about 25 mph I could keep up with them well into third gear. If I caught him off guard and he missed a shift, I might just be able to take him.

When the light turned green, I moved out smartly, but without too much show. He didn't dash off either, choosing instead to stay right beside me. He'd taken the bait. As soon as I hit 25 mph, which didn't take long, I nailed it, and an instant later I heard his V-Rod spool up like an angry bee. I've only actually run through the gears on my bike to the engine rpm redline a few times, but this was one of them. The shifts into second and third went perfectly but by the time I was approaching the redline again he was moving ahead. His bike was just too light and fast and he didn't miss anything, much less a shift. Still, it was close. By the time we both backed off, he was only about two bike lengths ahead.

When we pulled up to the next light we were smiling so broadly I thought our faces would crack. It was the feeling that middle-aged guys get when they act like teenagers, and know it, but can't contain themselves anyway.

After a few seconds of mutual admiration, he said, "Wow. She actually moves out for a big girl!"

And in that instant, though he didn't know it, he'd named my bike. She was indeed a Big Girl.

By the time we were all working on our final detailing touches, it was nearly sunset. I didn't really want to head back out and deal with the traffic, so I was relieved when I saw Jim and Larry passing out another round. We were obviously staying at the lodge again.

When Carrie and Nancy arrived, things actually started to get lively. Nancy was Alan's wife and Bill's mother. She was petite like Alan and every bit as much of a spitfire. The type of grandmother we all love: warm, witty, and a little bit irreverent in a way that only added to her charm. Alan, it was clear, adored her, and seemed even younger whenever they were close. Her eyes also twinkled whenever he was near. They were a generation older than all of us but looked like the youngest couple in the room. Within minutes, Alan opened up a bottle of red wine and poured Nancy and me glasses.

"I guess it's going to be a mixing night," I said to myself. First beer, now wine, and at some point, I knew, we'd get back to the scotch. Hector was already looking at me and miming putting ice cubes into a rock glass.

Carrie was Bill's wife. She was about forty, with dark shoulder-length hair, smooth skin, and curvaceous hips that were correctly highlighted by her tight jeans. A mother of three middle-school aged boys that were into motocross racing, she'd recently taken up riding herself. But she wasn't a real biker chick and didn't pretend to be. Charming and funny, like Nancy, she mostly did it because her husband and boys were into it, but she also had a little bit of an edge, and, I suspected, that helped.

Over time, the conversation became more animated—and slurred— and the stories started to multiply. Hector's were my favorite. He'd grown up in Mexico, the son of a reasonably well-off executive, but was ferociously bullied during his school years. To compensate, he learned to fight and became pretty good at it, particularly for his size. Once he'd gained the confidence of being able to hit hard, he'd take on anybody for even the slightest insult. He was in trouble so often that he constantly had to change schools. When it came time to think about a career choice, he wanted to be a fighter pilot, but his father convinced him to go into medicine. The pay was better and it wasn't as risky. After med school, he became a gynecologist. But he never did like private practice much, so after some years he took a job working for a major pharmaceutical company running their new drug testing process.

He owned two classic cars: one of those tiny, mid-seventies MGB convertibles and a 1971 Volkswagen bus with a "FunkenGruven" bumper sticker. It was his favorite car to bring to shows because the fans would always swarm it. Cindy added that he'd actually been propositioned several times in it by sixty-year-old women trying to relive their hippie youths.

We also regaled the newcomers with our riding exploits of the day, including how it seemed, whenever Jim was leading us, the "black cloud" would somehow cross our path. Having been to the Crazy Horse Memorial, with Native American culture fresh in our minds, I suggested that we start calling him "Chief Black Cloud." Larry loved it, and it stuck for the rest of the trip. I'm not sure that Jim appreciated the moniker. It was one of those half-mocking nicknames that somebody gives you and you never really like, but it was, at least to us, accurate. It was uncanny how he managed to find a way to continually ride us into rain—and hail.

There were other stories, including how Alan and Nancy met (it was their second marriage). The motorcycle races and injuries of Bill and Carrie's kids and Paul's work as a facilities manager for a major chemical company. Needless to say, I'll bypass the area where his plant is located if I ever drive through the Philly area again. Tom also told us a story about the first—and only—time he tried to commute to work on the New Jersey Turnpike. He was almost killed a half a dozen times.

As the evening progressed, however, it struck me that we all had something in common. It's something I've observed over the years about every biker I've ever met, whether male, female, young, old, novice, expert, "fake," or hard-core. Something that allows us to enjoy each other a lot more than any common background or political affiliation ever could. If you look beyond the bikes, the dress, and the jargon and observe, as a scientist, the way we interpret and respond to the world around us, you'll see it.

We all have a screw loose.

Day 6: A Parallel Universe

Tuesday was Bill's day in court. His lawyer assured him that it would be easy. After answering a few clarifying questions from the judge, his lawyer would make an argument for leniency. The judge would then knock it down to reckless driving, levy a fine, and offer some parting advice. They'd be in and out of the courthouse within an hour. And since he was first on the docket, he could be back at the lodge by ten o'clock and we could all take off on a relaxing day ride. It would barely slow us down. Even the weather seemed willing to cooperate. By the time most of us had slid out of bed and stumbled into the kitchen for our morning coffee, a rain shower that had overspread the area had moved on.

Not wanting to jinx a good thing, we decided once again to frequent our favorite spot for breakfast in Deadwood. Bill and Carrie were already on their way to the courthouse and Hector and Cindy had decided to sleep in and visit the Badlands National Park later in the morning. So the only change to the breakfast contingent was the addition of Alan and Nancy.

Alan's bike was a Sportster, Harley's smallest air-cooled model, and he'd added a taller sissy bar and backrest so that Nancy could ride comfortably on the back. Since it didn't have a windshield, he wore goggles, but they fit his personality perfectly. With his wispy gray hair, salt and pepper mustache, and swashbuckling good looks, he resembled a Golden Era aviator. Nancy wore a black Harley leather jacket, a bandana scarf, and a three-quarter helmet with a face shield that snapped down to deflect the wind. It was the perfect helmet set-up for a long ride on the back of a Sportster.

After a quick repair to fix a malfunctioning taillight, they were ready to go. Surprisingly the rest of us were as well. Even Jim, who's typical riding preparation ritual would test the patience of a saint, was saddled up and walking his bike backward out of the garage before Larry and me. Alan and Nancy, it was decided, would ride behind Paul. Tom would take up the rear, as usual. Everyone needed some gas, so we'd fill up at the station on the edge of town. The sun was already out and rapidly drying the driveway and waves of warmer air were rising from the ground, mixing with the cooler, wetter air left over from the rain. The weather forecast called for partly cloudy skies with a high of 80°F and a chance of an occasional passing shower, but nothing that was too threatening. We might just get lucky, I thought, and have a rain free day.

By the time we arrived back at the lodge, Bill's truck was in the driveway. Before we even reached the concrete driveway landing, we could tell it went well. The tension that he'd worn on his face since Sunday had evaporated. Smiling softly, he gave us a quick thumbs-up as we rumbled into the garage. Carrie was the first to say something.

Raising both of her arms in the air in a sign of victory, she blurted, "No DUI!"

Though I'm sure it was a relief, Bill seemed less enthusiastic. The charge had been reduced to reckless driving, but the fine was stiff. Counting legal fees and court costs it had cost him nearly two thousand dollars. What pissed him off the most, he lamented, was the truck had never moved. The "D" in DUI, after all, stands for "driving." He'd never even started the engine.

The original plan, hatched the night before, was to ride into Wyoming, visit Devil's Tower, and make our way back to Sturgis through the town of Belle Fourche. But the newcomers wanted to see Mount Rushmore and Bill wouldn't be deterred. They hadn't had a chance to ride yet, and Carrie, Alan, and Nancy wanted to see the famous monument straight away. Recognizing that they'd been through a lot, we agreed to dispense with the ride into Wyoming and head back to Rushmore. Larry wasn't happy because he knew, like the rest of us who'd been there yesterday, there was nothing more to see. I wasn't thrilled about going back either, but it was a small price to pay, I figured, to stay together.

There was one other complication that Jim had to consider and I could tell by the look on his face that he was pretty worried about it. Bill and Alan were fairly experienced riders, but Carrie had only taken the new rider course a few months back. She was a newbie. Bill had bought her a new Sportster as her first bike. It was matte black with very little chrome and was, as far as I could tell, completely stock. She'd ridden it less than a hundred miles since they'd picked it up.

This wasn't necessarily bad, we all have to start sometimes, but it would affect our average speed and range. With two Sportsters in the lineup and a brand new rider, we'd have to take it even slower and probably refuel before making it into Sturgis. Larry, I figured, would suffer the most. We all knew he liked to ride fast. It'll be interesting, I thought, to see how long he'll be able to take it.

The first step to making it easier for the new riders was to clear the driveway and assemble on the access road to the lodge. With a total of eight bikes, we'd need plenty of rooms to line up, so Jim pulled up close to the stop sign and shut down. It was a first test of patience, but no one seemed to mind. The weather certainly helped. The sky was clear, the air had just a touch of morning coolness left and a slight breeze was serving up scents of wildflowers. Two squirrels were chasing each other to my right, scampering across the mulch and up the trunks of nearby aspens. Even Larry seemed happy, staring off into the distance with a broad grin.

When we finally heard the pipes of Bill's Softail and the Sportsters, everyone turned back to see how Carrie was doing. While the mechanics of riding don't change very much with experience, you can always spot a new rider. You see it in their faces and in their movements, particularly at slow speeds. The predominant facial effects are those associated with fear, although it's not usually the fear of getting hurt that's on a rider's mind. More often, it's the fear of dropping the bike or doing something else that would be embarrassing. As Carrie was rolling down the driveway, I thought about one of the times I was most nervous riding my bike. It wasn't that long ago. I'd ridden out to another local high school to see one of my son's soccer games. After the match, his team and a large group of parents walked over to the area where my bike was parked. It must have been a novelty to see a "soccer dad" on a Harley because they were all watching me as I swung my leg over the saddle and prepared to leave. I tried to look unfazed, of course like I knew what I was doing, but I actually hated the attention. All I could think of as I started up and weaved out the parking lot was how embarrassing it would be if I managed to crash. I could see it in her tightly drawn lips. Carrie was going through the same thing.

Stopping naturally also takes time to master. At some point, just like on a bicycle, you have to put your feet down. It's not clear when you first ride a heavy motorcycle when to do it, or how to do it in a way that looks like you're totally in control. On a bicycle, you can usually come to a complete stop and balance for a moment before putting a foot down. And theoretically, on a motorcycle, you can do the same thing. But you don't want to. Given how heavy they are, as soon as you feel it starting to fall one way or the other, you want to stop it. So new riders tend to put their feet down too early and overcompensate from side to side as they slow. As she pulled up behind Bill, Carrie was doing this too.

But I had to admit, she had guts. By the time her bike stopped, she was smiling and trading barbs with Bill and Alan. She was going to show them, and us, she could do it. That's half the battle, I thought and turned ahead to look at Jim. He and Theresa had dismounted and were changing layers for a third time, necessitating another repacking of their remaining gear. I glanced back at Larry and he rolled his eyes. By the time we get going, I thought, it'll be in the afternoon.

After a few more gear adjustments, Jim started up again and we all coiled down the access road. After waiting a few minutes to make sure there was enough room for all of us to turn right without being broken up by traffic, we pulled out onto Route 14. We were finally heading towards Rushmore.

As I suspected, Jim backed off a bit on average speed so everyone kept up, including the Sportsters. If anything, our formation was even tighter than the day before. Larry, however, was driving me crazy. It was killing him to ride slower, so to compensate he kept dropping back and surging forward, at times riding barely a bike length behind me on my left. I tried not to think about what might happen if I had to swerve or stop quickly; convincing myself that he knew what he was doing, but I couldn't shake my nervous jitters. After a while, I stopped looking in my left mirror, choosing instead to focus on the scenery. Jim was slowing and it looked like we'd be turning into a scenic overlook by a large lake.

Walking casually, we all snaked our way down to see it. The view was spectacular. Surrounded by thickly forested hills and short, rocky cliffs, the water looked like a giant, shimmering mirror. A lone pontoon boat, far off in the distance, churned across its gray surface trailing a wake that sounded like a giant zipper. Although the sky was mostly overcast, the sun was illuminating the clouds in a way that was continually casting changing shadows on the water. It was so beautiful and serene it took someone else, a perky biker chick who had wandered onto the platform with her boyfriend, to suggest taking a group picture. It took a while for us to figure out how to assemble and we never did find Paul (he was off in the lone portable restroom), but she finally snapped a group photo.

Before we reached the entrance to Rushmore, Jim pulled over on a stretch of the access road with a wide shoulder. He wanted to give those of us who'd already been there a chance to avoid the fee and wait outside. It would help to keep the peace. Larry was the first to say he'd prefer not to go in and Tom quickly seconded. I agreed to wait outside as well. I just couldn't generate any excitement to see the famous faces again. Jim didn't really want to go back either but felt it was his responsibility as the Road Captain to lead the group. A few minutes later they rumbled off, leaving the three of us behind. We made a U-turn and stopped again on the opposite shoulder in a spot that gave us a good view of the distant hills. We didn't know how long we'd have to wait, but we didn't mind. Though now almost entirely overcast, the air was comfortably cool and the constant parade of bikes gave us something else to look at.

A short time later a park police patrol car moving in the opposite direction slowed to a near crawl across from us. The cop driving it lowered his window.

Pointing a finger at us, he said, "Hey . . . yeah, you guys; it's illegal to park on the shoulder. You have to get going."

After quickly scanning the road in both directions, we all had the same thought. Other groups of bikers were parked along the shoulder for as far as we could see and he hadn't bothered any of them. For some reason, he chose our merry little band to make his point. So instinctively, without collaboration, we conjured up the best show of contempt we could think of, which was to say nothing—other than Larry grumbling, "What a shithead"—and take much longer than necessary to make our riding preparations.

Larry started it by continually tinkering with his switches and lights as if something was wrong. I followed suit by taking a ridiculous amount of time to put on my gloves. Tom kept adjusting his helmet and playing with his chin strap, snapping it on and off again at least a dozen times. The cop waited across from us the whole time, getting noticeably more irritated with each passing moment, but that was the point. By the time we sped off, he must have been fuming.

A few miles down the road, after we were sure the cop was gone, we pulled over on the shoulder again to caucus. The first thing we had to do was let Jim know where we were, so I rang his phone.

As we talked, the sky darkened and a cool, damp breeze began to blow. A minute later a light rain started to fall. Figuring that it would be stupid to remain out in the open, I suggested that we ride ahead to Keystone and find a place for lunch. With a large group it would take time to get a table, so by the time the rest of them caught up with us we could all be seated.

"Good idea," Jim said approvingly. "The group's just approaching the viewing platform so it'll probably be an hour before we reach you."

"Perfect," I replied and slid my phone back into my jacket.

Larry and Tom liked the plan too and agreed to follow me. I had no idea what the town was like or what it offered, but it was easy enough to get there. Even I couldn't screw up this one.

Like many of the small ex-mining support towns in the area, including Deadwood, Keystone has a single main drag that's flanked on either side by retail shops, service establishments, and restaurants. Except for the tourist traffic visiting Mount Rushmore and some of the other local attractions, it's usually pretty quiet. The kind of small town with a hardware store, a diner, and a single traffic light. But on this particular Tuesday, it wasn't like that. Motorcycles were parked along the street on both sides in unbroken, angled rows, and bikers were surging along the sidewalks, packed like cattle. As soon as I made the left onto Main Street, I could see that finding a space was hopeless. It was hard enough to try and pick out a place to eat, much less see a gap that could accommodate three bikes. A place on the right side of the street, however, just before the last stop light, looked promising. It was a large, two-story restaurant of some kind that looked like an old hotel. Like many of the buildings in the town, it had a large outdoor balcony on the second floor and people were standing along the railing, drinks in hand, watching the parade of bikes rolling by. We could put our name in for a table and then wait outside along the railing, have a beer, and watch for Jim and the others. They had to roll through at some point. There was no other way into town.

When we passed the last stoplight, I noticed that a parking lot on the left, usually reserved for tour buses, was open to motorcycles. It was almost full, but towards the end, almost directly caddy-corner from the restaurant, was a space big enough for our three bikes. When I hit the engine stop switch, Larry was right beside me, on my left, with Tom slightly behind.

Larry unbuckled his chin strap and asked, "We going to that place?" He was pointing at the restaurant, and I could finally make out its name.

"Yeah," I replied, "Ruby House. It looks like fun. We can wait on the balcony, watch for the others and have a drink."

"Good," he replied, "I could use one."

The restaurant was on the ground floor and when we told the hostess that we had a group of ten, she said they couldn't seat us for an hour. Thinking we'd be angry, she followed up quickly with a suggestion to walk up the stairs to the outdoor balcony and visit one of the temporary bars.

"No problem," I said, "We were going to do that anyway. An hour is fine."

"Great!" she replied, "just check back in about forty-five minutes."

I could tell I'd chosen well as soon as we hit the second floor. The balcony was long almost fifty yards across. To accommodate all of the guests without everyone having to walk back and forth across its narrow width, they'd set up portable bar stations every ten yards or so. Small tables lined the railings with enough space between them for several people to stand. It was the perfect set-up to spend time watching the bike parade.

After we had found a table, I told Larry and Tom I'd buy the first round. A waitress greeted me before I could get to the first bar station and offered to take my order. Like a lot of the girls working the Sturgis rally, she was probably an import, but I was too busy checking her out to ask. She was wearing a Confederate flag bikini and white denim chaps, both of which I'd never seen before. Even more intriguing was her leather apparatus. It was a harness of some sort with a thick black belt and matching suspenders. Drink pouches were attached to the belt and loops sewn into the suspender straps held test tube shooters. She was also, I had to admit, pretty attractive. Not Luscious, but close. Young and cute with dirty blonde shoulder length hair and sculpted abs, she looked too athletic to be a working professional, maybe a cheerleader who was also an athlete. What really set her apart, however, at least to me, was her chest. It was actually normal, even petite. The waitress at the next station, besides being probably fifteen years older and not hiding it very well, was another cosmetically altered spectacle. I was beginning to be able to tell the difference and natural was winning.

After some small talk, she finally asked what we wanted.

"Three drafts," I said. Knowing immediately what the next question would be, and not wanting to listen to the list of options, I quickly added, "I don't care what kind, something pale and natural."

"Got it," she replied with a playful wink and scampered off.

I decided not to say anything about her when I got back to our table because I wanted to see Larry's reaction when she returned. Sure enough, as soon as she popped out behind a group of other bikers and reached our table, Larry lit up like a Christmas tree. After staring intently at her with his brown-gray eyes, he turned towards me, raised his eyebrows and nodded gently—the guy signal for "she's alright." Before she left, he asked her if she wouldn't mind if I took a picture of the two of them, and she accepted sweetly. A few seconds later we traded phones and places by her side.

As she walked away, he said, "Nice job . . . beers and the girl. You're hired."

I'd finally done something right.

When Tom walked away to call his wife, I was suddenly struck by the realization that I'd never had a one-on-one conversation with Larry. Then another thought slipped into my head. It had happened a few days ago, the morning after Bill's arrest when Larry had shot upstairs and yelled, "Whose fucking laundry is in the washer?!"

After I'd tried to poke a little fun at him by being overly careful, Jim had said, "Don't sweat it, he's just Larry. You've worked with the type. You ought to know."

It didn't take long to understand what Jim meant. As I quickly learned, Larry was a retired Air Force Master Sergeant, who'd spent more than twenty years setting up and operating mobile water distilling plants. After retiring, like most senior non-commissioned officers (NCOs), he'd continued to work, landing a job with a local water utility. He'd grown up in a tough neighborhood in Levittown, Pennsylvania, a working-class suburb of Trenton (on the other side of the river), barely one step ahead of the local law. In and out of trouble and without the grades or funds to go to college, he'd enlisted in the Air Force at the time that everyone was returning from Vietnam. The work was good, he said, indispensable to deployed air units and ground forces, but far enough behind enemy lines not to get shot at. And, as long as enough water flowed and no one got sick, the officers pretty much stayed out of his face.

More importantly, he added with a kind of sanguine reflection, the military had straightened him out. Most of his peers had drifted through life and accomplished little. He wasn't rich, but he had a house that was almost paid off, a few toys (the Harley of course being his pride and joy), a stable marriage, and some spending money. That was way ahead, he figured, of most of the guys he'd grown up within Levittown.

When I mentioned that I'd also been in the military his eyes emitted a sparkle and he asked, with genuine curiosity, how I'd served.

"I was in the submarine force," I said, "from eighty-five to ninety-two. Served on an attack boat and then in the Pentagon. Got out as a Lieutenant."

His reaction was what I expected, a mixture of surprise and respect followed closely, it seemed, with a look of suspicion. I always knew what the last look meant. He was wondering what kind of officer I'd been. Most NCOs never really like commissioned officers. They can tolerate and even admire the fair and competent ones, but the pompous, arrogant, and incompetent ones, particularly at the mid-levels, are the worst. At the same time, what they don't know, that we know, is that we almost universally admire them. After all, they do the real work, the stuff behind the glamor of flying or driving a ship that makes it all possible: the maintenance, the upkeep, and training of the crew. And they get paid a lot less, only because, it would seem, they didn't start out with a college degree.

But we also know, to get that work done, with green airmen, soldiers, and sailors fresh out of high school, they have to be strict—and direct. They don't have the time or patience to mince words, and it's probably the thing that we admire the most. Because at some point, after we rotate back to shore and take on our first staff job, particularly if it's in the Pentagon, we start to lose the edge we develop when we're deployed. High-level staff jobs, at least for officers, are more about selling than operating. About getting what the command needs (usually money), working programs for "stuff" (like planes, ships, tanks, etc.), and navigating the labyrinth of relationships necessary to keep everyone above you, and around you, happy. That's why, whenever you want to know what's really going on in a major Pentagon procurement program, you never ask the Program Manager.

If you do, you'll usually get an answer like, "The Air Force's new tanker will significantly improve our military's air refueling capabilities. While slightly behind the Milestone C approved limited production schedule, the program is meeting or exceeding most of its critical performance parameters."

Pull aside a Master Sergeant who's actually working on it and he'll tell you, "It's a fucking flying bathtub—utterly useless."

My favorite NCO, when I was in the Navy, was our Chief of the

Boat. A Senior Chief with over thirty years of experience, he'd been in just about every class of nuclear attack boat the Navy had put to sea since the 1960s. Tall and lanky, with jet-black hair that always seemed to be greasy, he was respected—and feared—by just about everyone, particularly the junior officers. As Larry and I continued our mutual scoping out discussion, a memory drifted into my mind regarding the one time I'd shown up for a command inspection in a sloppy uniform. Generally fastidious about my appearance, I'd partied a little too hard the night before and didn't have time to iron it. It was passable, but certainly not "four-point-zero squared away." Before we lined up our Executive Officer (XO), who was a rare combination of both competent and helpful, pulled me aside, frowned, and said he was disappointed. While I was one of his "most promising" officers, he wanted me to set a better example.

When the Senior Chief saw me, he only said, "Good morning, Sir. You look like shit."

His rebuke stung me a lot more than the XO's. I never forgot it.

By the time we'd drained our first beer and ordered another, I could tell I'd passed the test with Larry, whatever it was, and he'd certainly passed it with me. Jim, as usual, had been right. I did understand the retired Master Sergeant, and his "succinct" communications style didn't bother me. I just hoped he'd stop crowding me so much when we were riding.

After an hour at the hotel, well into our second round, just about the time when we were wondering where the hell the others were, the black cloud returned and it started to sprinkle. Most of the bikers on the balcony, like us, didn't move. It wasn't like getting a little wet was anything new—so we just watched, with amusement, as the riders below continued to roll by. Then, just as the rain intensified, four bikes led by a black Road King emerged from the squall. Tom spotted them first and we all burst into laughter, waving mockingly as they rumbled by. It was the rest of our group. "Chief Black Cloud" was leading them, and once again, he'd managed to find the worst of the rain. When they saw us up on the balcony, the girls waved back. The guys barely acknowledged us, except for Paul, who grinned and flipped Tom the bird. It was an appropriate greeting, I thought, given the circumstances.

During the lunch, the conversation inevitably turned to our riding plans for the rest of the day and what we were going to do after we got back to the lodge. Jim wanted to take off on another long ride back into the Black Hills National Forest. That wouldn't have gotten us back to the lodge until at least seven o'clock, but many of us, including me, wanted to take it easier. My ass still hurt and I was tired of riding in the rain. It was also, I figured, time to make a full evening of revelry in Sturgis, beginning with the venerable Full Throttle Saloon (FTS). After all, we had something to celebrate. Bill was free and for the first time we were all together. Given this, I suggested that we head straight back to the lodge, relax a little, and head out to the FTS around eight thirty. The others liked my idea better, which I could tell annoyed Jim, but there was one more thing to settle. Nobody, it seemed, wanted to take the chance of riding into town for the evening.

"We can take a cab," I suggested, "I'm sure they have vans and could take a group like ours and pick us up right at the lodge."

Nancy and Carrie asked enthusiastically, "Is that possible?"

"Hang on," I said, "I'll check."

Hector had given me a card for a cab service that had been left on the kitchen counter at the lodge. I pulled out my phone, dialed the number, and had a short conversation with the dispatcher. It was indeed possible. They could pick us up at around eight thirty at the lodge, drive us in, and pick us up around one or whenever we called—with thirty minute's notice. The fare was $60 each way, but if we split it, it would be almost as cheap as riding in and parking. Jim knew he was on the losing side of this one, so he offered up a pretty reasonable compromise. He and Theresa would take off on the longer ride he was thinking of and Larry would lead the rest of us back to the lodge, which was maybe a forty-minute ride. After Jim and Theresa arrived back, they'd head into Sturgis with the rest of us.

Larry didn't look too thrilled about being our Road Captain, but he nonetheless agreed, saying only, "OK. I'll lead the rest of the group back. It makes sense."

As the group assembled in the parking lot and we made our riding preparations, Jim pulled me aside. I could tell he was concerned.

Speaking softly, he said, "Hey. You know Larry likes to ride fast. You need to tell him, whenever possible, to take it easy. Carrie's a newbie."

"I was thinking the same thing," I said. "Don't worry about it."

When we were all more or less ready, Larry said to Alan and Carrie (the Sportster riders), "You guys have enough fuel to get back?"

"No, we don't," they said in tandem.

"OK, just follow me. We'll stop for gas in Rapid City before we get back onto I-90."

There were no assignments, but I figured I'd just ride on his right wing, as would be proper for the number-two position.

For the next half an hour or so, Larry diligently led the group, taking it very easy, as promised. We never rode above 5 mph over the speed limit. It must be killing him, I thought.

A while later, following Route 16 North, we hit the outskirts of Rapid City. Getting everyone through the lights as a group was nearly impossible, so every time we'd get split up, Larry would pull over and wait for the others to catch up. It was slow going, but mile after mile, we edged closer to the interstate. Finally, he pulled into a gas station with several islands of pumps and a large concrete landing. Larry and I didn't need to refuel so we pulled over in the adjacent area. The others inched up to the pumps.

When the Sportsters had filled up, Larry walked over and asked the group how comfortable they'd been with our speed. Several of the smaller bike riders (Carrie, Alan, Paul, and Tom) asked him to go even slower, no more than 60 mph. He looked at me and rolled his eyes, but nonetheless agreed. Itching to get going myself, I idled out onto the shoulder of the main road and shut down again, waiting for the others. As soon as Larry pulled up behind me, I heard it.

It wasn't nearly as loud as Chris's accident, but the sound pattern was eerily familiar. A harsh metallic bang accompanied by a muffled scream. Larry heard it too and we dismounted, spun around, and quickly scanned the pump area. Carrie's bike was lying on its side. She was standing beside it, still in a state of shock. She'd dumped her new Sportster.

It was a classic rookie mistake. She'd been following Bill out of the station when he'd stopped abruptly to let another bike go by. Turning slowly at the time, she'd hit the front brake hard instead of the rear. If you do this on a two-wheeler (try it with your bicycle at home), the bike will immediately drop in the direction it's been leaning. The only way to stop the fall is to quickly plant a foot and heave back. Instinctively, she tried to do this, but her foot hit the bike's footrest instead of the ground. From that point on, it was inevitable.

She did, however, do something right. Recognizing that the bike was going down, at the last possible moment, she jumped out of the way and let it go. As a result, she managed to escape injury, but not the embarrassment that comes with dumping a bike—particularly in a group setting—or the sting of disappointing her husband. He was, we could tell, struggling to control himself. It would be another unplanned expense. Trying to lighten the mood, we offered up some words of encouragement like "don't sweat it, it happens to everyone," (which is pretty much true) but when we said the bike didn't look too bad, Bill's face flushed with anger. We were apparently lying. The front handlebars were bent, the right mirror had broken off, and there were scrapes on the fuel tank and pipes. Still, it was fixable. Within a few minutes, we'd pulled the bike upright, straightened the handlebars and reattached the right mirror. She could ride on if she wanted to, but we'd all certainly understand if she wanted to call it quits.

But once again, she impressed us. With stoic determination, she pushed her helmet back on, buckled her chin strap, and remounted the bike. There was no way she was going to give up when riding meant so much to her husband.

Bill, still agitated, walked over to Larry and they exchanged a few words. I didn't hear what they said, but the tone didn't sound pleasant. If he's giving him any crap, I thought, it was unjustified. There was no way Larry could have prevented or even foreseen what happened to Carrie. In any event, just to be extra cautious, I walked over to Larry after Bill left and reminded him to take it easy. Carrie was probably still rattled and the others had asked to go slower. He nodded sullenly and we both mounted our bikes. When I heard Tom's chopper fire up with an earsplitting, "per-pop-bop," I knew we were all ready.

Two years earlier, during the Gettysburg rally, Larry had changed out his pipes. He went with a Vance & Hines set with a distinctive sound that was both sharp and crisp, particularly under hard acceleration. A few minutes after we all filed onto I-90, riding on his right wing, I heard them start to crackle. Glancing every five seconds or so at my speedometer, I watched as the needle climbed, rising quickly past 65, then 70, then 75 mph. For a while I kept up with him, but noticed, particularly when he hit 75 mph, the motorcycle headlights in my rear view mirrors getting distinctly smaller.

I couldn't believe it. Our Road Captain was ditching us. Even worse, he didn't seem to notice or care. Several times I fell back, thinking he would at least see that I wasn't keeping up and slow down, but he rode on, seemingly oblivious. Trying one more time to get his attention, I sped up and pulled to within a couple of bike's length distance, honked my horn, and switched my passing lamps on and off. Nothing. I thought about passing him, but he was riding close to 80 mph at that point, the crosswinds in the valley were swirling, and I didn't feel comfortable putting on even more speed. So I fell back again and signaled as best I could for a few more miles. By that time the group behind me had almost faded from view.

In the meantime, the sky was rapidly lowering and darkening, particularly to the west. Since we were riding northwest and most storm cells move in an easterly direction (though in the Black Hills they can come from anywhere), I figured we were going to hit rain again. Larry was now far ahead of me and the others even further behind. When the thunder started rumbling, I knew I had to make a decision.

Since speeding up and sticking with Larry wasn't an option, my choices were to slow considerably and wait for the others to catch up, or find a roadside shelter, stop, and flag them down. I thought for a fleeting moment about proceeding on my own but quickly dismissed it. If you lose the Captain, the number two's in charge. I wasn't going to shirk that responsibility. Plus, as usual, it had started to rain.

The only possible shelter at that point was a bridge about a quarter of a mile ahead. Beyond that, the road sank even further into the valley and stretched on for miles. Just as I was approaching the bridge, I glanced in my mirrors and saw the others rapidly slowing. They'd decided to go for it. Unfortunately, I'd missed the window. Now only fifty yards or so from the abutment, I was beyond the point of making a safe stop. So I rode on at my own reasonable pace, in waves of light to moderate rain, struggling to suppress alternating waves of anger, frustration, and guilt.

After what seemed like an eternity, Larry realized no one was behind him and started to slow. By that time, the rain had stopped but the sky was still confused and threatening. Finally, I saw his brake light illuminate and he pulled over onto the shoulder. When I pulled up behind him, my anger swelled to the point where I thought I was going to lose it. Not only had he ditched us, but he'd managed to pick the one spot to pull over on the twenty-five-mile stretch of I-90 between Rapid City and Sturgis that was probably the least safe. The shoulder was narrow, we were in the flattest part of the valley, storms were everywhere, and there was absolutely no shelter.

My executive training, however, kicked in. The Steven Covey stuff about how you're supposed to "seek first to understand." Maybe Bill had said something that had pissed him off. Maybe his speedometer had failed. Maybe his eyeballs couldn't adjust the eighth of an inch necessary to glance in his *fucking mirrors*. There had to be a reason. So I dismounted, took a deep breath, suppressed the urge to grab his neck in a chicken choke, and walked up to him.

"Where is everybody?" he asked.

Still struggling to control myself, I decided to open up with the facts.

"After we rolled on to I-90, you started riding faster than all of us and never slowed down. I tried to signal you. In any event, you left everybody behind. I saw the others stop under a bridge some miles back."

He stared at me for a couple of seconds, absorbing what I'd said, and knowing that I was pissed, wisely took some time before responding.

"Well," he mused, "then they'll have something to bust my balls about."

I couldn't help but smirk a little. It was vintage Master Sergeant.

When the group finally caught up with us, I decided to take the lead for a while. Still sensing that he was on thin ice, Larry slid in behind me in the number-two position and behaved himself, keeping a proper distance. When we were close to Sturgis, however, he bolted ahead of me, presumably to retake the lead. Figuring that he wanted to lead the group off at the proper exit, I fell back, scanning the signs.

A short distance from Lazelle Street, he switched into the left lane and put on more speed. Pretty sure that we were about to miss our exit, I raised my hand as a signal that conveyed "follow me" and veered off.

The rest of the group followed. Seeing in his mirrors that we were exiting, Larry made a wild lane change. He rode up over the V-shaped shoulder separating the highway from the off ramp and snaked his way up beside me at a stoplight. He was probably just daydreaming and forgot about the exit, I figured, but he'd screwed up as Road Captain—again.

My reaction this time, however, was different. Shaking my head the way that parents do when we watch one of our teenagers do something stupid and wonder if they'll ever turn out right, I just took the lead again.

"Larry is Larry," Jim had said to me once. "You get what you get."

My thoughts had also turned towards our plans for the evening and the stars, it appeared, were aligning. We were going to a great bar with a fun group, no one had to drive, and there were no commitments for the following day. The perfect ingredients for a good night of—as we used to say in the Navy—"steaming."

The Full Throttle Saloon has been an icon in Sturgis since 1999. Spread out over thirty acres of land two miles east of Sturgis. It's an enormous venue, with a huge outdoor covered stage, merchandise shops, a large indoor bar area with another stage. A half dozen auxiliary bars, zip line, a mechanical bull, a burnout "stage," and a parking lot bigger than an airport tarmac. On any given night during rally week the crowd can average fifteen thousand people. There's also an adjacent campground with rental cabins so you never have to leave the compound if you don't want to. I'd never watched the cable TV show about the FTS before reaching Sturgis, but apparently it's pretty entertaining. Since 2009, camera crews have been on site every rally to cover the exploits of the staff, entertainers, and patrons. With just the right amount of interesting characters (the owners, Michael Ballard and his wife, Angie, are quite famous), internal conflict, humor, and unpredictability that make these shows so popular.

But it's certainly not perfect, mainly because it's a tough business to run profitably. Since Sturgis doesn't have a lot of year-round biker crowds, particularly during the colder months of October through April, it's only open for the period of the rally. So they have to cover their salaries and all of the overhead of maintaining the place, plus marketing and operating costs, for a thirty-acre facility, in only *ten days*. Give that challenge to an average bar or restaurant proprietor and they'd laugh you out the front door.

Jim had decided we were going to visit the FTS long before we arrived in Sturgis. To him, and a lot of others I supposed, it was more of a tourist attraction than a bar, but how many biker bars have ten thousand Harleys you can look at? Another bonus was that Foghat was playing that night on the outdoor stage. They weren't my favorite rock group of the seventies, but at least they were a guy band. My wife and I had only been to one concert together in the past several years: Jewel. It was a smaller venue in downtown Washington, DC, packed with a lot of women who, I figured, had to drag their husbands and boyfriends along. My suspicion was confirmed when Jewel asked at one point what song the audience wanted to hear. Without missing a beat, I pulled out my lighter, flipped it open, and yelled, "Freeeeeebird!" Half the guys in the place erupted into laughter. Jewel was annoyed. So was my wife.

Our cab driver, Andy, arrived at the lodge in a small white panel van. "How many people do you have in your group?" he asked.

I'd already forgotten and had to take a moment to establish the count. Since Hector and Cindy had decided to go back into Deadwood and Jim and Theresa weren't back yet from their ride after lunch (he'd called me and said they'd meet us there), we were down by four.

"Eight on the way out," I replied, "but ten on the way back."

"Ten will be really tight. You'll have to get creative."

"No worries," I replied, "by then, that'll be the least of our problems."

I took the front seat so I could chat with him. He'd retired about ten years ago, moved to Sturgis and started his company as "something interesting to do." A hardcore biker himself, he knew a ton about the rally, the surrounding area, how to get things (presumably women, booze, and "stuff"), and what to avoid. He also had a wealth of stories regarding the people he'd picked up and what he'd seen. So many, in fact, that he'd written a book cataloging them. When he mentioned the book Larry shot me a look that conveyed, "Yeah right," but I believed him straight away. Intelligent, funny, and perspicacious, he was yet another example of a biker being what you might not expect. Intrigued, I asked him to tell a few.

The best one regarded our lodge. He knew it well, as did most of the other cab drivers, local girls, bar owners, and cops in the area. During one rally, according to Andy, a group of bikers with "real money" decided to host a party but realized, after they'd bought the kegs and liquor, they needed more female companionship. So they hired Andy to take them to some of the bars in Deadwood where they could scout recruits. The most willing were several of the imported "professional" barmaids. Andy, of course, dutifully shuttled them back to the lodge. Soon, however, they realized the party needed more kick. So they asked Andy to take them back into Deadwood again. This time, they invited every patron they could talk to. "Come on up," they'd say, "It's free and it's *rocking*."

Having set huge expectations, they then realized the single band they'd hired wasn't good enough. Once again, Andy came to the rescue. With his help, they quickly hired another one. By three o'clock in the morning, over four hundred people were on the property. With one band playing in the living room and the other one on the lower patio, call girls working the crowd—and the bedrooms—and expanded kegs rolling down the hills. Apparently it didn't break up until ten o'clock the following morning.

"That," he said, "was a *party*."

As we approached the FTS, the traffic thickened to almost a standstill. Inching forward, Andy finally lets us out on a sidewalk about fifty yards from the entrance. The procedure for picking us up was simple: just give him a call when we were ready, keeping in mind that it would take him at least thirty to forty-five minutes to get there. If it were after one o'clock, he could probably make it into the parking lot. When he handed us his card, I passed it around so everyone could enter his number into their phones. That way if we got split up and people wanted to leave at different times, we could make our own plans. Larry was already grousing about the cover charge.

It didn't look as big as I thought it would, at least from the outside, but for a long moment we all stopped and stared at the building. The front façade resembled a nineteenth-century hotel; with vertical, cedar planked outer walls, L-shaped rooflines, and a full-length Southwestern style porch. A large square center section, highlighted by rope lighting like the other edges of the building, jutted out from the walls. The front end of an old Harley had been mounted on it with the brightly lit words "FULL THROTTLE" and "SALOON" hanging above and below. But it was the backdrop of colors that really grabbed me: the brownish-red of the building set against the perfectly blue, softly fading summer sky. The orange glow of the setting sun washing across the thousands of bikes parked out front. It was so beautiful I almost didn't want to go inside.

The line to get in wasn't very long and one by one we paid the "extortion," as Larry called it, to get in. Apparently every year the owners experiment with different pricing schemes, but for the 2011 rally, the cover charge was $20. You also got two tickets for free drinks that could be used at any of the bars inside. Since all of the drinks were $5, as long as you had two, it actually only cost $10. To me at least, that seemed pretty reasonable. You'd probably pay a lot more than that just to see Foghat separately. And I was pretty damn sure I was going to consume a lot more than two drinks.

Like any time you walk into a large bustling place for the first time, it took a while for us to gain our bearings. Standing off to the side, we slowly rotated our heads, assimilating the layout. An area that looked like a pub was set off to the right. A band was playing on a small stage at one end of it. Bikers who were obviously enjoying themselves were stuffed into the area between the stage and a bar along the back walls. Not a single table was open. The left side contained more tables (all occupied) and an exit to the outdoor area, where, not too far ahead, there was a small pavilion with another bar. The center bar area, however, was where the real action appeared to be. Laid out in a giant rectangle, there were a half a dozen bartenders—all attractive females—working behind the counters with a ribbon of bikers at least six people thick hugging every inch of the perimeter. Since the space around the bar area wasn't very wide, maybe fifteen feet or so on each side, it was going to be difficult to work our way around it.

The other challenge, we quickly figured out, was how to stay together. With nowhere to sit and so much to see, it would be impossible to move around efficiently as a group, or, for that matter, to even talk. The noise was deafening. Bill, Carrie, and Paul were the first to defect.

"Keep your phones on," they shouted over the roar, "we'll text you later and hook up."

Larry and Tom were next. They were going to check out the concert area out back to scout out a good viewing spot. Already feeling a little claustrophobic and still missing the beauty of the settling evening, I decided to check out the nearest outdoor bar area. Alan and Nancy said they'd tag along. On our way out, Alan grabbed my elbow and bashfully asked if I thought the place served wine. It's all he and Nancy could stomach.

"Probably not," I said, "but I'll ask."

The first outdoor bar area turned out to be the only one that night with male bartenders, who, I quickly observed, were pretty rude. So I took great pleasure in inching my way up to the closest one and asking him, in an overly polite way if they served wine.

"No, not here," he responded in an annoyed tone, "just beer, in cans. Standard brands."

They were pulling them, I could see, out of giant iced coolers. Already thirsty, I handed him my two free tickets, a $5 bill and walked back with three ice-cold Michelob's.

Alan and Nancy shrugged off the bad news about the wine and we stood, for a long while, drinking our beers and further checking out the place. The outdoor stage pavilion, probably three stories high, was set about a hundred yards back. Even at that distance it seemed huge. A large crowd of bikers was packed fifty yards deep in front of it. Another more loosely coupled horde was milling around behind them. A large food cart and another outdoor bar were set upon the ground in the middle. To the left was "Angieland," where, for a fee, you could get your picture taken with her famous ass. Further up was a "topless bus" and a row of merchandise shops accessible from a raised walking deck. Bikes were parked to the far right and back areas, presumably for additional eye candy. I wondered how they got in.

Soon we discovered the first way the owners were controlling costs. The urge had hit Alan and me at the same time. Nancy took some pleasure in teasing us when we informed her.

"Jesus Christ," she said. "I expect it from the old fart, but I thought you'd hold up better. I think the line's back there."

The line was so long and crooked we didn't believe, at first, it was actually the one for the restrooms. I had to ask three different people before it sank in.

"Yeah," they all said with the same resigned exasperation, "it sucks."

Without many choices, we slid in behind the girl at the end. Alan, I noticed, started stroking his mustache as soon as he saw her. Barely old enough to be there, at least legally, she was strikingly pretty. With a rear end that was so perfectly formed—and highlighted—by her black leather pants, I couldn't help but stare at it. She was with her boyfriend, so it'd be tough to start a conversation, but we could continue to check her out when he wasn't looking. And for the next ten minutes, shuffling slowly along, we did.

I could tell we were getting close by the stench. Since we were downwind of the "complex," it was easy enough to pick up. Finally, we reached a staging table of some kind. Behind it were at least fifty tightly spaced, portable johns, arranged in a giant rectangle. The job of the guy at the staging table was to direct patrons to either side depending on sex, and, based on signals from runners on the inside, throttle the incoming flow. Once inside, runners led supporters to unoccupied facilities. For a tip, they'd even try to find you a clean unit. I didn't see anyone tipping them, and all I had in my wallet were $20 bills, so I took my chances. It was a bad call.

By the time I passed the guy at the table again, I was thinking, like most of the others I supposed, how I could possibly avoid going there again. The key was to adjust my drinking strategy. The beer had to go. Beyond a few pints, at least at my age, what goes in pretty much flows right out. I'd buy one more, just to quench my thirst while we found the others, and then switch to whiskey. It was a biker bar. They had to serve it.

Just then, my phone buzzed with what would be the first of many texts that evening. It was Larry "over at get jakkd," it said. I had no idea what "get jakkd" was, so I suggested to Alan and Nancy that we wander over towards the back area of the crowd where the bikes were parked. They decided to stay put. I could tell her interest in the place was rapidly fading. Alan also seemed to be a bit withdrawn. He was probably sweating bullets knowing she'd have to use the bathrooms. Their condition, he knew, as a husband, would somehow be his fault.

I found Larry and Tom about where I expected. They were both happy and infused, like I was, with the energy of the place. Tom was particularly bubbly, like a kid in a theme park, excitedly listing the attractions he still wanted to see. Larry was effusive in a different way, rattling off a steady stream of comments about the things he saw as his eyes darted around the place.

"Nice fucking ride," he'd say, looking at a bike. "No, that one's better" as a girl walked by. "OK, I'd trade her for that motorcycle, the Street Glide with the red paint job." Then, as another even hotter girl passed, "Holy shit, she'd probably kill me." Then staring at the bikes again, "What a beater," then, "Now that's a solid rack, real solid."

It was pure comedy.

I offered to buy the first round of whiskeys before the warm up band wrapped up. Larry accepted willingly, handed me a drink ticket, and said he'd take another beer as well. Tom suggested that I try the outdoor bar at the edge of the main bar, about thirty yards behind us. They'd passed it on the way over and it wasn't that crowded. A few minutes later, after studying some of the bikes myself, I found it.

The bartender, a little past her prime, was wearing a simple white bikini. A wedding dress veil was pinned in her hair. She was working her butt off. Alternately diving into two large tubs of iced beer that faced outward, towards the stage, and then, with a full twist of her body, grabbing shots of liquor on a table under the opposing counter. This way she could serve patrons from either direction. Seeing me approach from the back side, she leaned over one of the beer tubs and asked, somewhat breathlessly, what I wanted.

"A Michelob and three shots of Jack Daniels," I replied.

"No problem," she said, adding as she spun around, "just don't ask to marry me."

She probably gets that a lot; I thought and turned back towards the stage. Foghat was being introduced, precipitating another massive increase in crowd noise.

By the time I turned around again she was back.

Picking up that I was looking somewhat puzzled, she shouted over the crowd, "That's how we serve them."

It was, I quickly surmised, the second major way the owners were controlling costs. There, resting on the counter in front of me, were three tiny plastic cups filled with whiskey. They were so small they looked like thimbles. Trying to maintain a sense of humor, I picked one up and rotated it around, close to my face, examining it as an artifact. After a while, she caught on.

"That's its honey," she said. "It's not up to me. They're all pre-poured."

Trying unsuccessfully to summon something witty to say, I handed her Larry's drink ticket and a $20 bill. "Keep the change," was all I could muster.

Mostly, I was wondering how I was going to carry the drinks back without spilling anything, as well as how many FTS-sized shots it would take to get a good buzz on. My bet was at least a half dozen.

I rejoined Larry and Tom just as Foghat ripped into their hit song, "I Just Want to Make Love to You." Instinctively, we tried to move forward to get a better look, but it was impossible. The wall of bikers was impenetrable, and I wasn't sure I wanted to get any closer anyway. The sound was already horribly distorted and almost painfully loud. Even Tom, with his younger ears, was having a hard time enjoying it. When I showed him my empty thimble, he signaled he'd go back for the next round.

As soon as he got back, my phone buzzed. It was a text from Jim. He and Theresa were already passing the main bar and making their way outside. I tapped a note back saying, "meet u @back bar w/bbb" and showed it to Larry and Tom. Two seconds later, another text arrived. "bbb??" Grinning broadly, I typed out, "bikini bride bartender," and hit send. We all laughed.

I could tell right away that Jim was in a good mood. Their ride after lunch had gone well. He'd enjoyed the freedom of not having to worry about anyone else, and the scenery had been breathtaking. They'd even managed to avoid riding through any rain. After catching him up on our exploits, I asked him to hand me his drink tickets.

"Trust me, "I said, "You have to see this."

Standing with my back to him so he couldn't see what I was buying, I turned around and held up four thimbles of Jack.

"You gotta' be shittin' me!" he roared.

"Not much you can do about it," I said between breaths. "Just buy them two at a time and accept that it's $10 a drink."

We had forked over another $60 plus tips before Foghat finished "Slow Ride."

Larry and Tom were right where I left them. For the next hour or so, as the crowd and the band really spooled up, we wandered along the left periphery of the concert area, watching the show. Every twenty minutes or so, a designated runner would hit the bar in the middle and bring back more beers and shots. I lost count, but by the time we all agreed to head back to the main bar, we were walking with a distinctive wander. Theresa met us by the back entrance. She'd broken off sometime earlier to frequent the restrooms. I told Jim what to expect.

"Better than fifty-fifty we'll be leaving within an hour," I said, "she won't want to go back there." But I was wrong. Always the trooper, she'd figured out an even better way to obviate the need. She was going to stop drinking. It would also save money.

"Oh-kay honey," Jim said when she told him, "Whatever you want."

Theresa, now clearly the soberest, had the good sense to talk, and then grab, a small table about midway along the outer edge of the central bar area. It only had two stools, so I staked out a position on the level just below her and Jim. I tried talking to them by craning my head back and forth, but after a while, it got tiring. Larry and Tom had also wandered off. So I just stood there, with my whiskey-warmed face, observing the crowd.

The first thing that struck me was there wasn't a single person, of any age, color or sex, that wasn't wearing *something* that advertised their affiliation with Harley-Davidson. For some, it was everywhere: on their boots, pants, belt, t-shirt, jacket, jewelry, and even their bodies. For others, like me, it was more subtle (just a t-shirt). But I'd never seen, in all my life, brand loyalty like this. Even more impressive was the variety of costumes. The primary components were more or less the same. Lots of black leather exposed skin for the girls. Facial hair for the guys, tattoos, and chain jewelry, but the level of effort to be *different* was a step above, on average, what I'd seen so far at the rally. One guy had ponytails and braids not only in his hair but in his mustache, beard, and eyebrows. Another one chose to die his hair red and tie it up in shoots that looked like snapdragons. A younger guy with a bald eagle chest tattoo was walking around, shirtless, with an enormous pink rimmed novelty top hat. Face painting also appeared to be popular, from pure hearts and HD logos to whole face jobs that made people look like Halloween monsters.

The women had also stepped it up a notch. On the whole, they were younger and prettier than the downtown rally crowd and even more motivated, it seemed, to show off their curves. One particularly pleasing method I hadn't seen before was bare breast painting. There were all kinds of styles, from the whole breast storyboards to simple, tasteful designs centered on the nipples. At first I'd shrugged it off as a novelty because most of the women I'd seen, at least to that point, probably shouldn't have done it. But after returning from the bar to my favorite spot with a fresh round of shots, I changed my mind.

They'd taken up a space close to me just after I'd downed my "twins." And, surprisingly, they appeared to be alone. The blond was kind of cute and maybe a few years younger, but her friend, the brunette, just took my breath away. With over the shoulder length dark brown hair and a confident, slightly backward stance, she exuded a kind of sexuality that was powerful, understated, and classy all at once. She also had, I thought, the nicest pair of natural breasts I'd ever seen. The painting over her nipples was perfect: two blue hearts outlined with black rims that curved into the center. Before long, she noticed me checking her out. Her return glances were subtle, beginning with a simple acknowledgment, but over time, through the fog of the Jack, my brain started to process something different. She was smirking and touching her hair and looking back at me more often. The flirting had officially begun. Surprised that she might actually want to talk to me, I finally cracked a smile. When she smiled broadly back, my heart started pounding. Damn, I thought, even her overbite's cute.

Unfortunately, it was awkward. Jim, my wife's brother, was hovering above me. I trusted him as a road buddy (you know, what happens on a bike trip stays on a bike tour). I also knew that if I ever hurt his sister he'd break me in half. Theresa could also see my every move. She'd talk. In any event, I quickly dismissed the worries. Conversation in a bar was always within bounds, even with a beautiful, twenty-something half-naked female. But for some reason I continued to hesitate.

The truth was I was out of practice. I hadn't been to a bar with single attractive girls, without my wife, in a long, long time. A few gentlemen's clubs on business trips, but that didn't count. It was too easy. Strippers talk to you because it leads to money. This girl wasn't a professional, so I had to do it the hard way. A clever opening line, chitchat about the bar and where we were from, then funny opinions, and so on. But I didn't know where to start. In college, it was easy because the girls were all my age. She was probably twenty years younger. I'd probably slip up and mention Lynyrd Skynyrd or U2 and she'd look at me like I was from outer space. Or she'd say something about Beyoncé or Neon Trees and I'd ask, "Who the hell is that?" But mostly, I thought, it was a waste of time. Not because I might not have some fun, but because I knew, at the end, where it would lead: precisely nowhere. I loved my wife.

That was it.

In the end, I'd dithered for so long she wandered off with the guy with the goofy top hat. My mood plunged when I saw her go, but Jim, as usual, came to the rescue. Handing me another round, we went back to observing and talking about what was happening around us. It was getting even more bizarre. The costumes, in particular, were really starting to pump up the crowd. Whenever a good one would pass by, a burst of wild cheering and shouting would erupt. And there were more and more of them: a guy with a Kiss painted face and moon boots, a fifteenth century English Lord, Cat Woman. You name it. Along the bar, the mood was even livelier. A midget dressed as a Leprechaun was dancing a jig on the back counter, whipping the patrons around him into a cheering frenzy. Two girls on the back side of the bar, presumably off shift barmaids, were dancing in metal shark cages. The barmaids behind the counter were also starting to dance for tips. For $5 they'd turn around, give you a good wiggle of their ass and a few throws of their hair. For $10 they'd drop to their knees, stroke your head and then jump into a simulated pole dance. I didn't want to think what they'd do for $20.

Continuing to marvel at the spectacle, I struggled to put it all into perspective. It was as if we'd slipped into a parallel universe. Our new world was close to Earth, maybe directly below the surface, and similar in a lot of respects. But when our old world was flipped, the Earth's crust, like a warped mirror, had distorted it in certain ways. It reminded me of the famous *Star Trek* episode when the crew winds up on a different *Enterprise*. On the parallel ship, the crew dresses and acts differently. The men, sporting facial hair, are ruthless and mean. The women dress more provocatively and use their bodily charms to get ahead. But it wasn't exactly like that. The people in our new universe were certainly different, particularly in dress, but, on the whole, surprisingly tame. We had yet to see a fight, shoving match, or even an argument. And despite how half the women were dressed, not a single inappropriate grope or gesture. Mostly, I thought, our new universe was a universe where otherwise healthy adults could depressurize from the daily stresses of life. Assemble with a common bond, and act, at least in some way, unconstrained from the rules of the old universe. More than anything else, it was a world created to have *fun*.

Reinvigorated, we agreed that it was time to step up our own game. Going back to girl-watching was a good start. I'd noticed her when they all started dancing and pointed her out to Jim. She was on the other side of the bar, towards the main entrance. It was time to move.

On the way, my phone buzzed again. It was Carrie. They were looking for us. Larry and Tom were on the prowl as well. It was tough to respond because my elbows kept getting bumped, but after sending and interpreting some more barely legible texts, we all found each other.

After we'd all caught up, Larry asked why we'd chosen this spot. I pointed up at the barmaid. The guys immediately understood. She was by far the most attractive of the group. Tall and athletic with long, bleach blonde curly hair, she smiled in a way that was more natural than the others like she was really enjoying herself. She also had the best tan, although her spider web bikini top was at least one size too small. A rare case, I thought, where shrinkage was right.

Just after she'd delivered a round of beers to Bill, the biker standing next to me handed her a $5 bill. She gave him more than his money's worth.

When she was done, she stroked my cheek and whispered, "I'll do it better for you."

Carrie, who was by now the most visibly intoxicated of our group, stumbled over, grabbed my arm and sputtered, "If you buy a danssss from her I'll take your pixure!"

At that point, everyone started to egg me on.

Bill, Tom, and Larry really got into it, slamming their hands on the counter and shouting, "Come on! Do it!!"

Even Alan and Nancy were giving me a thumbs-up. Jim wasn't far behind.

"You gotta' do it, dude," he blurted, "and fassst because I'm fadin' . . ."

Overcoming some last hesitation, I called her over and asked her if she'd dance for me.

"Of course!" she replied, throwing her hair back to get ready.

As soon as I opened my wallet I knew I had a problem. The bills were all twenties. Jim caught me staring at them and turned back towards the group.

"Guys," he said with an increasing crescendo, "this is gonna be *good*!"

Not wanting to back out for fear of being labeled as a wimp or a cheapskate, I took a deep breath, extracted a $20 bill and snapped it up to her. When she saw it, her face lit up like she'd just opened the most coveted Christmas present of her life.

"Oh shit," I said under my breath, ". . . here it comes."

The speed of her start caught me by surprise. Within a second, she'd thumped her rear end down directly onto the counter in front of me, spread her legs out, and grabbed the back of my neck. Then, just as rapidly, she pulled my head forward straight into her crotch and started gyrating her ass up and down. The crowd went crazy laughing and shouting, but all I could think of was the oddity of the whole thing. A week ago I'd been quietly sipping a Diet Coke with my wife on a restaurant patio by the ocean. Now I was half a world away, in a parallel universe, hair deep in a bar maid's cooch.

Thankfully her pelvic muscles didn't last long and she jumped back up on the bar. The rest of the dance was more or less average, with an occasional dip to stroke my head again as the group stood back snapping photos. Towards the end, Jim grabbed my phone and took one so I could have my own record. When my daughter discovered it, sometime after I got home, she scowled, grabbed the phone and marched straight into the kitchen to show my wife. To her credit, my wife decided not to fuel her dramatics.

Holding my phone in one hand and a spatula in the other, she said, quietly, "She's cute." It was perfect.

Around one o'clock we made the call to Andy. I was the last to squeeze in and had to straddle the entry space just inside the suicide doors between the middle and front seats, holding myself off the floor with my arms. Jim couldn't believe that I was willing to travel that way, but it wasn't like sitting on somebody's lap was an option. The women were all with their husbands and I wasn't going to "ride bitch" with any of the guys, particularly when they were all pretty wasted. I'd just have to suck it up.

A variety of unplanned entertainment kept the fun going all the way back to the lodge. Carrie started the show with a series of drunken rants about all that was wrong with her soccer mom life and the FTS.

"Who doth she thinks schee is that team mom bitch . . . you know I could [hiccup] . . . do that too but I haff a life . . ." she'd say, then just as quickly change subjects to: "Shit those bathrooms were dist-custing, you know . . . [hiccup] . . . I mean why do they do that . . . they don't haff to do that . . . but I gotta admit that midget guy wuss really cute."

Theresa kept staring at her with her mouth half open, wondering what could possibly come out next. Tom, ever the kid, was giddily pointing out the fascinating things he saw out the window: the tricked-out bikes, the women riding topless, the wild costumes. Alan and Nancy, holding hands in the back, were still giving it to each other. She started it.

"I love you, but you really are a small man."

"There's nothing little about me baby, except my bank account," he laughed.

"You know you're pretty hot for a Grandma."

"Yeah and you still can't handle me."

And so on. But the most amusing thing other than Larry's drunken snore, particularly to Jim, was watching me deal with my leg cramps.

Every couple of minutes, my hamstrings and calves were knotting into balls. The only way out of them, given my strange position, was to flop around like a hooked game fish.

Andy suggested that I drink some water at one point but otherwise didn't say much.

He's probably seen a lot better than this, I thought. I doubted we'd even make his book.

Day 7: Uneasy Feeling

Jim had mentioned it to me when we got back to the lodge. "Tomorrow," he said, "is the day I want to take the long ride into Wyoming and visit Devil's Tower."

It was hugely tempting. An ardent fan of the movie *Close Encounters of the Third Kind*, I'd wanted to see it all my life. But I was exhausted. I'd been riding for six straight days. My ass was still throbbing and my leg muscles were a mess. The mental strain was also starting to get to me: the unpredictable weather, the close calls. After more than two thousand miles, I needed a day away from it. Not wanting to punctuate the evening on a sour note, I stalled, saying only, "Sounds good, but let's talk about it in the morning."

Jim bounced out of bed at eight-thirty like the prior evening's debauchery had never happened. The others were still sleeping it off and in no condition to do anything. While he was showering, I wandered into the kitchen. Hector and Cindy greeted me warmly. They were going to spend the day in the Badlands National Park. When I asked how they were going to get there, he replied, "By Monte Carlo, of course!" He knew by now that his bike wouldn't be coming and there were no rental motorcycles available anywhere in the area. They'd taken the news well, considering the situation, but I felt sorry for them. It wasn't the vacation they'd planned for. Since I'd already decided to take the day off, I offered them my bike. Hector was tempted, I could tell, but politely declined. You have to be pretty close friends with a man to take his motorcycle on an all-day ride and feel good about it. He had too much class for that.

When I finally screwed up the courage to tell Jim that I wasn't going, he launched into a vigorous sales pitch.

"Dude, I can't believe you're going to miss this. I checked the weather and it's going to be perfect. Low eighties, no rain, and light winds. And my tour guide says the Tower is *the number one* thing you have to see around here. Come on. I promise we'll take it easy."

I wavered for a while and at one point almost gave in, but something strange was telling me not to ride that day.

"Even the Lord had to rest on the seventh day," I finally said, "and if it's good enough for Him, it's good enough for me."

Dejected, he turned towards Theresa and said, solemnly, "He's not going."

She did her best to act disappointed, but I could tell that she didn't mind. It would be another great day with just her husband.

What I really wanted, more than anything, was time to think.

The best way to get my mind in gear, I figured, was to take a long hike. There were supposed to be some mountain trails nearby. It would also help to stretch my legs. So after downing a light breakfast and saying goodbye to Jim and Theresa, I laced up my new riding boots, grabbed a water bottle and stepped outside. It was the nicest morning yet. The air was already warm and rapidly drying. The sky was cloudless and brilliantly blue. Skeptical that it would stay that way, I pulled out my phone and checked every weather source available. The forecasts were all the same: sunny with a high of 82°F. The radar was clear for hundreds of miles in every direction. It figures, I thought. The one day I won't ride will be the best weather day of the entire trip.

Ten steps away from the lodge, I stopped dead in my tracks with my first practical thought of the morning. I hadn't left a note. Jim and Theresa knew what I was doing, but they were already on their way to Wyoming and wouldn't be back until dinner time. I hadn't mentioned my hiking plans to Hector and Cindy and the others were still asleep. If anything happened to me, no one would know where I was. Quickly deciding that it wasn't necessary, I started out again at a brisk pace. I've got my phone, I thought, and it's fully charged.

Before long, at the far end of the road loop that led back to the lodge, I found the start of a dirt logging road. It was wide enough for a pickup truck to travel and had some old tire tracks, so I figured it had to lead somewhere. I'd have to stick to it because shortly beyond the edges of the road, the hills were steep and thickly forested. But at least it would be easy to follow. By the time I'd passed the first pile of cleared timber and branches, I was ready to put all things motorcycle and Sturgis behind me.

Some time later, as I rounded another turn, my thoughts turned to what had been bothering me. A conversation with my wife the day before had triggered it. Or, more accurately, had added enough incremental concern to generate an uneasy feeling. It wasn't anything she'd said that was out of the ordinary. Usually, our "away" conversations revolved around our kids and managing the house and our chat before my FTS adventure had indeed fit that pattern. But something had been particularly off. She'd been more focused than usual. Very organized and authoritative in recounting the day's events with the kids and the next to-dos on the house, but at the same time more emotional, almost spiritual, when it came to our closing affirmations of love. The words I'd heard a thousand times before spoken this time with more tenderness, conviction, and reverence. My first thought, after we hung up, was that she must be really missing me, but it was more than that. It was as if she was trying to crawl in even closer to my soul, perhaps to protect me. While at the same time fulfilling a more intense need to be even more protected, coveted, and loved herself.

It hadn't always been that way. For me, it had been love at first sight, but for her, falling in love had taken a good deal of time. In fact, considering how our first date started, it's a wonder we ever saw each other again. So as I walked along, still pondering why she'd acted that way on the phone, I thought about our courtship.

It began in the spring of 1986. I was in the second phase of Naval Nuclear Propulsion training, called "prototype," after six months of Nuclear Power School, which is essentially a Master's Degree in Nuclear Engineering and Reactor Plant Operations crammed into six months. The next step is another six-month training period where you qualify to operate an actual reactor plant. The Navy has some operating nuclear power plants on land, either prototype units for future submarines and surface ships or previously operational units extracted from retired boats. And the worst—the one nobody wanted to be assigned to—at least in the 1980s, was the S3G prototype in West Milton, New York. It was the oldest plant, made by cutting up the *USS Triton (SSN-586)*. The only twin reactor plant submarine the Navy ever produced (and there were good reasons for that. Heavy, slow, noisy, and temperamental. It didn't last long in the fleet). By the winter of 1985-86, when I arrived, it was already on its last legs. The standing joke at S3G was when you gave the order to "bring steam into the engine room," you brought *steam into the engine room*—because it was coming out *everywhere*.

As an officer, we had to learn how to do everyone's job, so we had plenty of opportunities to get hot and sweaty. And we also had to learn to do our own job, which was giving all of the necessary orders to correctly start-up, operate, and shut down the plant. That required knowing it backward and forwards from an engineering standpoint, as well as all of the operating and casualty procedures (what to do if something goes wrong). It was also our first chance to supervise a crew.

The plants ran continually—or at least they were cycled continuously. So we worked shifts: either days, "mids," or nights, ten hours a day, with, on average, seven days off a month. The whole thing was, by and large, rather miserable, but the best part was when you pulled mids. You could sleep in, arrive for work at around three in the afternoon and be off by about eleven o'clock. And then, after a quick dinner and shower, walk into town and hit the bars by midnight. In the State of New York, they stayed open until four in the morning. That made it tolerable.

The closest decent town to West Milton was Saratoga Springs, home of the famous Saratoga Racetrack. So after "nuke school," I rented an apartment within walking distance of the downtown area with another junior officer in my prototype class. Square shouldered, big-boned, and handsome with sandy blonde hair and thick forearms, he would have made a great lifeguard. But more than anything, he looked like the famous University of Michigan football coach Bo Schembechler, so we called him "Shemmy." And Shemmy and I loved to drink "jenny screamers" (slang for a local beer called Genesee Cream Ale) at an Irish pub in Saratoga.

But one cold night, after a mid-shift in early April, we decided to try a different place. It was a small bar, a street or two behind the pub we were used to frequenting and had the reputation of being more of an eclectic, college-aged hangout. I'm not sure what drew us there, but sometime after midnight we paid the small cover charge and started scouting for a table. The music was deafening even to a couple of twenty-three-year-olds, so we positioned ourselves as far away from the DJ and his eight-foot floor speakers as possible. Even then, it hurt just to listen to it, and the conversation was nearly impossible.

At some point over the roar, I spotted her on the dance floor. Wearing pink painter's pants and a white blouse, with neck length shag, cut light brown hair, I started studying her more carefully. She was with a friend who was taller and more of a traditional "blonde bombshell," but for some reason I wasn't the least bit attracted to her. The petite one had already caught my interest. But I couldn't really see her face. So I told Shemmy to hang on for a minute, stood up, and started moving towards the dance floor. A few paces later, I finally got the full picture. And when I saw that cute, coy smile beneath her greenish-grey eyes and those sculpted, oversized hips, I stopped breathing. Some say it hits you like a thunderbolt or an arrow, but for me, it was more like a sudden realization that I'd found a great treasure. She was the one, my future wife and the mother of our children. I saw it right then. Somehow, I knew.

Cutting in closer, I screwed up the courage to ask her to dance. She politely declined, saying, "No, thank you, I'm just hanging out with my friend."

Fresh off of a painful breakup with another boyfriend, the last thing she wanted was to start fishing again. I was also one of those "Navy guys." She could spot them a mile away. Though we didn't wear our uniforms in town, the tapered sideburns gave it away. And we were all the same. Arrogant, cocky, and interested, it seemed, in only one thing: a few months of good romping before blowing town. In that, she had "zero interest."

Crushingly disappointed, I sat back down with Shemmy and ordered another beer.

"Hey, I saw you asked that girl to dance . . . no luck, eh?" he said.

"Yeah," I replied, "and it's too damn loud in here. Let's go."

As we chugged the last remnants of our "screamers," her friend, the tall blonde, approached our table and grabbed my arm.

Pulling me closer, so I had at least a chance of hearing her, she screamed, "Hey . . . I've been talking with my friend . . . and she thinks that maybe she was a little hard on you . . . maybe you should ask her to dance again."

I had a second chance.

After a few dances, with her mostly looking at other things while I tried to make small talk over the ridiculous amount of background noise, she said she had to go. Terrified that I might lose her again, I quickly asked for her phone number. I figured I had about a one in ten chance. Staring at me for a moment, struggling with the decision, she reached into her pocket, extracted a cocktail napkin and a pen, and scribbled it out. It was the first and only time she'd ever given out her phone number to a man in a bar. And to this day, she'll tell you she doesn't know why she did it. But I was elated.

Stumbling home, after one too many screamers, I slapped my arm around Shemmy's broad shoulders and slurred, "You know thhaat girl I met . . . the cute one in the paainters paaannthss . . . *hahhtsss* the woman I'm gonna maaawwy."

He just chuckled and rolled his eyes.

A few days later I called her and we set up our first date. It was after a day shift, on a Friday evening, and I was to pick her up at her sister's house in Ballston Spa. The plan was to have dinner at a restaurant in Saratoga called Lillian's and then maybe walk the town. She didn't sound too excited about it, and I was nervous as hell, so to blow off steam and calm myself, as part of my getting ready ritual, I washed my car. Everything had to be perfect.

I could tell she was anxious as well, so when I arrived at her sister's place, I did my best to put her at ease and be the consummate gentlemen. I introduced myself, handed her some flowers I'd bought, made some small talk, and walked her to the car. I'd purchased it five months earlier. A 1972 Oldsmobile Cutlass Supreme Convertible, and though it was only a year newer than my LeMans, it'd already been meticulously restored by its previous owner and looked brand new. It was also the best looking car I ever owned, equally attractive to both men and women, with radiant green metallic paint, color-keyed wheels, and a white top and interior. And, like my LeMans, it had a column shift and a bench seat, which I loved (much better for snuggling with girls). So after I opened the door for her and she got in, I was hoping she'd sit reasonably close to me. But she positioned herself as far towards the passenger side door as possible. And, sitting with her hands folded, said nothing as I pulled out of the driveway and drove down the hill that led to the main highway into Saratoga. Not a single opening line—nothing.

Wondering why she was so quiet, I pulled onto the highway and started accelerating. It wasn't that hard of a takeoff, I certainly didn't floor it or spin the tires, or, for that matter, even strain the engine. It was just a brisk run up to the speed at which I generally drove, which, in those days, was almost 10 mph over the speed limit or more. Just about when I'd passed 60 mph (it was a 55 mph zone), she spoke.

"So, are we going to fire?"

"No . . . sorry . . . I didn't mean to scare you . . ." but my voice trailed off. She apparently wasn't pleased. I suppose it could have been worse, I thought. She could have insulted my car. But by the time we got to the restaurant, stung by her sarcastic chide, I was already questioning whether or not I wanted to go through with dinner.

Our table wasn't ready so they asked us to sit at the bar and wait, which was fine by me. Our small talk ever since her "going to fire" comment had been strained, and she also had a maddening habit of looking at just about everything but me when I was talking to her. So when the bartender asked for our drink orders, I let her go first, which was proper, but quickly followed with a request for a Jack on the rocks. I needed something with some bite to steady myself. She never gave me the chance.

"So," she said as soon as he left, "you drink *liquor.*"

Thinking oh no, I've screwed up again, I tried to soften the blow. "Yeah . . . sometimes, usually wine or beer . . . but . . . I do like a Jack every now and then."

Glancing away again, she didn't say much, so I just drank my whiskey, waiting for the bartender to return so I could order something else and possibly redeem myself. Or, increasingly, I thought, just keep going, get shit-faced, and be done with it.

When he saw that my drink was nearly empty, which didn't take long, he leaned over and asked, "You want another one?"

"No thanks," I responded, "I'm going to switch to wine, maybe a glass of Merlot."

Before he could even spin around again, she cocked her head to the side and said, more playfully this time but still with disapproval, "So, now you're *mixing*."

A week earlier, when we'd first met, I was sure she was the one. Now I wanted to throw my drink in her face. No other woman had ever cycled my emotions this way. Maybe she does have what it takes to be a good wife. I reached out for her hand. She squeezed it back with a sly smirk. OK, I thought, I'm starting to get this girl. But one thing for sure. If she is the one, it's never going to be easy . . .

And it never was. It took a full three-year pursuit before she finally married me. With a couple of near-breakups (always precipitated by her, usually after one of my visits), a few trials of my own with other girls (which she *still* gives me grief about), long separations (two deployments and one local special operation), and other miscues. But the turning point came two years later after I got home from my second deployment.

It was a special operation to a "northern operating area." In 1988, before the Berlin Wall came down, we were still chasing around Soviet submarines, and "way up north," as we called it, was pretty much where they lived. I never did understand why everything was so super-secret. It's not like they didn't know we were up there snooping, or we didn't know when and where they were snooping. It was just part of the game. And our "spec op" was more or less typical. Get up there, skulk around, come back, and report. Two months of continuous operations, most of it submerged, without a port call or a chance to call home. Our only contact with the outside world would be through "family-grams."

Before leaving, we handed out four of the forms to every member of the crew (The policy was you got two for each month of a deployment.). No one got more or less. The instructions, being the Navy, were precise. No more than forty words and a prescribed total number of characters, punctuation included. All of them had to be sent to the squadron communications office for screening, and they had the right to edit or not send one at all if they decided it was improper. Inappropriate meant anything that would unnecessarily depress a crew member or interfere with him doing his job (In those days submarine crews were male-only.). So if your girlfriend or wife wanted to send a family-gram that said something like, "CAN'T TAKE IT ANYMORE. LEAVING YOU. WILL LEAVE YOUR THINGS IN APARTMENT WITH YOUR DEAD DOG," it wasn't going out.

There were good reasons for the limited length of the messages, as well as the limited numbers, and we all knew them. In those days, attack submarines could only receive radio traffic at periscope depth (PD) with a receiving mast up. And staying at PD for any length of time was undesirable. Not only did it slow transit progress (with a mast up you can only do about five knots maximum speed), but it was dangerous. Nuclear powered submarines today are nothing like the fleet boats of World War II. They're not designed to "crash dive" and get down quickly. And you can't turn a seven thousand ton boat at slow speed quickly. Thus, they're very vulnerable at PD. So to minimize the interruption in transit time and the risks, you wanted to spend as little time there as possible. And that meant limiting the amount of "radio traffic" you had to receive and transmit. Today, we snarl if we don't have ten megabytes per second download speed with our internet connections. In 1988, on an attack submarine at sea, it was about a thousandth of that. And operational traffic, instructions on where to go, what depth to run at, and so forth, always took precedence. So limiting the amount of "personal bullshit," as our Chief Engineer called it, was critical. That's why we were only allowed, on average, less than three words a day.

Sensing that we were at a critical point in our relationship. I gave my girlfriend, who I was still hoping—someday—would be my wife. Two of the forms, together with an instruction sheet, and asked her only to send me one every three weeks. In the meantime, I planned some surprises. I arranged for two dozen roses to be delivered to her on her birthday (about three weeks after we left), and wrote her two love letters that would hopefully, if Shemmy got it right, be mailed in time so that she'd get them before I got back.

I gave the other two family-gram forms to my Mother and briefed her on the rules and procedures by phone, because I knew the written instructions would be too detailed for her.

"Remember Mom," I recalled saying as we hung up, "you can only send in these two."

Two days into our outbound transit, during a nighttime excursion to PD, the first family-grams came in. The radioman was surprised that we'd received a batch so soon (most people waited at least a week to send one). And was particularly baffled by the fact that three of the five, amongst the entire crew of 108, were for Lieutenant McPherson. They'd never seen that before.

When they informed me that I'd received three—news that was already spreading through the crew faster than word of future port calls—I was surprised but excited. One of them had to be from my girlfriend. But when they handed me the messages, I quickly realized they were all from my family: one from my Mother, one from my sister Kathleen, and one from my brother. It didn't make sense. I'd only given my Mom two of the forms.

About a day later, during another PD excursion, another batch came in. A total of fourteen.

"You're not going to believe this Sir," the radioman said as I opened the door to the communications shack, "but two of them are for you again."

Now more angry than surprised, I grabbed the messages and scanned the last lines. One was from my Mother—again—and another one was from a high school friend. What the hell is going on here? I thought. And, most importantly, where are the ones from my girlfriend??

I never got another one—after five, I figured the squadron cut me off. So for the next two months, while just about everybody else got some emotional reassurance from the woman they loved, I couldn't do anything but wonder if she really cared for me, or, for that matter, if anything I'd planned—or was planning—would ever come to fruition; if the flowers had arrived or if she got my last love letter asking her to consider moving to Norfolk when she graduated with her nursing degree so we could be closer. Even though I worked harder during that deployment than any other time on the boat, with the responsibility for four divisions (reactor controls, damage control, main propulsion, and communications), she was never far from my mind. By the time we pulled up in Norfolk again, exhausted by the workload and the emotional turmoil caused by our communications blackout, I was ready to collapse.

So the last thing I wanted to hear, once we shut down, as I worked frantically to tie up all of the loose ends so I could escape and call her, was that the squadron communications officer had boarded and wanted to see me. He was a Lieutenant, like me, but had already completed his sea tour and taken a job at squadron headquarters. It wasn't exactly a plumb assignment, more or less a parking lot for someone who probably wouldn't even make Lieutenant Commander. And he had the reputation, as almost all squadron staff officers did, of being a "weenie."

A few minutes later, with crew members from my divisions coming in and out of my shower-sized stateroom in a frenzied hurry, he wedged his way in and started talking. It was one of those conversations where you respond to everything very professionally—while secretly thinking something else.

"Wow, I'm glad I caught you."

"Yes, it's great to see you." [*No it's not. I've got a thousand more important things to do right now to get the hell off this boat, including figuring out if I still have a girlfriend, and you're in my way.*]

"You seem to have had a problem with family-grams this deployment."

"Yes, I got five if that's what you're referring to." [*You know damn well I got five. It was certainly the talk of our boat for a week.*]

"Are you aware of the policy?"

"Yes, I'm well aware of it." [*I'm the Communicator, you idiot. I briefed the crew on it. Of course, I'm aware.*]

"Well, I did all I could, but there were way too many forms that came in."

"I appreciate that." [*You didn't do anything, you dweeb. You just followed the procedures. And, in fact, you were probably too stupid to catch that you let five go out instead of four.*]

"Have a good weekend!"

"You too." [*Piss off.*]

And with that, he handed me a stack of over fifty forms. It had to be my Mother, I thought, my sweet, clueless Mother. She hadn't understood my instructions—or just ignored them—made over fifty copies of the form, passed them out to my family and friends, and asked them all to write to me. And if that was true, then maybe, just maybe, within the stack, were the forms I'd given my girlfriend. They might have arrived after I'd already hit my allotment.

With my pulse racing, as quickly but carefully as I could, I rifled through the pile. And there, towards the bottom, were two forms of her handwriting. Ordering everyone out of my stateroom, I shut the door, locked it, took a deep breath, and started to read.

By the time I was done, I was completely renewed. She'd received the flowers and they were beautiful. She'd been thinking a lot about us and really missed me. But more importantly, she was going to take me up on my suggestion to move to Norfolk when she graduated. And, finally, the words I'd longed to see—or hear—for two years. She was in love with me.

It was the happiest single moment of my life.

A year later, on a postcard-perfect day over the Memorial Day weekend, at the Norfolk Naval Base Chapel, we began our life together. And as I rounded the next turn on the path, passing another pile of cleared trees and brush, I thought about how far we'd come. We'd worked hard but had been very fortunate. Our kids were doing well in school, staying out of trouble, and making good choices. We'd moved to our dream location, started a new home, and achieved financial security. She was well liked and had a close circle of loving, vivacious friends. Our marriage was still strong and neither of us had ever strayed.

But still, something wasn't right. Over the past three years it had hit her in waves, nothing too horrible. But enough to periodically sap her energy and cause her to wonder and worry, to dull her outlook and turn her towards pessimism. And for the past few months, as I prepared for the Sturgis trip, her depression had grown more frequent and intense with a few bouts of crying. When I'd catch it, I'd only squeeze her hand, and she'd dab her eyes and wave it off as a likely premenopausal symptom. But I could tell she didn't really believe that, and neither did I.

So as I continued to hike along that mountain trail, thinking about her worsening bouts of depression and our most recent conversation, for the first time, it dawned on me that something could actually be wrong. And, more strongly than any time I'd ever been away before, including all my years of Navy and business travel, an intense, near despondent revelation washed over me.

I needed to *get home.*

My plan had always been to stay another three days, with four days riding back, to make it an even two-week vacation. There was still a lot to see, including the Buffalo Chip, the Badlands National Park, and—if Jim was willing to go back again—Devil's Tower. Each of which would have taken a full day to properly explore. But by noon on the seventh day, I was done. The only question in my mind was which route to take back.

When I got back to the lodge, I grabbed my Harley tour guide, a pad, and a pencil and snuggled up to the kitchen table. A few of the guys were in the living room watching an old Clint Eastwood western, but the house was otherwise quiet.

The first thing I decided was that I-70 through Missouri was out. There was no way, even if the weather cooperated, that I was doing *that* again. So there were only two choices. A more northerly route that would take me to I-90 East again and into Illinois and down through the Ohio Valley to the Southeast. Or, a more southerly route that would take the back way out of Sturgis to the south, down into and across Nebraska, then south through Kansas and Oklahoma, and more directly east through the southern tier of states back to South Carolina. The southern route would have the advantage of following at least one recommended "scenic" road, Route 2 through Nebraska, which I'd wanted to take on the way out to Sturgis but couldn't because of the flooding. It was a little bit longer in terms of total miles, but spread out over several days that wouldn't make much of a difference. The choice turned out to be easy. I'd ride south.

The next, more difficult part was figuring out how to break the ride up. While I wanted to get home as soon as possible, I wasn't going to shoot for a three-day trip again. Since the total distance was just over 1,900 miles, three days would require successive "cannonball runs" of better than six hundred miles a day. I wasn't doing that again either. So over the next hour, using Google maps and the calculator on my phone, I started to carve out what I thought would be more reasonable segments. The objective for the first day would be to make it to Grand Island, Nebraska, a ride of about 450 miles. From there I'd travel due south, through Wichita, Kansas and into Oklahoma. The best stopping place would probably be somewhere east of Tulsa. That would require about 500 miles. The third day would be the longest, from eastern Oklahoma to Little Rock, to Memphis, and then down into Birmingham, Alabama. A total run of about 550 miles. And finally, on the fourth day, I'd ride from Birmingham to Atlanta, and then home, a distance of about 400 miles.

It all depended, of course, on the weather. A massive cold front had formed in the central Rockies and was moving east across the Great Plains, touching as far north as Nebraska and stretching all the way to Texas. It was a slow mover, crossing about five hundred miles a day, so if I left the next morning, I'd probably catch up to it by the end of the day. And then each successive day, as I moved south and then east, I'd be more or less staying on its trailing edge. If the timing were right, I wouldn't have to ride through it, but I'd probably be chasing it all the way across the country. The only other option was to wait a day to give the front more time to advance, but something else could always pop up as the warmer air tried to filter in again behind it. At least I knew where this enemy was.

Having learned on the way out how *not* to pack, I spent the next segment of the afternoon bettering my technique. I'd brought along too many pairs of jeans and never realized how heavy they were, so the first thing I did was leave the ones I liked the least in the dresser. I could live with two pairs going home. Next, I organized each item by weight and placed the heaviest items, like my passenger backrest and computer, in the large travel bag. This would put the bulk of the weight further forward and lower since the big bag rested directly on the passenger seat. The lighter clothes, including what I'd need to change each day, I placed in the smaller tour pack bag. The scotch was already long gone so I could put my bathroom bag, which was nearly as heavy, where it had been in the left saddlebag. My heavier rain gear would fit neatly into the right one.

After giving Big Girl another quick wash and detail, I loaded everything according to the new plan, swung my legs over, and rocked her from side to side in the garage. She was certainly heavier but still felt stable and balanced. Overall, it was a tremendous improvement.

When Jim and Theresa arrived back from Wyoming, they pulled into the garage, dismounted and studied me carefully. I must have looked determined and driven, "on a mission" as we used to say in the service, while at the same time a little guilty and anxious. The tour pack and the large travel bag were also back on my bike. Something was obviously up. In hindsight, it must have been obvious.

Taking some time to assemble his thoughts, Jim finally said, "I didn't think you'd last much longer. It's OK. I'm personally ready to go home too."

He was letting me off the hook. Relieved, I suggested that we have a last quiet dinner together in Deadwood. The others were already spooling up to hit Sturgis again, but with a long road trip ahead of me beginning first thing in the morning, I didn't feel like partying. Jim and Theresa readily agreed. Their Devil's Tower ride had been exhilarating, the best day ride of the entire trip, but they were sunburned and tired. We'd ask the others to be nice but doubted anybody would want to come with us. As we suspected, they all declined. Larry's response had been the best.

"Are you fucking kidding me?" he snorted. "Last night was just a warm-up!"

I let Jim pick the place, and after talking to a few bikers on the street to get advice, we found a table on the roof of a restaurant overlooking the main drag. The food was pretty good and we spent a lot of time talking about our kids, but the mood was subdued, the conversation mostly quiet. When we finally did return to motorcycling talk, Jim asked me what route I was going to take. Having already studied it in great detail, I drew it on a cocktail napkin. Theresa looked away for a moment and when her head turned back, I could see water in her eyes. She was worried. After that, I tried to keep it livelier, but it was a lackluster performance. I was worried as well, not only about the long, lonely ride ahead and the unforeseeable dangers and obstacles that I knew would arise, but mostly about doing the unthinkable—letting my wife down. However long it took, I had to get home unharmed.

And as I laid in bed, on my last night in South Dakota, thinking of how much I missed her and the ride ahead, I realized how different it was all going to be.

Part IV: Riding Back
Day 8: Starting to Lose It

I woke up to the smell of brewing coffee around six o'clock. For once, someone had managed to get out of bed ahead of me. When I stumbled into the kitchen, still yawning and rubbing my eyes, Hector and Cindy were buttering some bagels.

"We didn't want to miss saying goodbye," they said.

Over the past several nights of sipping scotch, smoking cigars, and sharing our childhood stories, we'd all become good friends. Aside from my brother and sister-in-law, I'd miss him and Cindy the most.

When Jim and Theresa wandered in we all tried to make small talk and crack a few jokes, but everyone seemed to be infected with a palpable nervousness. After a while, I realized why. They were all worried that something bad was going to happen to me. At first I was touched, but after a while it started to get on my nerves. The way that happens when you're about to do something dangerous, someone who cares about you is anxious about it, and it makes you even more nervous because they're nervous.

They made it even worse by following me out to the garage and walking beside me as I rolled Big Girl down the gravel drive onto the access road. Obviously, they weren't done saying goodbye. After adjusting my gear, shaking hands with Jim and Hector again, and enduring several more "Please be careful"s from the girls, I finally hit the starter. Aside from the ride out of Manchester Harley-Davidson on my first bike and watching my son Chris ride out of the Kawasaki dealership for the first time, I couldn't recall a time on a bike that I'd ever been as nervous. Knowing my luck, I thought, I'll dump her on the first turn. But I made it.

Before long I was through Rapid City and heading south on Route 79. It was one of the best roads of the entire trip. Two lanes wide with big shoulders, lightly grooved concrete and long, natural curves. It ran along the seam of the valley that separates the Black Hills to the west and the Badlands National Park to the east. Traffic was light, with only a few massive rigs every now and then traveling in the other direction. I kept Big Girl at 72 mph with my feet on the highway pegs and surveyed the nearby hills, still covered with late summer grasses and wildflowers. Farther away, to my right, the Black Hills were fading into hazy, purple colored apparitions. To my left, the Badlands were rising in small, distant, tan colored mounds. The air was cool but rapidly warming, the sky a light pastel blue with little nodule-like clouds. It was a near perfect ride.

Aside from the small sign that welcomed me to Nebraska, it was easy to tell when I'd crossed the border. The landscape turned markedly different. The distant hills and the rich palate of colors that defined South Dakota were gradually replaced with endlessly rolling fields of gently swaying summer wheat. Later, I found scenic Route 2 and turned east, hoping that my Harley Tour Guide wouldn't let me down.

Unfortunately, I didn't get a chance to think about that much longer. The storm front located over North Texas and Oklahoma that I'd so diligently tracked the day and night before had indeed moved to the east, but its massive counterclockwise wind rotation had picked up even more steam. When I'd been traveling on Route 79, mostly to the south-southwest, its winds had been directly behind me. Which, I now realized, was one of the reasons why the ride had been so enjoyable. But now, moving to the east-southeast, directly perpendicular to the wind flow, I was in for a rude awakening. And rude it was. Within seconds after turning onto Route 2, fierce, spasmodic wind gusts of 30 to 45 mph slammed into my left side. Instinctively I backed off on the throttle a bit, slowing below 70 mph, but they kept coming at me, with maddening unpredictably, mile after mile. Sometimes they jerked my head so violently I could actually hear my neck crack.

There was, however, a silver lining. I'd noticed the BNSF (Burlington

Northern Santa Fe) coal trains paralleling the westbound side of the road for some time. At first they seemed out of place—long, rusting leviathans that were marring what a sublime Nebraskan countryside was—but with each passing mile I found myself studying them with an increasingly wondrous fascination. The first thing that struck me was the number of open freight cars filled with black coal that were sitting along the miles of tracks that ran parallel to the road. There had to be thousands of them. Every now and then I'd pass a few engines, usually hitched together in groupings of two to four, but they were also idle. When I finally did spot a train that was moving, it was poking along to the west at no more than ten miles an hour, barely moving the endless line of cars in front of it. Whoever needed the coal obviously didn't need it very quickly. But after a while, the thought that increasingly came to me was how the two were perfectly blending together. The blackness of the coal and the hardness of the steel with the pastel colors and softness of the earth. An oddly but strikingly beautiful juxtaposition of industrial might with bucolic grace. Despite the crosswinds, I couldn't keep my eyes off of it.

It was so mesmerizing, in fact, that I forgot about my fuel situation. I'd noticed once I'd turned east that it was low, but once I started watching the trains, I never looked down again. By the time I did, somewhere well to the east of the running point onto Route 2, the needle was pegged low. Luckily, there was a station just ahead on the westbound side, so I rapidly slowed and turned in.

The station was bigger than I expected for such a remote location with five or six islands, each with two pumps, and a minimart that was big enough to be a full-sized grocery store. The parking lot surrounding it was also huge, with roughly a hundred or so motorcycles parked in various spots. It was obviously a favorite stop for Sturgis travelers. Still a little agitated at not being able to ride as fast as I'd wanted to, I picked an island that had only one car and pulled up behind it, hoping to refuel quickly. As soon as I did another car pulled in behind me to grab the other pump. A quick scan of the other islands revealed no better options. They were all full. I'd have to wait.

The car ahead was an older mid-size Japanese sedan with a faded paint job and missing hubcaps. Though there weren't any school stickers on it, for some reason, it struck me as a kid's car, probably a high school hauler. Sure enough, two teenage boys were in the back, trading candy and occasionally punching each other. Completely self-absorbed, they didn't notice me pull up. Already annoyed at having to wait, I immediately spotted something that caused a rush of blood to surge to my face. There was no fuel nozzle in the tank.

One thing you learn at a bike rally is gas station etiquette. And a good way to spark a fight, or even a riot, is to violate the number one rule. Never, *ever*, under any circumstance, leave a bike or a car at the pump if the station is busy. If it's at the pump, a person should be with it, shoving in fuel. If anybody has to do anything else during the stop, buy a drink, use the restroom, have a smoke, or just kill time, they should do it before or after gassing up. Leaving an unattended vehicle at the pump while people are waiting is simply beyond rude.

Figuring there was no way the kids in the back couldn't at least hear me, I pulled up closer and blipped the throttle a few more times. They looked back at me briefly, but just as quickly turned back to trading candy again. That was strike one.

A minute or so later, with anger building even further, another kid exited the store. He was taller and thinner than the other two with long, wavy brown hair, a faded t-shirt, and pants sagging low enough to expose half his underwear. The kind of teenage boy that responsible adult males see and instinctively want to smack in the head with a two-by-four. Carrying a tray stuffed with sodas, some candy, and a few small bags of chips, he sauntered over to the car. Unable to shout at him over the roar of my V-twin, I decided to just gun the engine a few more times, figuring he'd get the message. Just before he opened the front passenger door, he stared at me for a brief moment but conveyed nothing. No smile, smirk, apology, or even a simple, "We'll just be another minute." Within seconds, he was inside and trading the crap he'd bought with his friends. Still with no other pump options, with anger spreading to every limb in my body, I squeezed my hand grips even tighter, feathered the clutch, pulled up so close my front tire almost touched the car's rear bumper, and gunned the engine nearly continuously. Not one of them even looked back. Either they were so completely self-absorbed they were actually unaware of how rude they were being, or they were intentionally ignoring me. I couldn't decide which was worse. In either case, it was undoubtedly strike two.

After another long minute, a boy who I figured to be the driver emerged from the store. The oldest of the four, with big, dark eyes and the beginnings of a scraggly mustache and sideburns, wandered over to the car holding one of those ridiculously oversized fountain drinks. When he was abreast of the driver's side door, I did my best to put on as mean a face as I could muster. The kind of squint that could fire bullets but chose, at least at that point, to say nothing. When we finally made eye contact, we connected in a way that I hadn't with the others. It was obvious that he knew I was there, waiting, and that I was sorely pissed—but he chose, like the others, to do nothing. Yet he was different. There was something even more sinister about him, a more intensely disrespectful manner in the way he was dismissing me.

And at that moment, it all started flooding back. The accumulated frustrations of raising four teenagers: the self-absorbed behaviors, the inability to recognize and assess risks, the fights over chores and keeping the kitchen clean. As one of my friends likes to say, "Teenagers are like farts. You can barely stand your own." I could put up with my own kids out of love and the hope that they were going to grow into responsible adults one day, but with somebody else's kid it was nearly impossible. And this particular teenager—this *punk*—was infuriating me to a level I'd never experienced. It was time to teach him a lesson.

I noticed that a car on the island adjacent to us had moved off. I pushed Big Girl back far enough to just get by his rear bumper, gunned the engine a final time and pulled up to the pump directly across from his car. Since he was now inside his vehicle and didn't seem to be in any hurry to leave, I took my time removing my helmet, thinking about how I was going to confront him. The first thought that came to me was what Jim would probably do in a situation like this, or Larry or any of the other hotheads I knew. They'd probably walk up to his car and plant their right boot heel as hard as they could into the driver's side door, reach in through the window, grab the kid by his neck, pull him out, stomp on his chest, and shout something like, "You see me now, punk?!" But that wasn't my style. I had to make sure, at least at first, that he knew what he was doing was wrong.

So I made the first decision of our altercation.

Helmet in hand, I walked a few paces towards the driver's side window, stared at him for a long moment, cocked my head, and said, indignantly, "The next time you gas up, try moving your car away from the pump after you finish so that *OTHER PEOPLE* can use it."

I was expecting a taunt back, a half-scared, half-challenging, "So what's your problem?" or maybe even a weak apology, but his reaction completely threw me. He just stared back at me without the slightest change in expression or movement. At first I thought he might have been drunk or high on drugs, but the telltale signs were missing. His eyes were bright and his body was rock solid steady. My next thought was that he might be crazy, but he didn't have wild eyes and most of the guys I'd encountered in my life who were stupid fighters would take on their opponent almost immediately. This kid wasn't baiting me, but he wasn't scared of me either. And that didn't make sense. I was older, yes, but in the best shape of my life, certainly no pushover, with twenty more pounds of muscle. I was also dressed in full motorcycle gear with body armor. Dozens of other bikers were also close by and if I got into any trouble, they were sure to back me up. None of that seemed to matter. He just kept staring back at me, expressionless, with a cold, hidden confidence. I wondered what was behind it.

A moment later, I started to figure it out.

His left hand was on the steering wheel and I'd thought that his right hand, at least at that point, was gripping his horse-sized soda. But I could see his drink in the console now, the straw sticking up almost to the level of the dashboard, and his hand wasn't on it. It was hidden between his legs, down low in his crotch, the wrist above it cocked at almost a ninety-degree angle. There was only one reason why his right hand would be there—in that position. And it damn sure wasn't because he was holding himself.

He had a gun.

My mind at that point switched into hyper-drive. He was apparently waiting for my next move and I had to figure it out, fast. Calmly, but with a speed driven by adrenaline, I ran through the options. Turning my back on him was out of the question. So was mounting a forward charge. While most people with a pistol can't hit the broadside of a barn. Knowing my luck, before I could close the ten feet or so to the car, the kid would probably squeeze off a perfect Dirty Harry like shot straight through my forehead. And there I'd be, collapsed on my back, my brain slowly shorting out . . . contemplating my last epic failure . . . a vision of my wife floating over me, shaking her head, saying in a partly disdainful but mostly pitying way, "You sure screwed that one up."

But I also didn't want to let him off the hook. I was still wounded and angry with too much testosterone and pride to back down. So I just stood there, staring at him. The two of us caught in a frozen moment of time, the next second of which, when it resumed playing, carrying the potential to forever alter each of our lives.

My next words—and how I said them—would be crucial. Something overly angry and aggressive might lead to the gun coming up. Something weak and scared could embolden him to go on the offensive. Finally, perhaps willed in some way by my deepest desire, which was at that point for him to just go away, I swept my right hand to the left in front of me as if pushing his car forward and said, sternly, with just a hint of contempt, "You can *leave* now."

Frozen again for a few moments, he continued to stare, but then, still expressionless, turned his head forward, and slowly . . . mercifully . . . drove off.

When I walked the few steps back to my pump, I expected to be profoundly relieved. Instead, I was overcome with a wave of intense, searing anger. The kind that comes when you back down and immediately question your decision. A toxic mix of shame, remorse, and guilt that causes you to replay things and contemplate what you should have done if you had more guts or weren't so maddeningly responsible. Yeah, I thought, I was pretty sure he had a gun, but I still could have done a hundred other things differently to have taught him the lesson he sorely needed. And so, as I stuck the fuel nozzle in Big Girl's tank, my mind unexpectedly launched into a fantasy, replaying the whole scene as I wished it would have happened, and, more importantly, ended.

The replay had started right before I waved him off. Instead of saying something lame like, "You can leave now," I reached into my jacket pocket with my right hand and extracted my Zippo lighter. Magically full of lighter fluid now (it was, in fact, dead), I clicked the lid open, slowly, so he could see what I was doing, flicked my thumb over the flint wheel, and ignited the flame. With his face now showing some signs of curiosity, I grabbed the pump nozzle with my left hand and moved it towards the lighter, smirking. The boys in the back seat were watching me intently now. Their facial expressions turning from mocking amusement to fear, and with my smirk broadening into a deliciously self-confident smile, I squeezed the handle as hard as I could. With gasoline now shooting out in a tight, powerful stream, I slowly brought the flame closer. A second later, with a distinct "WHUMP!!" the gasoline ignited into a vicious ball of boiling fire.

As people around the station gasped, screamed, and ran for cover, I swiped my flamethrower back and forth between the pump islands, close to the teenager's car but not yet touching it, testing its limits. I had to make sure they recognized that they were about to be incinerated.

As soon as the boys in the back turned forward and started frantically slapping the shoulders of the boys in front, screaming, "Get out of here!!" I leveled the roaring stream of fire at the back of the car.

With the sound intensifying into a deep, reverberating rumble, the fire quickly enveloped the rear bumper, trunk lid, and taillights. Thick black smoke rose from the edges of the flames in great swirling eddies. Soon afterward, I could see the car's silver paint blistering and hear its taillights popping.

Their exit from the station, this time, was not as controlled. With its engine straining under full power and its rear tires on fire, the little Nissan squealed back out onto Route 2, fishtailing wildly.

Calmly, confidently, I let go of the nozzle's handle, dropped it gently to the ground, pulled my helmet down, buckled my chinstrap, and restarted Big Girl. There was a need to hurry. They'd be easy to catch on the open road.

Running through the gears smartly, hunching over a little to shield myself from the force of the wind, I kept accelerating until I spotted a small, charred-looking sedan ahead on the horizon. Traveling at over 110 mph, it didn't take long to close the distance. A couple of hundred yards back. When I was sure the boys in the back of the car could see me, when I knew that what they were about to see would shove them into a full-fledged, stark raving terror, I started the transformation. A simple flip of the ignition switch cover was all it took.

The center headlight retracted first, exposing a multi-barreled machine gun. The passing lamps dropped down next, extending themselves with a series of precise mechanical clicking sounds into left and right missile launchers. Two missiles, miraculously popping out of the frame rails, snapped into place below them. The lower part of the windshield then grew into a hardened steel fairing, while the topmost portion thickened into a thin strip of smoked, bullet proof glass. Then, with rapid precision, a shell of light armor grew up from the floorboards, over my boots, up my legs, across the gas tank and back over the engine vitals. To make her look even scarier, as a last evil touch, conical spikes sprang outward from the saddlebags.

She'd become a Screamin' Eagle death machine.

Now recognizing that they were in deep, deep shit, the boys in the back seat implored the driver to put on more speed. But it was hopeless. The Nissan's mouse motor was no match for the death machine's 110 cubic inch V-twin, now supercharged for added measure. A slight twist of the throttle was all it took to maintain a constant distance behind them. Besides, closing the final gap could wait. It was time to amplify the fear factor.

The left switch cluster controlled the machine gun. Calmly with cold, mechanical precision, I pushed down on the upper part of the high beam switch, now labeled, "Gun Arm" and pushed the horn button, now marked "Fire." The sound was distinctive like an enormous buzzsaw spitting nails. A fraction of a second later the first bullets tore into the Nissan's rear bumper with the sound of shredding plastic. The following rounds walking rapidly across the rear decklid with a thudding *pup pup pup pup.* The rear window blew out next with startling ease. Its thousands of tiny glass shards falling mostly inward onto the boys ducking below the top of the seat. The last remnants of its attached headliner flapping helplessly in the wind.

Having survived the initial machine gun burst, the boys in the back seat lifted their heads again. But this time they didn't look consumed with fear. Their eyes were aflame, their facial expressions tightened with anger, and they were screaming something and swinging their arms and hands back and forth in significant cupping motions. They wanted me to come closer. Curious and knowing that I could dust them off at any time,

I rolled on some throttle and closed to within thirty yards or so. They were more confident now, more assured in the way they were waving me forward, and for a moment I thought it might be a trap. Perhaps they had the driver's gun, some other weapons, or a few good hurling objects. But it didn't strike me that way. No, they wanted to say something, a last disrespectful, defiant insult—a teenager tough guy line—before I waxed them for good. So leaning forward even further, with a final twist of the throttle, I closed the last bit of distance necessary to hear what is was. Finally, the taller, pimple faced one opened his mouth.

"Come on the old man," he hissed, "you got nothin' . . . ."

It was time.

Releasing the throttle to open up the distance, I snapped the Off/Run switch, now labeled "Missile System Power," upward. An instant later the speedometer face flipped over to reveal a small video screen. The Nissan was more or less in the center of it and two red circular reticules were superimposed above it, the kind you see in spy movies that are probably nothing like real missile aiming systems. Taking my time to get it right, I reached down with my right hand and twisted the trip computer knob to center the reticules over the back of the car. When they were close enough, I hit the start switch, now labeled "Missile Enable." A second later the two red circles collapsed onto one another, flashed brightly, and a blinking red "Missile Ready" LED illuminated on the screen. Then, with a final smirk, I pushed both turn signal switches—the launch commands—inward.

The right missile whooshed off the rail first. A heatseeker, it flew straight up the Nissan's tailpipe. The left missile, carrying a proximity fuse, shot through the open space that used to be the car's rear window. Within a fraction of a second both of them had what their sensors told them was necessary to detonate.

The explosion was thunderously deafening and it shook the ground so violently I was nearly bounced off of the death machine. The force of it was staggering, blowing the Nissan's engine block two hundred feet into the air and its four wheels laterally across the highway, deep into the surrounding fields. The heat was intense enough to instantly vaporize most of the car's remaining metal and everything in the interior, including the occupants. With no time to avoid the fireball, I lowered myself even further onto the gas tank and rode straight through it, avoiding because it was a fantasy, the ten-foot crater below. Seconds later the car's engine block thudded deep into the pavement of the highway behind me followed by its hood. The lighter piece failing to pierce the surface, spinning instead, charred and smoking, in the fresh Nebraska breeze.

Now it was my turn to a tough guy line.

My first thought was, "Eat that zit face!" but I didn't like it very much. And I was out of time. Gasoline was spurting out of Big Girl's tank and spreading rapidly down her right side onto the concrete. I was overflowing her tank, poorly. The fantasy had come to an end.

But it helped—a lot. By the time I was wiping up the spill with some of those blue gas station paper towels, I couldn't control my laughter. A few of the bikers milling around saw me and looked back with quizzical expressions, probably wondering what the hell was so amusing. Or, more likely, what kind of an idiot would overfill his tank so badly. But it didn't matter. I had a full tank and with the help of my fantasy, I'd put the altercation behind me. It was time to get back on the road.

After a while the coal trains stopped following the road, the landscape flattened even further, and the ride became an endless slog across country wheat fields. Every half an hour or so I'd have to slow to roll through a small town. Usually with a country store, a church, farm equipment/supply outfit, and maybe a place or two to eat, but other than that, there wasn't much to see. Some time later, I found a "biker friendly" restaurant and stopped for lunch. But soon afterward, still rolling east, the towns became increasingly pathetic. One of them only had a single blinking caution light. I wondered why they even bothered to lower the speed limit and raise it again. It seemed like a waste of good signage.

By late afternoon, already tired and sunburned, I was nearing Grand Island. About twenty miles out, I saw a line of traffic ahead that was rapidly breaking. A black and white "ROAD CLOSED" sign was blocking both lanes. An orange "DETOUR" sign with a black arrow pointed to the right. Annoyed at the inconvenience, I momentarily contemplated turning back, but I couldn't think of any better routes. At least this one was marked, and if trucks were following it, it had to lead back to the east. I'd give it a shot.

Following the line of traffic, I slowly turned right. Moments later, enormous clouds of red dust swirled up from the vehicles ahead of me. At first I didn't know what it was, maybe the dirty wash from an open dump truck, but when my front tire started squirming I knew I had a problem—a *big* problem. The road had turned to dirt, a fine, soft, powdery red dirt with no shoulders or turnoffs, and the tall summer wheat fields that lined each side were acting like vertical walls preventing the dust that was being kicked up by the traffic moving in both directions from spreading out across the fields, turning it instead into a swirling, side laying dust tunnel. Whoever had selected the detour route hadn't thought one iota about motorcyclists. It was almost impossible to see, particularly when a truck passed moving in the opposite direction, and even tougher to breathe. It was a death trap. I had to punt.

Squinting tightly, choking on the dust, I simultaneously pushed and held both turn signal switches to turn on my hazard flashers and slowed Big Girl to a stop. Another bike and a pickup truck were behind me. For the next several minutes, for what seemed like an eternity, I tried to turn her around. When I'd attempted a similar maneuver in Missouri, some days back, on the ride out, the issue had been a slippery surface. This time it was like turning around on a bed of flour. I turned the front fork slightly to the left, feathered the clutch, and slowly inched forward over the crown of the road. Once the front wheel was over and I tried to push back, I couldn't make it over the humps of soft dirt again. She wouldn't budge. The only way out was to get off and try to push her forward or turn even sharper to the left in the soft powder under power. If I didn't make it and had to hit the front brake, in all likelihood, I'd dump the bike.

It was unbelievably tricky, but somehow, slowly, I managed to make the tighter turn. Once I was facing the other way, the guy on the bike behind me, who was now on my left, asked me what I was doing. Somewhat breathlessly, I said. "This is way beyond my ability. I'm going back."

Five minutes later, trailing a cake of red dust, I was back on Route 2, heading west.

After about six miles, I stopped at a crossroad with a gas station on the southwest corner, filled up, and pulled out my iPhone. A few minutes later the guy on the bike behind me rolled in. He smiled and said that I'd made the right decision. He'd broken his ankle last year on a similar road and it wasn't worth it. After comparing maps on our phones, we realized that the crossroad to our immediate right, a paved single lane job that ran north-south across more wheat fields, would lead back to I-80. It would also allow me to bypass Grand Island and get to Hastings, which was my alternate "stretch" destination for the day. Even closer to Kansas, it would make the next day's ride that much shorter. He planned to stay a while longer at the convenience store, so we said good-bye. And with the sun lowering to my right, with the wheat fields softly glowing, I pulled out onto the crossroad, heading south.

The speed limit seemed terribly low for a reasonably straight, paved country road—only 40 mph—but I willed myself to relax. Riding slower would help reduce the wind wash from the steady stream of heavy rigs rolling north in the opposite direction, no doubt using, like me, the alternate route. For a while passing them was even fun.

A short time later, however, I rapidly closed the distance to an old white Chevy pickup. The driver, probably a local farmer, was poking it along at no more than 25 mph. Some plywood boxes with what looked to be built in shelves were in the back, stacked next to each other. Since the road was divided by only a single dashed white line, I wanted to pass. But the steady stream of trucks moving north didn't provide a big enough window, even for a bike as quick as mine. Frustrated at being boxed in, I downshifted into third gear and waited for my chance. But the line of trucks was unbreakable. Mile after mile, I had to wait.

Just when I thought there might be an opening and was about to nail it, the pickup truck hit a large bump and the lid on one of the boxes in the back bounced off. It came back down askew, not sealing the top anymore. One of the drawers had also slid out. Curious as to what it was, I momentarily hesitated and lost my chance to pass. As a result, I wound up stuck behind him again, this time even closer. For a moment I thought I saw something buzzing around the back of the truck, but then I heard it. A distinctive, rapid "bzzzzzzzzzttttt" accompanied by the slightest sensation of my neck being brushed. Focusing on the back of the pickup more intensely, I could just make out some flying insects nervously darting around the top of the box. Shit, I thought. He's got bees.

I told myself not to worry, to relax, that they were probably just harmless farm bees, but the memory of my most recent run-in with the six-legged little bastards was increasingly dominating my thoughts. It had happened only a few years back.

We were living in Northern Virginia at the time. My wife had asked me, as part of a final late spring cleanup, to remove an old tree stump on the edge of an island in our back yard. I started with some other chores first but finally got around to grabbing our biggest shovel and walking over to the stump. It'll probably take about a half an hour of hard work to get it out, I thought, and went back to the garage to find my work boots. I'd need the extra cushion to jam the shovel into the ground.

When I came back to the stump, I took a deep breath, aligned the shovel to a spot on the ground that seemed like a good place to start, and shoved my boot down as hard as I could. The blade penetrated the ground with a crunching noise and slid in so quickly I almost lost my balance. Wow, I thought. That was way too easy. A moment after I pulled the shovel out, still thinking where I was going to place it next, I noticed a small black and yellow spotted ball that appeared to be growing up out of the ground. Mesmerized by the way it seemed to be expanding out of nowhere, I stood, watching, as it continued to inflate in size. When it got to be the size of a softball, a ribbon of flying objects seemed to take off from its surface. A fraction of a second later, I felt the brush of tiny wings followed by a steady stream of angry "bzzzzzzzzztttttt"s.

Flooded with adrenaline, I dropped the shovel and took off running for the back door of the house. I suppose if a wall had been put in my way I would have run straight through it, but on that day, I ran into something worse. We'd hired a contractor a few months back to build an outdoor porch, and he'd dug a five-foot deep drainage ditch that ran parallel to the back of the house between the island and the back door. It was marked off with yellow "DANGER" tape, as it should have been, but in my wild flight of panic I forgot all about it. So as soon as I broke through the tape, I fell straight into it, with my head hitting the upward sloped side so hard the right side of my face buried itself in the mud. Stunned and feeling the bees descending on me, I started wildly thrashing my legs and feet to regain any possible foothold, and, with the help of my hands digging upwards, clawed my way out. But I'd lost precious seconds. By the time I could accelerate again, they were all over me. An entire swarm of angry yellow jackets, the first attack force from a hive of over five thousand workers, all intent on doing one thing: exterminating the awkwardly flailing human dipshit who'd dared to breach their nest.

Swinging my hands around me wildly, trying desperately to fend them off, I changed direction and decided to make for the pool. Before diving, I managed to reach into my pocket, grab my iPhone, and throw it back onto the grass. Surprisingly, it landed undamaged.

I wasn't so lucky. By the time I hit the water, at least two dozen were in the process of thrusting their stingers deep into the tissues of my back, shoulders, and legs. Figuring that increasing water pressure might cause them to back off, I strained to make it to the deep end, but it didn't work. At eight feet deep they were still stinging the living shit out of me.

By the time I emerged for air, most of the swarm had retreated back towards the hive. My wife, having observed most of the attack from a window, was waiting for me by the back door. When I stumbled in, she tried to look sympathetic at first, but with her hand over her mouth, she quickly burst out laughing.

"Oh my God," she said through laughs that were increasingly unconstrained, "I wish I could have captured that on tape."

After drying me off and applying some Cortisone, she counted twelve stings. My only solace was that it could have been worse. She liked the fact that I'd saved my phone.

With the yellow jacket attack still fresh in mind, I studied the behavior of the Nebraska farm bees in the pickup more carefully. What bothered me the most was the way they seemed to be checking me out. The first bee was probably a scout, a single soldier sent out to see whether or not the human riding the loud two-wheeler was a threat. So after buzzing around me two or three times, he flew straight back to the box. But after he returned, another group came out, this time larger in number, maybe a squad. They flew around me in more places, past my eyes, around my neck, over my exposed hands, and even around my torso and legs. Then they flew back. Thinking that I was getting a little paranoid, I fell back about twenty yards, hoping they might forget about me, but a short time later, a third squad came out. Sure enough, they flew back to my now more distant position; buzzed all around me, and then returned to their box-hive, transmitting, no doubt, further intelligence. They had to be massing for an attack.

I knew that probably wasn't the case—honeybees usually only attack when they are directly threatened—but no matter how hard I tried, I couldn't shake the thought. They were in there . . . planning something. With the initial scout and the two other squads back from patrol, they'd probably already briefed their bee-Sergeants, who had updated their bee-Lieutenants, and they were in a huddle now, briefing their bee-Commander. A decorated Lieutenant Colonel, a favorite of the Queen; he was taking it all in, smoking a stubby little bee-cigar, and had already started to summarize.

"OK, men. I get it. We got a human male, middle-aged, riding one of those mechanical horses, fifty yards to our rear. The outer blue denim skin over his legs looks tough to penetrate, the shiny black skin impossible. But his eyes are vulnerable and we might just get a few Special Forces guys up his air holes. Alpha Company will go for his face, backed up by Bee-Team Four. Bravo Company will go for his neck. Charlie Company, the white skin through those stupid looking half-gloves. Once we have him thrashing, he'll probably wreck the machine. As soon as he hits the dirt, we send in Battalion reserves. Sound the call. We attack in two minutes."

Trying to overcome my growing anxiety, I fell back even further and waited . . . and waited . . . with sweat beads forming on my forehead, for a chance to pass. Finally, after a huge fuel truck rolled by, a large gap opened up. Determined to get away, I jammed the top of my left foot down on the shifter peg and cracked the throttle open so hard I thought the hand grip might spin off. By the time I'd passed the old Chevy, left the bees behind, and moved back into the southbound lane, I was already into fourth gear and passing 80 mph. After slowing, for the next ten minutes, all the way to I-80, I kept listening for any pursuers. If there were any, they never caught up.

Having put up with asshole teenagers, a death road, potentially killer bees, and over five hundred miles of highway travel, by the time I rolled into Hastings I was starting to lose it. Too tired to even read any billboards, I pulled into a Comfort Inn right off the highway, unpacked, and walked to a sports bar across the street. The waitress was college-aged, perky, and cute, so I let her talk me into a large pizza. I couldn't even finish half of it.

An hour later, after a short phone call with my wife, I was already in bed, my trusty iPhone at my side, watching time-lapse weather radar images. A front was swooping down from South Dakota behind me and would be on top of Southeast Nebraska by morning. I'd have to get out of Dodge before it hit or I'd be stranded, waiting for it to pass, for hours.

As usual, it was going to be close.

Day 9: Scorched Earth

I woke up well before six and immediately turned on my phone to check the weather. It wasn't good. A strong line of thunderstorms was just to the north, running from a northwest to southeast line and heading to the southeast. The main front, the one I knew I'd probably be chasing all the way across the country, had slowed and stalled over southern Missouri. It was possible that the two fronts over the course of the upcoming day could combine and join forces. That definitely wouldn't be good.

The hotel room they'd assigned me had two doors, a front door that opened into a hallway and a rear door that opened into the parking lot. Wanting to see what it was like outside, I walked over and opened the rear door. As soon as I did, a rush of wind blew into the room and caught the curtains on the single window. For some reason, it startled me. If it had been that windy, I should have heard something during the night. But the room had been surprisingly quiet, the only sound a soft humming from the air conditioning unit. I was also expecting to see some light. It was less than an hour to sunrise, a time when the sky is usually brightening, but it was still pitch black outside except for the light coming from two parking lot lamps. On the edge of the lot, the branches of two large maple trees were thrashing angrily, their leaves rustling slowly in the stiff breeze. It was creepy enough that I actually shivered.

My most immediate concern was the front swooping down from the north. A quick time-lapse replay of the weather radar showed that it would overtake my current position within an hour. Thus, I had two choices: leave as soon as possible and try to outrun it before I turned due south to Wichita or wait until it passed Hastings entirely. Waiting it out would cost me at least two to three hours and I wouldn't be able to leave until late morning. On the other hand, if I left right away and averaged at least 50 mph, the storm would never catch up. The prudent decision, of course, was to wait. But I wanted to get going, to keep moving, to *get home*.

Thinking that some food and a good cup of coffee would help to make up my mind, I quickly dressed and walked over to the breakfast room by the entrance. They'd just opened up so I was the first one in. Too antsy to sit, I downed a cup of coffee, an English muffin, and a banana while pacing the floor. All the while, my eyes were glued to a television set mounted high in a far corner. One of those nasty red banners was sliding across the bottom of the picture. I couldn't read it, but I knew what it meant. The area was under a severe thunderstorm warning. I kept telling myself to calm down, that waiting it out would be no big deal, but something kept tugging at me, pulling me, like a massive tractor beam, towards the southeast horizon. It was time to go.

By six-thirty I was on the road, heading out of town on Nebraska Route 6. Though it was still dark outside, the security lighting from nearby buildings, parking lots, and industrial facilities was making it easier to see. But after I left the glow of the town behind and rode out between two large corn fields, a thick, scary darkness returned, made even more foreboding by the fact that it was now close to sunrise. That meant that the cloud cover overhead had to be dark, very dark, and that meant that the severe thunderstorm line was closing in. My only hope of outrunning it, since I was heading due east, was to make it to Route 81, my next objective, and turn south before it overtook me.

A few minutes later, lightning started flashing to my left, and then, unexpectedly, to my right. Somehow, the storm had spread over me. Fierce gusts of wind then slammed into me from both sides, howling on and off in entirely random sequences. It was like I was back on Route 2 again, only worse. Even ducking behind the windshield as far as I could for cover, the best I could manage was between 50 and 55 mph. Soon afterward, still between the corn fields, the rain started. It wasn't too bad at first, but once the sheets intensified, I knew I had to get off. I hadn't even made it the twenty miles to Route 81 and my plan to get out ahead of the storm had failed.

But there was no time to feel sorry for myself. I was out in the middle of nowhere again with a severe thunderstorm line bearing down on me, and after my experience in Missouri, I damn sure didn't want to ride through another one. So my thoughts turned to survival and finding shelter—any shelter. I passed a few homes, mostly ranches with narrow front porches and detached garages, but they looked deserted. If one of them had even a single light on I might have stopped, but I didn't want to pull up to a dark house and run under a stranger's porch. Dressed the way I was, in full motorcycle gear, I'd probably wind up scaring somebody to death. So I passed them by, ducking behind the windshield, squinting through the rain and the windblown spray as best as I could, struggling to see.

Finally, I saw a Phillips gas station up ahead on the opposite side of the road. The tall marquee was brightly lit and the attached convenience store, while not exactly lit up like a church, had some visible lights on. It was open. As soon as I started to slow, the rain intensified into a pounding deluge. By the time I pulled up under the overhang over the pump island, thunder was booming nearly continuously. I'd missed the worst of it by seconds.

Relieved to be safe for once, I took my time removing my helmet and sat on Big Girl for a while, watching the storm. The Rain was hammering the metal roof of the overhang with a deafening roar and spreading across the road in high, sweeping sheets. Now past sunrise, the sky was just bright enough to see the bottoms of huge, dark thunderclouds moving ominously over the fields with smaller, dark gray chaser clouds racing along their edges. Lightning was still flashing on the horizon, from both the north and south, with an occasional cloud-to-ground strike to keep it interesting.

Figuring that it'd probably take a while for the storm to pass, I decided to check out the convenience store. Not wanting to leave my bike at the pump—after all, that was rude—I scanned around, looking for a better place to park. To my right, closer to the road, a single diesel pump was set up to service large trucks, but it had no overhang. The rest of the parking lot was wide open. If I wanted to move, I'd have to park Big Girl out in the weather and then run back into the store. I didn't want to have to deal with that.

Looking around some more, I realized the island had plenty of rooms. There were four pumps, laid out in pairs facing outboard along the near and far ends, so if any other cars pulled in they'd have easy access to any of the other three. And it was empty. Just past seven o'clock and still abnormally dark, no one appeared to be in the mood to gas up. So I decided though I knew it was "verboten" to leave Big Girl at the pump, I'll keep an eye on the island, I told myself, and if it starts to get busy, I'll come back out and move her.

The store was poorly lit, probably still in the process of being opened, with the brightest light behind the counter. A single clerk appeared to be in the process of opening the cash register. He was older, close to seventy, with an excellent number of blackish-brown age spots and a large, pitted, rosacea marked nose. Opening things up with great care, he went about his business, more or less ignoring me. Probably the owner, I thought. After a while, I caught him looking my way, moving his head up and down. He was checking me out. The only reaction I could discern was a slight upward arc on one side of his mouth. I knew that look because I'd used it yesterday on the teenagers. It was the look of contempt.

Almost tripping along some poorly lit aisles, I finally found a large coffee urn on a table that was wedged up into the back of the store. The coffee smelled freshly brewed, so I grabbed a small Styrofoam cup, filled it up, and walked back towards the front.

When I was abreast of the counter, I said, "Good morning," respectfully but without cheer, and asked him how much I owed.

"Thirty-five cents," he replied, gruffly.

Struggling to suppress a smirk, I pulled a quarter and a dime out of my pocket, handed it to him, and turned back towards the aisles, thinking that he'd been a little rude. He could have at least said hello. On the other hand, the coffee was a good deal. At Starbucks, they'd probably charge you thirty-five cents for a stirring stick. Then again, I thought, after taking a first sip of his brew, Starbucks coffee is actually good. His swill tasted like dishwater.

Figuring that I ought to buy something else to keep the peace, I started wandering the aisles again, keeping a watchful eye on Big Girl through the window. A couple of cars had pulled in, but one at a time. She didn't seem to be in the way of anybody, so I spent a little time in-between window scans studying the merchandise. Every item had one of those little stick-on price tags. I wondered if he had a little elf that ran around marking them.

When I was back towards the front again, holding a small box of Motrin, he pointed his finger at me, cleared his throat, and barked angrily, "You need to move that bike! It's time for you to go!"

Caught off guard by his stern rebuke, especially considering how careful I'd been to monitor the situation so that I wouldn't, in fact, bother anybody, I shot back with a lawyerly defense.

"I've been watching my bike very carefully," I said, "and it hasn't blocked anyone."

"That's not true!" he roared. "A car came in here a while ago, had to circle the island several times and then drove off!!"

Stunned by his quick retort, I stood there, my face flushing red, wondering if I could have missed it. No, I thought, I've been watching the pump island the whole time and a car never drove in, circled and took off again. There had only been two vehicles, and they'd pulled right up, refueled, and left. He was lying. And by now something else was clear. He didn't like bikers, and he didn't like me. He just wanted me out of his store.

My first instinct was to attack his lie, but he'd probably just double down with even more venom, and our argument would escalate into a shouting match. And in the end, he'd win. It was his store. If I started to make trouble, he'd call for help. And that could only mean more delay. I was in rural Nebraska. His brother was probably the local Sheriff and his brother-in-law the Municipal Judge. If I turned into a smartass, which I probably would, they could hassle me for hours. And if they were dirty, which was possible, they could plant something and I'd spend days in jail and thousands of dollars trying to unscrew it all. He wasn't worth it.

So after staring him down a bit, struggling to suppress alternating feelings of anger, frustration, and helplessness, I quietly dropped the Motrin and walked out. When I reached Big Girl, I mounted her saddle, somewhat lethargically, and studied the sky. While the rain had moderated and the lightning had moved off to the south, it still wasn't safe enough to proceed. I'd have to find another way to kill some time. The good news was that it was considerably brighter out. And after scanning the parking lot for shelter again I realized, for the first time, there was a Subway sandwich shop attached to the right side of the jerk's store. So I started up Big Girl, put her in first gear, goosed the throttle a little, nudged her over to a space directly in front, shutdown, and walked inside.

The Subway clerk greeted me with a cheer that immediately improved my mood.

"Good morning!" she bubbled. "If you want to wait out the storm you can take a booth in the front. Take all the time you need. And if you want something to drink in the meantime the coffee's fresh and we have cold drinks in the refrigerator over there!"

It was such a stark contrast to how I'd been treated on the other side that I felt like jumping over the counter and giving her a big bear hug. But I didn't do that. Instead, I offered up a warm, "Thank you, that's very kind," and purchased a Gatorade and a water bottle. Within a minute, I'd spent ten times the money that the jerk had been able to get out of me on the other side.

For the next twenty minutes or so I sat in a booth, watching the storm, checking the weather radar on my phone and sipping water. A young Hispanic guy came in to buy some donuts at one point, but otherwise it was quiet. Eventually, between the coffee at the hotel, the jerk's dishwater, and my new water bottle, the urge hit me.

Still anticipating my needs, as soon as I stood up, the clerk said, "The restroom is right through the opening at the back of the shop."

Man, I thought, she's good.

As soon as I walked through the opening I realized that the two establishments shared a common bathroom. On any other day, this might not have mattered much, but still smarting from the sting of the jerk's discrimination, I realized it would give me the cover I needed to fight back. After all, I'd moved my bike away from his pump island and I was waiting out the storm in an adjacent shop. And since I'd bought a drink there, I had every right to use the bathroom—which was also his bathroom. And if I had the right to use his bathroom, I certainly had the right to go back and shop some more. And that would drive him bananas.

So after washing up, I left the restroom and walked back into his store. As soon as he saw me his face stiffened and turned beet-red. Another clerk had joined him, presumably after I'd left, and I saw him jab the new guy with his elbow. He'd probably mentioned our little run-in, boasting how he'd fearlessly kicked out some degenerate biker. The new guy was about the same age but shorter, with whiter hair and a pale face that made his blushed cheeks stand out even more. Almost immediately, the two of them started to whisper and point at me.

For the next twenty minutes, I played a cat and mouse game across the store. When they were watching me, which was almost all of the time, I'd pick up various pieces of merchandise, read their labels, and harmlessly place them back on the shelf. But they couldn't see me, or watch me, every second. The aisles were too tall and closely spaced together and they had to attend to other customers. So when they weren't looking, I took every opportunity to screw up their inventory. I placed stuff back where it didn't belong. I peeled the little price tags off of things and switched them around, trying my best to put low-priced labels on high priced items and vice versa. If I couldn't get the tag off, I'd flip it around so nobody could see it. When I got to the beverage refrigerators in the back, I opened the doors and studied the inventory, slowly, letting all the cool air spill out. I even thought of breaking the plastic seal on some of the twist-off caps, but that'd be too detectable. My sabotage had to be discreet. The best part was they knew that I was up to something but couldn't, at least yet, figure it out.

After a while, however, I started to feel a little guilty—that it was wrong and I was immature. So I walked back towards the bathroom. The new guy, who increasingly reminded me of pictures I'd seen of the gangster Whitey Bolger, almost tried to block me, gearing up for a confrontation, but at the last moment, he let me pass. It backfired. The fact that he would even consider getting in my face made me even more determined to do everything possible to annoy them.

Trashing the bathroom, or better still, making them *think* I was trashing the bathroom, was an excellent place to start. So I spent the next ten minutes inside with the door shut and locked, purposely hitting the walls with my elbows, making noise. For added measure, I ran the sink water continuously and flushed the toilet at least five times. When I finally emerged, Whitey was standing right in front of me. He was quaking with anger, moving his head right and left, straining to look beyond me, to see if I'd damaged anything. I hadn't.

As soon as we passed each other, I noticed there was a small lounge with a few simple card tables and chairs on the other side of the hallway. It was another shared space between the two stores. Grabbing an old newspaper off of the floor, I slumped into a chair, lifted my legs up and dropped my boots at the center of the table with a loud thud. The paper wasn't the slightest bit interesting—all local farm community news—but I knew that when Whitey came out of the bathroom and saw me nonchalantly reading it, with my feet up, it would piss him off to the moon. Sure enough, a few minutes later, after another angry conference with the jerk, he marched over.

"How long are you going to stay?" he asked.

"I don't know," I replied, "probably until the storm passes, but I may stay for lunch and have a sub."

That got him. They both looked at each other, incredulously, trying to figure out their next move.

Finally, Whitey said, this time with more resignation, "We'd appreciate if you'd just be on your way."

It was all I needed. They recognized they had no real power over me. I'd won.

Itching to get going again, I walked back through the opening of the Subway store and peered out the front windows. The rain had ended and the sun was just emerging from the clouds. A quick scan of the weather radar on my phone showed the storm continuing to move to the southeast. Knowing that my saddle would still be wet, I asked the young lady behind the counter if I could grab a few napkins to dry it.

"Of course," she said. "Take all you need, and be careful out there."

I wanted to hug her again.

When I walked out, Gatorade in hand, I immediately looked up to scan the sky. I'd never seen anything like it. The cloud cover was perfectly split in half from the northeast to the southeast horizon, with dark gray thunderheads to the south and a brilliant, cloudless blue sky to the north. It was if a giant hand had planted a compass in the ground on my exact spot, drawn a line across the dome of the sky with a pencil, and neatly pushed everything over to one side. While wiping my saddle down, I debated whether or not to don my rain jacket. The road was rapidly drying, but I'd still have to endure a lot of sprays. And if the front decided to turn more to the south, along Route 81, anything could happen. Choosing to be prudent, I reluctantly put it on.

For once I made a right call. Soon after turning south, the rain started again. But it was light and sporadic, so I kept rolling at a leisurely 65 mph. A half an hour later, I was in Kansas.

After a quick stop near the town of Salina to gas up and shovel down some food, I checked the weather again. The storm was still a good thirty miles ahead of me, so if I continued to take it easy, I wouldn't run into it. But something else was bothering me. The way the air was heating up was odd. Every time the sun would peek out from the leftover haze, it ignited a microburst of steam heat that almost burned my exposed skin. I'd experienced this kind of heat before in the engine room of a ship, but rarely outdoors. The type of weather that people in the Southeast call a "three-shirter" (requiring you to change shirts three times a day if you work outdoors), or in the Northeast, a "real steam-ah." And it was barely one o'clock, the hour when afternoon temperatures start their final climb. Over the next several hours, it was bound to get worse.

As it turned out, 2011 was the second hottest summer in the United States on record. Texas and Oklahoma were particularly hard hit. By September 13, Dallas had endured seventy non-consecutive days with temperatures exceeding 100°F. Parts of Oklahoma suffered even more, with conditions competitive to the Dust Bowl years of 1934 and 1936. By August 3, several locations had recorded forty-three consecutive days exceeding 100°F. Multiple high-temperature records fell in Tulsa and Oklahoma City during the first week in August (each city hit 113°F), with heat indexes approaching 140°F. It was also painfully dry. Aside from a brief respite the week before I rode through, rainfall was well below normal. The combination of the heat and dry conditions had devastated crops. By mid-August, vast swaths of Oklahoma and Texas farmland were designated to be in a destitute condition, ultimately resulting in billions of dollars of crop losses.

Though I'd missed the worst of the heat by about a week, by the time I crossed the border into Oklahoma temperatures were still well into the nineties. Stillwater, close to my route when I turned east towards Tulsa, hit 99°F that day. And because I was following the back end of a storm front, the humidity was higher than it had been the week before (on average nearly eighty percent) so the heat index was almost as bad, well into the "extreme danger" zone.

Conditions close to the road surface were even worse. The interstate I'd merged onto (I-35) was paved asphalt. On a hot summer day in direct sunlight, asphalt temperatures can quickly hit 150°F. This warms the air even further, particularly close to the road surface. A foot off of the ground, where my feet were resting on Big Girl's highway pegs, the air temperature was probably ten to twenty degrees higher (110°F to 120°F). Another foot up, where my rear end was sitting, it was probably five degrees higher (105°F), not counting the heat from her engine. Running at a constant 2,800 rpm to maintain 72 mph, her cylinder fins were dumping additional heat into the air stream, washing over my left leg and inner thigh (the way the exhaust pipes come out the engine on a Harley V-twin, most of the air rushing over the cylinder fins expels out of the left side) while the heat from her oil tank was radiating upward, through the saddle, into my rear end. It was like riding in a convertible car with the top down on a hundred-degree sunny day with the heat on full blast, the seat warmer on high, and a blow dryer aimed at your groin.

My first concern, other than cooking my vitals to a point where they might not work again, was dehydration. So I pulled over to the first available rest stop, drank as much water as I could from an inside water fountain, and refilled my empty Gatorade bottle. Thinking that it would be better to keep my jacket on to minimize water loss from evaporative cooling, I put it back on when I walked outside. But within seconds I was baking again. There was no way I could continue wearing it. When

I rolled back onto I-35 South, I was down to a single dry-fit t-shirt, at least above my waist.

Over the next hundred miles, I rode as fast as I could stand, hoping that the extra rush of wind would cool me down, but it was still a miserable trip. My socks became soaking wet and the sweat from my groin and rear made it look like I'd urinated in my jeans. My t-shirt was covered with salt stains. I could tell that Big Girl wasn't enjoying it either. The air pouring onto my left inner thigh kept getting hotter, pulsing it seemed, with every stroke of her cylinders. She was panting like a sweating race horse. If we hit traffic, her oil would overheat and I'd probably collapse from heat stroke.

"Come on girl," I started to say, "we're in this together. Just keep rolling." And mile after mile, mutually enduring the discomfort, we did.

But what really dominated my thoughts was the landscape around me. In the weeks before I'd rolled through, during the hottest and driest periods, grass and brush fires burned uncontrollably across the central and northeastern counties. I never knew how many acres were affected, but entire sections of the land on the part of I-35 I was traveling on, including the center median and fields on the north and southbound sides, were totally charred. As black as crude oil, for as far as I could see. With the smoke still rising in spots in knee-high, swirling twists, it looked as if a nuclear blast generated firestorm had completely laid waste to the area. The only signs of life were the hammer oil pumps that dotted the fields, their heads rhythmically seesawing, oblivious, it seemed, to the devastation around them. It was truly a scorched Earth.

When I turned onto Route 412 East towards Tulsa, the effects of the grass fires were less severe, but I had other things to worry about. It was a turnpike, and after a short time, I ran into a line of traffic waiting at the entrance to a toll booth. Sweating profusely, with big Girl idling roughly, struggling to dissipate the heat that was slowly crippling her, I waited for my turn to get a ticket.

When the toll booth operator finally gave it to me, I quickly ran Big Girl up through her gears and back up to highway speed. Just as I dropped her into sixth, I noticed a sign that said "No gas/food for 35 miles." Remembering that it had been a while since I refueled, I nervously looked down at the fuel gauge. She was on empty. Somewhat panicked, I quickly checked the miles remaining on the trip computer. It read forty-five. If I didn't make it, I'd have to walk the remaining distance to the station in hundred-degree heat. Thankfully, she got me there. But it was close. She holds six gallons and I filled her up with 5.6. After downing another Gatorade, I wiped myself down with one of my detailing rags and restarted, hoping to be east of Tulsa by dark.

Ten miles from the city limits, the sky turned dark again and high wind gusts rocked me from the southwest. The trees by the road were swaying wildly and debris was swirling across both lanes. It was time to get off. Thinking that I'd probably just caught up in the storm I'd been following all day, I stopped at a McDonalds and checked the weather radar. A huge, nasty-looking yellow and red line of "blobs," running northwest to southeast, was just to the north of Tulsa and descending to the southeast. Severe watches and warnings were up and there was a possibility of large hail. Figuring that I'd be delayed at least an hour, I checked the local traffic. With the start of the Friday afternoon rush hour, it was already a mess. The storm would just make it worse. There was no way out. I had to quit.

Luckily a Hampton Inn was just up the road, so I mounted Big Girl a last time, fired her up, and quickly closed the distance. Before shutting down again, with the wind swirling around me in the parking lot, I looked down at the trip computer. I'd logged only 443 miles, the lowest cross-country daily mileage total of the entire journey. She had a few bug splatters, including a butterfly of some sort that was still partially attached to her left side mirror, but what bothered me the most was the heat we'd ridden through. It could easily have fried her oil. But there wasn't much I could do about it, at least for now. So I quickly unpacked and walked up to my room.

After watching the storm pass, calling my wife, and catching up on the news, I walked down to the lobby and asked the clerk behind the desk if there were any restaurants within walking distance.

"You bet," he said enthusiastically. "There's a sports bar next door just across the parking lot."

Eager to quench my thirst again—with anything—I walked over to it, but quickly stopped when I saw the front façade. The windows were blacked out and the front door was covered with vertical steel bars. A guy sitting on the curb a few feet from the door must have seen me hesitate. He was wearing jeans, probably forty-something, with scraggly facial hair and a nondescript t-shirt. A cigarette dangled from his cracked lips.

"It's OK," he assured me. "A good place."

His encouragement made me feel a little better, but I probably would have tried it anyway. There was no way I was riding again that day.

When I opened the door, the first thing that struck me was how big the place was. A half-dozen pool tables were spread out on either side of the entrance and a similar number of circular poker tables were arrayed closer to the bar. On the right side, there were some game machines, the kind that kids beg their parents to use but we generally avoid. Several of the poker tables were filled, I assumed, with regulars. The people were mostly older: the men with worn craggy faces and cowboy hats; the women, probably grandmothers, wearing cheap summer dresses. A few younger guys were playing pool, but the bar was mostly empty.

I took a seat at the bar near the cash register. A Little League baseball game was showing on the bar TV. Maybe some of the grandkids of the people playing poker were playing in it, I thought. The music was delightful, first a Patsy Cline song and then an AC/DC ripper. I chuckled at the mix but liked it. Finally, the barmaid approached me. She was older, with white, gray hair that looked like fine wire with just a hint of some bad hair coloring that hadn't washed out. Her face had deep wrinkles, but her eyes still sparkled.

"Do you serve dinner here?" I asked.

"Yes," she replied, "we certainly do... some of the best food around, so you'd better try it."

Confident that she'd already made a sale, she handed me a menu.

"Would you like to start with a drink?" she asked.

The beer refrigerator behind her looked like it had some decent choices, but my stomach already felt bloated from all of the water and Gatorade.

So I quietly asked, "Do you have any red wine?"

"Not much," she replied with a hint of disappointment, "but I do have some Merlot."

"I'll try it."

Too tired to look at the menu, when she returned with my wine, I asked her for a meal recommendation.

"The pork chops," she said without hesitation. "They were cut fresh this morning. I saw the cook do it. And he knows how to grill them, Texas style, which is what keeps all the regulars coming."

"Regulars?" I asked, wondering who would keep coming to a place that shows Little League baseball games on the bar TV.

"Oh yes, a whole bunch. Some from as far as fifty miles away."

While pork chops aren't normally my favorite meal, she was too nice to turn down.

"OK," I said. "I'll try them."

She was so excited she could barely scribble the order, and after handing it to the cook she came back to reinforce, probably three more times, that I was going to love them.

While waiting for my meal, some time later, a guy took the bar chair two seats to the right of me. It was the right place to sit if he didn't want to initially intimidate me but still wanted to talk. He was husky, early forties, with a round face, thin lips, and long rows of small but straight teeth. Not in great shape, but formidable. He ordered a shot of Jack Daniels and slowly sipped it, quickly disgusted, as I was, with what was showing on the bar TV. Soon, as I suspected, he opened up.

"Hot enough for ya today?"

"Yeah, just awful."

"Last week, parts of Oklahoma City hit 116°F. But today's been better."

"Doesn't seem that way. When I crossed the border this morning, it looked like I was descending into hell."

"Yeah, it's been causing all kinds of problems."

"Like what?" I asked with genuine curiosity.

"The main breakers in people's electric boxes are tripping, particularly if they're mounted on walls that face the sun. And grass fires are everywhere."

After that, he scanned me more carefully, probably saw my new riding boots, and asked, "You ride in on a motorcycle?"

"Yeah, I'm on my way back from Sturgis."

"Really? Sweet. Where ya headin'?"

"Hilton Head Island, South Carolina."

"Not sure where that is. But whud da ya ride?"

"A Harley Screamin' Eagle Road King. Oh-eight model."

"Daaaay*aaam*!" he exhaled in a perfect Oklahoma twang.

After that, I figured I was in.

The pork chops came next, and as the sweet old lady had promised, they were delicious. I devoured them, along with the grilled squash and baked potato, in less than ten minutes.

Meanwhile, we continued to make small talk.

"Do you ride too?"

"Used to, I was even a member of a club some years back."

"You got out of it?"

"Yeah, when I was about forty."

I sensed a lot of conflicted emotions when he answered. Maybe he couldn't afford it anymore, maybe his wife finally put her foot down, or maybe he'd had a severe accident. At any rate, he quickly changed the subject.

"Now I just run my business. Industrial parts. Mostly for the oil business. Whud da you do?"

Caught off guard, I said, "Oh, well . . . ahh . . . I just retired from my second career."

He looked at me for a few awkward seconds and then said, in a lower voice, "You look awfully *young* to be retired."

I tried to make light of it and brush it off, saying, "Well it just worked out. I was a partner in a large management consulting business. It did well, so when the time was right, I cashed out."

But it didn't work.

Increasingly and obviously agitated, he looked back towards the bar, twirled his shot, and replied in an even lower voice with a hint of anger, "So you're a white collar biker."

I chuckled and said, "Yeah, I guess you're right. You could say I'm a 'white collar biker' . . . I mean, I don't belong to a real biker gang, and I'm just a guy seeing the country."

But I knew I'd said something wrong. And sure enough, over the course of the next minute or so, his whole demeanor changed. His neck muscles tightened and his teeth clenched. He twirled his shot more and flexed his forearms. After another long silence, he started to say what he felt about white collar bikers, how he and his gang had hated them, that we were fakes and were ruining the sport. The conversation was deteriorating, fast.

Having already paid for my meal, including the tip, I got up and said, "Well, I'm tired, so I'm going to go," and started to walk out.

When only a few paces from the bar I heard him say from behind me, "So, are you going out to put on your colors, man?"

It was an insult, a cheap shot, and for a moment I considered walking back and punching his fat head. But he wasn't worth it. It'd turn into a bar-wrecking brawl, I'd probably lose a few teeth and we'd get arrested in the process. And more than ever, I was worried about my wife. She'd been melancholy when we'd spoken before I'd left my room. She wasn't feeling right and felt depressed. I needed to get home. So I half turned, shot him a dirty look, and walked out.

On the short walk back to the hotel, and for the next hour or so in my hotel room, I brooded. Not about having been insulted, but about what it meant to be a real biker. My brother-in-law Jim had told me many times that the beautiful thing about riding a Harley and sampling the culture was that the vast majority of people don't judge you. They really don't care where you're from, what stage of life you're in, how you look, or what you wear. As long as you ride a Harley-Davidson and you're not a complete dweeb (there are some unwritten rules), you're in. Most of the people are friendly, courteous, and helpful. And so far, in all my riding experiences, including in and around Sturgis, I'd found that to be true.

But I had to admit to myself, the guy at the bar had stung me, and even worse, I was developing my own prejudices. While I certainly thought the guys with the tattoos, the braided hair, the scars, and the jackets with the right colors, patches, and pins were real bikers. I was beginning to think less of the weekend warriors. The folks who, previously like me, took their bikes out once a month on a perfect day for hour long rides. The folks who towed trailers behind their bikes (do they really need all of that stuff?). The folks who rode Honda Gold Wings with their rows of switches, neon lights, heated doodads, navigation systems, and twenty extra wind deflectors (more like convertible cars than motorcycles, at least to me). Were they real bikers too?

In the end, however, I decided that it didn't matter. All bikers have something in common. We love to ride motorcycles, and that ought to be enough. More contented, I went back to thinking about my wife and the remaining trip ahead.

"Two more days," I kept saying to myself. "Just two more days."

Day 10: Through the Demilitarized Zone

For once I woke up to good news. While the line of thunderstorms that had doused the Tulsa area the night before were still formidable (in fact they had grown in size), they had moved towards Little Rock. Another line had also formed and was over Oklahoma City, but I'd easily stay in front of that one. With luck, I would roll through Little Rock, well behind the storm. And since I was heading to the northeast towards Memphis and then back to the southeast again, I might just do a northern loop over the storm and enjoy a rain-free day. My objective for the day, assuming the weather held, was to make as many miles as possible before stopping, possibly to, and even through, Birmingham, Alabama. My Maps application said this was over 675 miles, which I really didn't want to tackle, but having made only 443 miles the day before, I decided to try and push it.

After a quick shower, I walked outside to check on Big Girl. Mainly to make sure that the guy from the night before hadn't decided to take out his wrath on white collar bikers and scar her in some way. I remembered that I'd told him what type of bike I was riding and she was still parked reasonably close to the bar next to the hotel. It wouldn't have been hard for him to put two and two together. In any event, she was unharmed, just soaking wet. The leather on the tour pack was wavy—it had probably absorbed a lot of moisture from the heavy rain the night before. On the positive side, however, the rain had actually washed off some of the road grime and she looked a little brighter. I winked at her, went back inside to down a quick breakfast, and was back on the road by six forty-five.

The first step of the day's leg was to ride through the city of Tulsa. It was a Saturday morning and the city and sky looked like they both had a hangover from the night before. Everything was blue-gray, faded, and forlorn, especially the sky. Long, flat bands of gray clouds blocked out the sun's light except on the edges of the horizon as far as I could turn my head to either side. It looked like a massive pot lid had been placed on top of the city. Later, as I rode on toward Arkansas, the sky looked even more confused. It was a mixture of every cloud type that I remembered studying as a kid. Cumulus, stratus, and light wisps of cirrus in white, dark, and gray, all mixing in a strange living cocktail. It was one of the most unusual skies I'd ever seen. Soon, I rolled onto I-40, heading due east again.

A while later, I crossed into Arkansas. Like so many other areas of the country on this trip, it wasn't what I expected (at least the West Central part that I was riding through). It looked like Virginia or any other of a dozen different landscapes in the East close to low mountains. There were great bands of deciduous trees, rolling hills, and the blue-gray hint of low mountains in the distance (the Ozarks). For some reason, I had in my mind flat farmland interrupted by pine forests and craggy, bare soil plateaus. Maybe I picked up that impression up from one of my favorite car guy B-movies of the 1970s, *White Lightning*, which was shot in and around Benton, Arkansas.

At any rate, as the miles rolled by the weather improved, and with the number of trucks on the road increasing, I worked on my passing technique. I was moving at about 72 mph in a 70 mph zone, and with the rolling hills slowing the big rigs on the long inclines, there were plenty of potential victims.

The major thing you have to manage when passing a heavy truck at highway speed on a motorcycle is the characteristics of the air wash surrounding the truck. Heavy trucks at highway speed push a large dome of air in front of them as they move along, creating a positive pressure wave that fans out behind the cab at an angle much like the bow wave of a ship. They also leave behind a lower pressure area behind the trailer that collapses with the air around it in great vortexes, creating more turbulence.

Thus, as you approach from behind on an open motorcycle, even a heavy one like Big Girl, the first thing you notice is the swirls of air from the collapsing low-pressure area behind the trailer. It's like riding rows of big invisible vertical car wash brushes made of air though. They rock you from side to side in a quick motion, occasionally slapping you in the face as they overlap. Once you're beyond the trailing edge of the trailer, you enter the zone just before the main positive pressure wave from the cab. The resulting change in air pressure and the flow tends to want to suck you in towards the wheels of the trailer, so you have to lean a little to the left to counter it. Once you encounter the main pressure wave, which is usually just behind the driver's side door and lasts until you're just in front of the cab, it tends to want to push you outward, so you have to lean in. Once you exit that wave, you encounter fresh air again, but you're usually going faster, so you get buffeted by that. You might also, as you leave the front of the truck, get hit by strong crosswinds, so you have to be prepared. Daniel, the biker at the Chili's bar in Sioux City, Iowa, told me a story about this as we were ordering our third round.

A friend of his, a cop, and a relatively inexperienced rider were on a ride with Daniel and his group on a very windy day. One by one, they all passed a slower moving truck at a relatively high rate of speed. The cop was the last to pass, and just as he emerged from the front of the truck, he was hit by a huge crosswind blast. Daniel looked in his side mirror to check on him and watched as the cop was "flicked" off the highway to the left like a great hand had just swatted him out of the way. Daniel immediately slowed and watched the cop's headlight bob wildly up and down as he fought to maintain control in the grasses of the median. Somehow he managed to keep his bike up, and moments later he emerged back onto the left lane of the highway. Daniel said he and the rest of the guys in his group laughed their asses off, but I'm sure the poor cop wasn't amused. He might have even had to change his underwear.

Aside from the air wash of the truck, the next thing you have to manage is the risk that the truck won't see or hear you as you approach and will move over into your path. If that ever happens, particularly quickly, you're in big trouble. With all of this in mind, the passing technique I developed went something like this: As I approached from the rear and encountered the air wash, if the cruise control was on, I turned it off. This gave me finer, quicker throttle control for the ultimate pass. I also moved my feet from the highway pegs (if they were there) and placed them on the footboards, reducing the time it would take to hit the rear brake pedal if I had to slow rapidly. Next, I signaled and moved into the left lane and adjusted my speed so that I could do a moderately quick pass. You don't want to go too slowly because you could get stuck in the air wash adjacent to the truck and the driver might forget that you're there. And you don't want to go too fast because the turbulence when you hit the fresh air in front of the truck can be enough to make you lose control (like the cop). At any rate, once in the left lane and at the right speed, I moved my thumb from the turn signal switch (lower on a Harley), rested it on the horn button (just in case), and began the pass. Once abreast of the truck and right before the cab, I quickly rolled on more throttle. Once ahead of the truck, I signaled, moved back into the right lane, slowed, and placed the cruise back on.

I have no idea whether or not this was "textbook," but it seemed to work, and I kept practicing it until I had it down to military-like precision.

As I approached Little Rock, the temperature appeared to cool a bit. The sky cleared, with just a hint of leftover white, wispy clouds to let me know that a front had been through sometime before. I was really starting to enjoy the day, good weather, nice roads, decent scenery, and light traffic. I afforded myself the luxury of using the highway pegs more, and with winds light, wound Big Girl up another few notches to 74 mph.

East of Little Rock, it was time for gas and groceries again. As was the usual routine at this point, as soon as I stopped, I checked the weather radar on my iPhone. The line of storms that had passed through Little Rock earlier in the morning had moved on to the southeast. But a new, thin line running north-south had formed around Tupelo, Mississippi, right over Route 78. They were, however, moving east, so by the time I rolled through Memphis and back down to the southeast towards Tupelo, they'd be well to the east of me.

Given this, there was no need to hurry. So I took my time eating my fast-food lunch, noticing, as I did so, that the kitchen of the place didn't look very clean. The floor was covered with a thin layer of grease, and fries and other food remnants were everywhere. Definitely, as my wife would say, "sketchy."

About an hour later, as I was nearing Memphis, my stomach started cramping. Feeling flushed, with sweat beads dotting my brow, I swallowed hard and tried to shrug it off, but as I crossed the Mississippi River, staring at the lone tugboat churning through its muddy waters, I had to choke back a gag reflex.

A short time later, I entered the northeastern part of Mississippi. My usual custom when entering a new state was to blow the horn a few times as long as there was nobody around me, a spirit lifter of sorts. This time, however, when I pushed the button, it remained silent. I tried it several more times, but it was dead. An hour before I had used it when entering Tennessee. Now, with two days to go, two major cities to ride through, and Island tourists still left to dodge, I wouldn't have a horn. There was no chance of getting it fixed for the rest of the weekend—it was late Saturday afternoon and the service departments at Harley dealerships are almost never open on Sundays. I wondered if it would come back to haunt me.

By this time, in addition to my stomach, my rear end was beginning to really ache, so I practiced the body exercises that motorcyclists make up when riding on long trips. My routine was probably like so many others: I placed my feet on the footboards, lifted my rear up slightly, and rolled my hips backward and forward a few times. Then I lifted it up again, shifted it a little to the right side of the seat, and then back to the left again. Then I moved my feet to the highway pegs and flexed my hamstrings down, straightening my legs as much as possible. Finally, I leaned forward and arched my back, ducking my head behind the windshield for a moment to take a short but welcome break from the wind. It's routine, but it works. The blood starts to circulate again and you can make another thirty miles or so.

As the afternoon advanced, I rolled into Alabama. And somewhere between Tupelo and Birmingham, on what seemed like a road to nowhere, it happened. Riding along at 74 mph, still gulping from time to time to push back the acid reflux that wouldn't seem to go away, a sudden urge hit me to throw up. Getting it right would be significant. One misstep and I'd puke inside my helmet, or worse. Slowing as fast as I could, I pulled over, ripped off my sunglasses and dropped them to the left, unbuckled my chin strap, pulled my helmet off, leaned over to the right—and vomited all over the shoulder.

After shutting off the engine and expelling a few more times, I rolled forward a little, threw the kickstand down, turn off the ignition and dismounted. It had been pretty gross, but at least I'd avoided getting any spew on Big Girl or myself. So after calming down, fishing a rag out my saddlebag and wiping my mouth, I found a guard rail, leaned up against it and took my time to rehydrate. And as I stood watching the few cars and trucks that passed, water bottle in hand, I thought about how much, of all the things that parents have to put up with, I hated puke. I could take poopy diapers, even when they leaked all over. I could take broken bones and injuries, asthma attacks and runny noses and fevers, but the thing I hated the most—far and away—was vomit. And my kids were masters at blowing it, particularly my oldest son. Though it had happened over fifteen years ago, the memories of his most infamous episode were still fresh enough to cause me to chuckle.

We were on our way back to our home in Massachusetts from a short Thanksgiving vacation at my Mom's house in Maryland. We'd decided to take our new car, rather than my wife's station wagon since it got better gas mileage. I'd picked it up a few weeks back. It was a 1994 Volvo 850—the quintessential New England yuppie car—and my wife wanted it more than I did, so my compromise had been to get the turbocharged version of the handling package, with leather seats and all the goodies. It didn't even have a thousand miles on it yet, but I was already a convert. It was smooth, solid as a rock, and surprisingly fast.

When we reached Connecticut, we stopped for lunch at a Friendly's restaurant. The kids had the grilled cheese sandwiches they always ordered, but I noticed that my oldest son wasn't eating much.

"You feel OK, buddy?" I asked.

"Yeah Daddy, I'm OK. I just weally want a stwah-baewwy milkshake. Can I have one—please, please, please!"

Little boys, I thought. They're so cute when they can't pronounce "r"s. Something told me that I ought to say no, but my wife interjected and agreed. We were less than two hours from home and, she had to admit, they'd been pretty good. They could share it. But my oldest son, when he saw it, positioned it as far away from his brother as he could and consumed just about all of it. One of the largest shakes I'd ever seen, probably made with at least four full scoops of ice cream.

A few miles from home, on the last stretch of the interstate before our exit, I heard him say, somewhat meekly from just behind me, "Daddy . . . I don't feel so good."

Figuring we'd be home within ten minutes, I didn't register much worry but looked back to see if everything was OK. They were both tucked neatly in their car seats with their favorite "bankies" fluffed around, and the younger one was still asleep. My wife had also been nodding off and barely had the energy to look at me. Everything seemed fine. We only had a few miles to go.

The road was three lanes wide at that point and I'd just moved over into the left lane for a final pass of some slower moving cars and trucks. Concentrating on getting back over in time so I could make our exit, I missed the barely perceptible gulps coming from my oldest son. And then, with a revolting, *"PUHWAAAAUUUUUGGGHHHHH,"* it shot straight out of his mouth.

The force of the stream was so powerful it momentarily pushed my seat back forward and, after expanding its initial energy, it ricocheted almost everywhere else. Thinking, oh my God, this can't be happening, I tried to concentrate on pulling the car over, but it was difficult to see out of the puke-splattered rear window, and it was already dripping off the headliner. So I pushed the flasher button and just started moving over—to the sound of horns blaring—and when I hit the right shoulder, I slowed to a stop as fast as I safely could.

But I was too late. My younger son, when he woke up and realized that he was covered in puke, immediately started hurling all over his lap. And my wife, before I had a chance to warn her, looked back. Already six months pregnant with our third son, it didn't take much. It'd been her most difficult pregnancy so far, with debilitating sickness almost every day. Slapping a quick hand over her mouth, she spun her head forward again and tried to hit the power window button, but it wasn't located in the same place as the station wagon she was used to driving—and the doors were locked. A second later the first batch shot out between her fingers all over the center console, probably a good pints worth, while the rest of her stomach contents expelled into the windshield.

The smell was just staggering. Fighting back a gag reflex myself, I hit the door unlock button and stumbled out of the car with my back towards the traffic. At that point, I wouldn't have cared if a truck picked me off. Taking a few more paces backward towards the left rear of the car, still in shock, I tried to calm myself, but the kids were crying and my wife was already screaming at me to do something. So I opened the trunk, grabbed the only cleaning rag I'd brought along, took a deep breath, and, holding it over my nose and mouth—opened the left rear door.

It was a total horror show. My oldest son was holding his two hands outward, watching puke drain from his fingers onto the seat in a mouth-wide-open, face-crunched-up prelude to his next shrieking cry, while my younger son was pulling his blanket up, watching the puddle that had formed in his lap slosh onto the floor. Spew was dripping from the ceiling like rain from a tree canopy, and the main bulk of it was pooling in the creases of the seats and draining over the edges onto the floor. Still dry heaving, my wife had the glove box open, desperately trying to find some napkins. But the mess on the dashboard was draining into it while the spatter from the windshield was sliding into the defroster vents. As an added bonus, right after I'd bailed out, she'd lowered all the windows, and Volvos being boxy, the spew from the ceiling was dripping straight down into the door sills.

Sacrificing one of the bankies, I did my best to at least get the bulk of it off each of their hands and faces, but the best I could do was to suck it up, drive home and get everyone inside. For the last mile into our neighborhood I sped pretty badly, hoping that I'd be pulled over. The poor cop, I would think as he walks up to the car and looks inside—for that matter, takes his first *whiff* of what's inside—he will never make another traffic stop again.

We all recovered, of course, after rinsing our clothes off in the laundry room washbasin and some long, hot baths and showers. But our car—our first nice new car—even after six hours of painstaking cleaning with sudsy ammonia, fresh water rinsing, and blow drying, was never the same. I traded it two years later when the weather was mild enough so the dealer wouldn't have to turn on the ventilation system.

And as I put on my helmet, slid on my sunglasses and restarted Big Girl, feeling a lot better, I realized there was another advantage to traveling by a motorcycle that I hadn't thought of. They don't have interiors.

A half an hour later, running on fumes again after a search that led me several miles away from the highway, I found an old convenience store and pulled in. Still thirsty, I walked into the shop and grabbed a Gatorade. The woman behind the counter seemed genuinely pleased to see me. She was in her mid-fifties with dark hair and newer style glasses that made her look younger. Wearing an attractive summer blouse and decent jewelry, she struck me as a southern belle who was strangely out of place in a backwoods convenience store.

"I'll take this please," I said and handed her the Gatorade. "And is it OK for me to leave my bike at the pump?"

"Why that would be *faahine*," she replied in a proper antebellum timbre. "Where are you heading?"

"South Carolina," I said. For once, it didn't seem that far away.

As I was paying for the drink, we both turned our heads to watch another pickup truck. An older but well maintained Chevy carefully backed up to the pump ahead of the one where Big Girl was parked. The driver was young, really young, maybe sixteen, and he looked absolutely scared to death—his round face pale, his lips trembling. He probably figured if he hit the bike behind him some tough guy biker would fly out of the store and slit his throat. We both chuckled at the spectacle.

Back on I-78 East, the afternoon started to get very long. The sun was getting low in the sky behind me, casting longer and longer shadows in front of Big Girl. Every now and then the air would suddenly cool and I'd see patches of water on the highway, a reminder that the storm front I was following was probably no more than twenty or thirty miles ahead. I crossed six hundred miles for the day, still making good time.

Finally, I saw a major split in the road ahead. The right lane was labeled "Route 78 – Birmingham" and the left lane was labeled "Route 78." I was confused. The last time I'd studied my Google Maps application

I seemed to recall that there was only one road to Birmingham, so why was it now splitting into two? There were a few trucks ahead of me and I saw them move into the right lane and brake for the exit, so I figured that had to be the one. They'd know where to go. In any event, I followed them off.

It didn't take long for me to question my decision. The road was still two lanes on either side, but the lanes had narrowed and the shoulders had disappeared. There were more traffic lights and I seemed to be passing an endless array of cheap shopping centers, pawn shops, check cashing places, and lower quality fast food joints. I considered finding a hotel, but there were no signs or advertisements for any of the usual chains. Some time later, I passed a hotel adjacent to a shopping center with a sign hanging at an odd angle that just said "Hotel." It was two stories high and constructed out of painted white cinder blocks. All of the room doors faced the parking lot, which was empty except for a 1980s style Chevy Caprice with ridiculously oversized chrome wheels. I wasn't staying there.

Just as I was considering pulling over to check the route, the cityscape changed into a demilitarized zone (DMZ). If there were tall high-rises with broken windows and laundry hanging outside, it could have been the Bronx in the 1970s. Abandoned railcars were everywhere on the left, their graffiti-stained sides rusting on tracks covered with weeds. I passed a few neighborhoods on the right with small, wood frame houses with dingy white peeling paint. In between two of these, a house had collapsed, its roof caved in a surprisingly uniform flat looking "U." I thought of stopping and checking to see if I was on the right road, but I didn't want to take the risk of someone approaching me. Finally, after several more traffic stops I saw one of those confusing road signs ahead with multiple interstate and state route markers. They were all piled on top of one another in a grotesque looking inverted tree, the kind we don't have to interpret anymore because of GPS-based in-car navigation systems. It was hard to study because there were a few trucks ahead of me, but I was finally able to see a sign for I-20 East to Atlanta. It may not have been the best route to get there, but I'd found the next road I needed to get me home.

I downshifted Big Girl a few times and started to exit, noticing that the exit ramp was tightly coiled and the maximum recommended safe speed was 15 mph. A small Honda coupe was behind me, tailgating so closely that I could see the driver in my right side mirror. He was a kid, maybe twenty, with dark hair, dark eyes, and a thin mustache. As soon as I left-signaled to move onto the interstate, he charged ahead on my right, passed, and switched lanes two more times to the left, missing me by no more than ten feet. For the second time on the trip I wished Big Girl was equipped with rocket launchers.

My sole objective at this point was to find a hotel. The sun was setting. I'd now clocked 675 miles, my rear end was aching, my face was burning from the combined effects of sun and wind, and I was having trouble reading road signs and concentrating. The billboards lining the road at this point were particularly inscrutable. Located high up on bluffs that lined the road, hundreds of yards on either side, I couldn't quite make them out.

Still straining to read one of the billboards, I completely missed what must have been a deep, jagged pothole in the center of my lane just ahead. The road surface hadn't up until that point offered a clue that those hazards existed. It was concrete, stained dark in each lane from years of city traffic, but otherwise smooth. Big Girl slammed into it with a bone-jarring "whamm!" and the unmistakable metallic creaking sound that springs make when compressed to their maximum limits. She momentarily dipped, taking me with her, my rear end lifting from the seat, my hands instinctively squeezing the hand grips with all the force I could muster. An instant later we were through it. I held my breath thinking about the rim and the tire. It had to be bent, the tire was probably blown. I let go of the throttle, downshifted into fifth, and just rode her straight for a few seconds, looking down at the fork and the front wheel assembly to scan for damage. She rolled on. Still in disbelief, I leaned left and right to change position in the lane and tested the front brake. Nothing. She seemed completely nonplussed about the whole thing, with no new vibrations or shudders. She was one tough girl.

Ten minutes later I was able to make out a billboard with some recognizable hotel chains, including a Hampton Inn. It said, "Exit Now!" which was helpful because at that point I just needed to take orders without thinking. I rolled off of the exit, now just east of Birmingham.

The hotels were located high on a bluff that overlooked the highway. A Holiday Inn to the left was at the highest elevation, precariously perched on a rocky outcropping. A Quality Inn and a Hampton Inn were further up on the left just off of the main road. I quickly chose the Hampton and followed the signs into the parking lot. It appeared to be nearly empty, so surely they'd have rooms. I swung around to the front of the hotel under the lobby portico, shut off Big Girl and walked into the lobby.

The reservation counter was on the left and a clerk was in the process of checking in another guest. He was dark skinned, with smooth jet black hair and dark eyes, probably Indian or Pakistani, a bit younger than me. He was entirely focused on the computer screen, his face dour with a look of stern concentration, so he never made an attempt to acknowledge that another potential guest had arrived. He just stood there, tapping away at his computer keyboard, the soft glow of the screen illuminating his face. For the next few minutes, he kept on tapping . . . tap tap, tap tap tap tap, Enter, Enter, Enter, Enter, tap tap tap . . . and I realized I was witnessing one of the things I hated the most about checking into hotels: the two thousand keystroke check-in.

In all of my business travel, I could never understand how it could possibly be so complicated to check a guest into a hotel. There just weren't that many choices. Most of the nicer chains were non-smoking these days, all you had to decide was king or double queen. It was probably a disgruntled employee, I thought. A way to get back at the Man. Her assignment had been simple enough: create a check-in system for all of the individual hotels. But she'd been given one of those "solid citizen" performance reviews a few years back, the kind that companies give when they want to keep exploiting your labor without a decent raise or a bonus, and she was howling angrily about it. So her payback was to design the system to be as painful as humanly possible for the front desk clerks. I could see her handiwork, the brilliance of her subversion:

Make them have to check the entire inventory of rooms, one at a time. If they skip ahead too fast, make it default back to the beginning. Require verification to continue after every room check with at least five "Enters." It'll grind them to a halt. And the best part is, company "leadership"—the same clowns who shaft us every year while reward-

ing themselves—don't know shit about systems. It'll take them years to figure it out. And by then I'll have found a better job. Maybe further screwing up airline reservation systems, if it's even possible to make those worse . . .

As I was pondering this, the tapping continued. Tap, tap, tap, tap, tappity, tap tap . . . Enter, Enter, Enter . . . tap tap, tap . . . and even the guy ahead of me started to get annoyed. He was shifting his weight, moving his feet, and cocking his head from one side to the other. At one point, he half-glanced back at me and shrugged his shoulders. Still the tapping went on without a word of encouragement or a moment of eye contact with either one of us.

My anger growing and my patience wearing thinner, I started to fantasize again. I thought of the Screamin' Eagle death machine, but it didn't seem to fit the situation. No, this time it would be something simple. I'd just hurl my full-faced helmet at his head and clock him so hard he'd instinctively look up to see where it came from and finally see that two human beings were standing in front of him. But I'd probably get arrested for assault and there'd be lawsuits, so like so many other travelers that endure this kind of crap every day, I just stood there, taking it.

A few minutes later, still tapping . . . Tap, tap, tappity tappity tap, Enter, Enter, Enter . . . he mumbled that he had to check into something, turned around, and walked into a back room. The counter was still. The hotel was eerily quiet. Additional minutes passed. The guy in front of me lifted his hands in an exasperated gesture, but at that point, I'd had enough. Borrowing a line from Larry, I muttered, *"Fuck this,"* spun to the left and marched out of the lobby back towards Big Girl.

Steaming, I threw my leg over the seat, slammed down my helmet, snapped the ignition switch clockwise, smartly clicked the run switch to "On," and simultaneously hit the starter. I think Big Girl knew I was pissed because her V-twin fired on the first stroke of her cylinders, without the usual "cheauh, chauh, chauh, per-pop! bada-bup-bup" that was her usual starting cadence. I pushed in the clutch, stomped on the toe shifter to put her in first, and roared out of the parking lot, realizing as I did so that even if the missing clerk heard the racket, he probably wouldn't care.

Back on I-20 East, I scanned again for hotels, staying in the right lane and riding under the speed limit. Another set was available at the next exit, so once again, I rolled off to the right. Up ahead to the right just down across the road was another Hampton Inn, a carbon copy of the last one, backed up against a low bluff. Not wanting to indict an entire hotel chain because of one rude clerk, I decided to give it a shot. I pulled what looked to be an exact replica of the portico that Big Girl had been under just before and scanned the parking lot. It was even emptier than the last one. I killed the engine and walked inside.

Refreshingly, I was immediately greeted by two counter clerks, both women, one young with medium blond hair and a cute smile, the other much older. As I approached, I saw the older one take a half step back, her lips quivering ever so slightly as she did so. She was scared of me. Not wanting to shatter her likely perceptions of bikers, I addressed the younger one who seemed eager.

Helmet in hand; I asked her gently, "Do you have rooms?"

"Yes!" she responded enthusiastically and blurted out the room rate, "Seventy-nine dollars a night."

But before she could start her check-in routine, I leaned over and asked her the next logical question on my mind.

"Are there any restaurants that are within walking distance of this hotel?"

"No," she replied in a very professional manner, "all of the food is four miles further up I-20 at the next exit."

I stared at her for a long moment and I could tell by the sly smile that was forming on her now blushing face that she knew what question was coming next.

Leaning in towards her even closer, with all of the charm and humor I could muster, I said, "So . . . are there any hotels up there too?"

With just a hint of a chuckle, she said, "Yes."

"Well then," I said, "I guess I have four more miles to go."

A few moments later I was rolling on I-20 East again. It was now past sunset and the sky and the surrounding countryside were darkening rapidly. Big Girls' headlight and her passing lamps were starting to illuminate the road signs and the blacktop. A strange feeling came over me—creeping fear, that sixth sense that something wasn't right. It was critter time. Still riding under the speed limit, in the right lane, I repeatedly scanned the tree line adjacent to the shoulder for any signs of lurking animal life. To heighten my fears, a few moments later, I passed a deer lying on its left side, its curved back resting on the white line separating my lane from the shoulder. It had been freshly killed. I'd seen enough dead animals while riding on a motorcycle by now to be able to tell the difference. There was no smell; it hadn't started to decompose yet. For the next three miles, I tried not to let my imagination get the best of me. Instead, I just silently prayed: please God, keep the animals at bay and please let me get off.

Soon enough, I slowed for what would be my third attempt that night to find the magic combination of a decent hotel within walking distance of a restaurant. This time I was glad to see that there was a lot more infrastructure around, including restaurants and gas stations, but I couldn't see where the hotels were. I guessed they were to the right and turned south, discovering sometime later, as would be my luck, I was wrong. Pissed again, I pulled an illegal U-turn and headed the other way. As I crossed I-20 heading north, I could tell I'd reached the tipping point, the point when you just can't ride another half-mile, the point when it starts to get really unsafe, the threshold I'd crossed on Day 2. To make matters worse, I was riding into one of the most confusing situations you can encounter on a motorcycle—or a car for that matter—trying to find something while traveling through a densely packed area. People were lined up to make left turns in one of those dual-use center lanes. Entrances to parking lots were everywhere and cars were darting in and out. There were multiple traffic lights spaced closely together, all turning different colors. While processing all of this information, trying not to make a mistake, trying not to get killed, I had to scan the side of the road and find the hotels that still remained illusively hidden.

Finally, out the corner of my eye to the right, I spotted a sign for a Quality Inn. It appeared to be off a service road close to the interstate. I slowed to make a turn at the next traffic light and noticed the sign for a Ruby Tuesdays in the same area. Bingo. Still not knowing if the road was the right one, I turned right, passed the restaurant, followed the road to the left and spotted a Quality Inn. Even better, there was a Best Western at the end of the road, so I had two choices. The parking lot of the

Best Western was illuminated better—a major plus—but when I saw two Harley Electra Glides parked in front, that was the clincher. It was biker friendly. I pulled under the portico, exhaled sharply, shut off Big Girl, and glanced down at the trip computer. I'd ridden 690 miles, the same total as Day 1. The exhilaration, however, was gone.

It had seemed infinitely more exhausting.

Day 11: Guardian Angels

I met them at the hotel. Since it was my last day with only 420 miles to go, I'd taken the liberty of sleeping in a little more. So by the time I walked into the breakfast room, it was already bustling with activity. Two men were sitting at a small table towards the back, quietly chatting. Both about the same age, with white-gray hair and alabaster skin, they were alternately trading a pencil and a napkin, drawing a map. Probably the guys on the Electra Glides, I thought. A quick scan of their clothing confirmed it. They were both wearing riding boots, jeans, and Harley t-shirts—the standard outfit. And like so many other bikers, including me, they had goatees: one fuller, snow-white and perfectly trimmed, the other more straggly and salt and pepper. But there was something else about them, a subtle kindness in their demeanor, an approachability that I'd rarely seen in other bikers. Feeling a little lonely, I chose a table close to theirs and sat down.

I wasn't even through my first sip of coffee when the shorter one greeted me. With my full riding gear on, it must have been easy to figure out.

"Good morning," he said. "You on your way back from Sturgis?"

"Yeah," I replied, "Last day . . . can't wait to get home."

"Where's that?"

"Hilton Head Island."

"Nice. We're from Myrtle Beach. My name's John and the taller guy here is Mike."

"Nice to meet you both," I replied, but quickly realized that I was probably holding them up. So I gave them an out.

"Looks like you guys are finished," I said, "so if you want to get going that's no problem. I've still got some eating to do."

"No, no," they both replied politely, "we're in no hurry. And it's good to talk to someone from home."

I'd never met a pair of bikers who were easier to talk to. For the next twenty minutes, through at least two more coffee refills and probably the largest breakfast I'd consumed on the trip, we talked about riding. They'd been all over, to almost every one of the major rallies, usually traveling alone, but sometimes with their wives.

"Bringing the women along," John said with reflection, "is a double-edged sword. It's certainly nice to have female companionship, but we can't make as many miles in a day. And storage space gets tight—really tight. If an average Electra Glide with a tour pack, like mine, can carry about eight cubic feet of luggage, my wife takes seven of it, so I have to stuff what I need—clothes, bathroom bag, booze, everything—into a cigar box."

"When I travel alone," Mike added, "not only do I get all of the luggage space, but I can carry a cooler where she normally sits. John and I stock it with everything: beer, water, Gatorade, food—the works. It's our portable refrigerator."

"Tough trade," I said jokingly, and they both burst out laughing.

"Not really," said Mike, "I'll take the cooler any day."

After some more small talk about their riding club in Myrtle Beach, I pushed my chair back and started to rise. It was time to get going. When we were all standing and shaking hands to say good-bye, John's face lit up with an idea.

"Hey, why don't you ride with us? We can stay together at least as far as Atlanta."

"I don't know," I said anxiously, "I don't like to ride very fast—seventy-two tops—and I don't want to hold you guys up."

"That's not a problem. We'll ride at your pace. Just follow us to Atlanta."

"How are you guys on gas?" I asked.

"We topped off last night, but if you need to stop, just let us know."

"OK," I said, "you got me. Just give me five minutes to get my stuff and I'll meet you in the parking lot."

Brimming with excitement, I was back outside and packing my bike before either one of them.

They were parked about thirty yards away, towards the back of the hotel. When they finally did emerge, small duffle bags in hand, they took their time walking over to their bikes, packing, and adjusting their gear. The sun was rising behind them above a band of shale-colored clouds, its rays illuminating the margin between the clouds and sky with a reddish-yellow glow. It was a beautiful summer morning sunrise, the kind that's designed to provide a break from the haze, heat, and humidity of the ensuing day that starts to suck the life out of everything on the ground. Breathing easy in the flower and grass scented air, enjoying the repose, I made my own final adjustments and looked back at them, waiting for a signal.

And at that moment, as my eyes focused on their faces, something unexpected happened. The sun had just risen above the edge of the clouds and its rays, shooting to the east, began to illuminate their hair. I'm not sure why, perhaps because it was mostly white with just a little bit of gray, the thickness was just right, or they used some kind of special hair gel. Maybe the bandwidth of the incoming rays was within some perfectly tuned range. Within seconds, both of their manes were glowing yellowish-white and channeling the light into sharper, prism-shaped beams that spread out laterally in all directions.

Struggling to understand what I was seeing, a strange feeling started to spread. My skin erupted in goose bumps and my lips began to quiver. My nerves were tingling, almost humming from my toes up through my torso. I gasped for air once, choking up, but the sensation wasn't at all frightening. To the contrary, it was subtle and soothing as if an ethereal blanket of grace had gently descended on my shoulders. Smiling broadly, I began to understand.

We'd had one of our best conversations on the entire trip the night before, or, for that matter, our whole marriage. Full of humor, hope, and playfulness, but at the same time interesting and honest. Not much about little things like the house or upcoming kids events, but a funny recast, almost a comedy roast of our life together. Like so many other couples, we'd been through a lot. No money to start off with, working multiple jobs, putting ourselves through college, four kids, big moves, big risks, and dumb mistakes, but a lot of rewards too. But no matter how crazy the road had been, at least so far, we'd done it, what we said we'd do—the vow we'd taken on that beautiful spring day in Norfolk over twenty years ago—to build a *life* together. And part of that commitment, she'd remind me from time to time, was to be there for her and the kids. If I got sick, she'd understand and take care of me, but otherwise, I had a responsibility to live, to not do something stupid and get myself killed.

She didn't say she was going to do it as we closed our conversation. But standing in the parking lot, staring at the sight of the wondrous beams of light reflecting off of the heads of my two new friends, I knew she had. It was something we all recognized.

My wife carries a quiet spirituality that those of us who know her well understand and in many ways, envy. It's a relationship that has deepened, over time, through self-study and reflection, into something well beyond a once-a-week remembrance. She doesn't push it on anyone or wear it on her sleeve, but it's always there, mystically lifting her, like an additional buoyant force. And part of her own ritual, as with so many others, is that she prays. Never for anything material or mundane, but for what really matters to her, the health and welfare of the people she cares about the most. And strangely, she almost always gets her way. It's something we laugh about from time to time in our family, something that my oldest son best encapsulated once at dinner. It was just after we got the word from Chris's orthopedist that his knee was going to fully recover. She was pleased of course and profoundly relieved, and reminded us that her prayers had been answered.

"Of course, Ma," he said, "We'd expect nothing less. Everyone knows you stand in right with the Lord."

So to me at least, it was obvious. After we'd talked last night, before trailing off to sleep, she'd prayed for me. Prayed that I'd return home safely, unharmed so we could continue our life together. And as usual, her prayers had been answered. John and Mike, the two white-haired biker gentlemen on the Electra-Glides, were my protectors, my Guardian Angels. Somehow, they'd been sent to guide me home.

The hotel was right off of the interstate, so before long we were rolling east on I-20, directly into the sun. John took the lead, riding to the left side of the right lane, with Mike and I staggered behind. I couldn't tell how fast we were going because of the glare off of my speedometer, but it was quickly apparent they'd forgotten about my request to take it easy. They were moving—actually moving. The construction cones that lined the shoulder in the left lane were flying by in a nearly continuous stream of orange and black. The tree lines on either side of the road were rushing behind me in a dizzying blur. Knowing that it was Sunday, I could understand why they weren't that concerned about speeding through construction zones. But I would have thought, particularly when a lane was choked off, that they'd at least slow a little. But they never slackened the pace. We had to be riding at close to, or well over, 80 mph. Maybe she had another motive with her prayers, I thought. I do have a pretty nice life insurance policy. Still, I kept up.

Since I only started with a third of a tank, I knew it would be an issue within a relatively short period of time. But at the speed we were traveling, Big Girl was consuming even more fuel than usual. Not wanting to hold them up, I held off as long as possible. When the trip computer was down to forty miles, I downshifted into fifth, sprinted ahead of Mike, changed into the left lane and pulled abreast of John. When I pointed at my tank, he nodded his head in recognition. Before I could even drift back to behind Mike, his right turn signal illuminated and he started to peel off at an exit. I thought they'd at least continue on for a few more miles, but I guess that wasn't his style. If you need gas, you need gas. And on a bike it's always best to get it as soon as possible. I still hadn't learned that.

After topping off and visiting the store, I walked back out to where their bikes were parked. Mike opened the top of his cooler and offered me a Gatorade. It was just as he said it was, a rolling refrigerator that took up the whole passenger seat and stuck out a couple of feet on either side.

"The weight doesn't bother you?" I asked.

"Still lighter than my old lady," he replied with a wink, "and it never talks too much."

By the time John walked up, we were half way through our drinks. Another natural conversation ensued. The morning was beautiful and the traffic had been light. We were making good time and could be in Atlanta by noon. Assuming that I'd continue to follow, I was about to bring up the speed issue, but Mike caught me off guard.

"Listen," he said, "when we ride we always trade off being Road Captain. And since John led last time, it's somebody else's turn. I'd prefer to follow since I have to carry this casket on the back of my bike, so why don't you lead? We'll follow you and split at the I-20 and I-75 junction. OK?"

Shocked that they would offer me, a new rider with their group, the honor, I hesitated. It would be my first time as a Road Captain and I'd be leading a pair of guys with probably ten times more experience. I knew I could do it, and probably well, but I didn't want to let them down. But I also didn't wish to seem like a wimp. After an awkward pause, considering the responsibilities, I finally spoke up.

"Sure," I said, "but I won't be going as fast—maybe seventy-five tops. So if that's OK with you guys, I'll be happy to lead."

"No problem," they said in tandem. "We'll follow you all the way, *Captain*."

It was official. I'd been spot promoted.

Leading turned out to be a lot more fun than I thought it would be. Besides being able to set the pace, I enjoyed pointing out the road hazards to my fellow riders and navigating through the construction zone lane changes. John and Mike turned out to be good followers and stayed right with me, usually in a perfect position. Even the occasional dead animal did nothing to slow us down.

Before long, we were on the outskirts of Atlanta. When the road widened to four lanes and the traffic increased, staying together became more challenging. So when I passed a slower moving truck or car, I made sure we all had plenty of time to make the lane change and get back into position. If we got split up, I'd adjust my speed so they had a chance to quickly catch up.

When a huge overhead billboard indicated that I-75 was approaching, I almost didn't want to see it. But a mile from the final split, as I changed into the right lane, I knew it was over. John was the first to move over to the left and Mike closed the gap so they were almost riding tandem in the same lane. Since I was slowing to veer off and they put on a little more speed, it didn't take long for us to converge. When they were right beside me, on my left, they momentarily slowed and turned their heads. Grinning broadly, John gave me a salute and Mike followed with a downward, two-fingered Harley wave. A good-bye, a thank you, and recognition of a job well done all wrapped into one. The latter is what got me the most. I'd passed the Road Captain test with flying colors. And I realized something else. Earning the respect of a couple of bikers I hardly knew felt better than any professional "atta-boy" I'd received in a long, long time.

Choosing to stay as far away as possible from any heavy trucks, I moved into the HOV lane and set the cruise at 70 mph. It was well above the speed limit, but no one else seemed to be paying attention to it either. In fact, for a Sunday morning, people appeared to be in one hell of a hurry. Cars were passing me at times like I was standing still—even moms in minivans. A small church van, one of those big boxy Dodges that carries a dozen or so people, zipped by doing at least 85 mph. At first I thought maybe everyone knew the police had the morning off. Every now and then I'd pass a patrol car sitting in a construction zone, idling with its lights on, presumably just to warn people. But there were no construction workers and none of the squad cars ever moved. The cops inside them were probably reading the paper and sipping coffee. They apparently didn't care. So taking a cue from everyone else, I sped up.

The hardest part turned out to be I-16 again. It's a long, lonely road and by the time I passed Macon I was already mentally finished with it. Willing myself to press on, I tried to think of anything but the highway. My wife, sleeping in my own bed again, my wife again, sleeping with my wife in my own bed, my kids, the puppies—anything. But the demands of riding kept bringing me back to keeping Big Girl in the right position in the lane, dodging road hazards, passing trucks safely, and managing the wind. Except for, as usual, I forgot one thing. When I finally did look down, I slapped my knee in a gesture of exasperated disgust. I was almost out of gas again.

Remembering the lesson that John taught me earlier in the morning, I veered off at the first available exit. A quick left turn and a few hundred yards later, I pulled up under the sagging portico of an older station. Since it was my last gas stop of the trip, my last top off before the final leg home, I decided to visit the restroom. Staring at the weather radar on my phone, not really paying attention, I walked into the store. The bathrooms were off to the left and there was a line. Initially frustrated, I realized it would give me more time to study the images. Thunderstorms were popping up all around me and a huge north-south line was just to the east. By the time I hit I-95, I'd probably be on top of it.

When it was finally my turn, I reached for the doorknob and noticed a paper sign that had been hung on the door. It looked strangely familiar. In large black and blue block letters it read: "RESTROOMS ARE ABSOLUTELY AND STRICTLY FOR THE USE OF IN-STORE CUSTOMERS ONLY." Surprised, I read it again and turned my head backward to scan the store. I couldn't believe it. Shaking with laughter, with the other patrons looking at me like I had some kind of a mental problem, I opened the door and walked in. Yep, I thought, everything's the same. Somehow, I'd managed to ride two thousand miles across the country and back again and wind up, unknowingly, in the same crappy gas station. The first stop outbound and the last stop back. What were the chances? Wondering what other surprises could possibly be in store for me, I fired up Big Girl and accelerated back onto the interstate.

Mile after mile, as I closed the distance to the coast, the weather deteriorated. The sky was confused, angry, and changing rapidly, particularly over the highway. One minute a disorganized thunderhead would pop out from the white cumulus clouds on the left, while the next minute a smaller, darker thunderhead lined with fast moving gray chaser-clouds would appear on the right. Rain sprinkles would start and stop randomly while thunder rumbled all around. It was as if the sky was trying to organize itself into a more uniform, more menacing storm and whoever was putting the pieces together was angrily grumbling because they kept falling apart again. Ten miles from I-95, however, a real threat emerged.

To the east, probably no more than five miles ahead, the clouds had organized into a solid dark gray band all the way down to the horizon. The trucks and cars heading west, towards me, all had their headlights on. A few minutes later, a couple of lightning strikes to the east flash illuminated the darkness. The claps of thunder that followed were sharper and more carefully timed. I'd finally caught up to the front I'd been chasing across the country for three days.

Though all I wanted to do at that point was close the last distance and get home, I knew the prudent thing to do was to stop and let the front pass further to the east. So I pulled over under the large bridge over I-95 at the I-16 interchange, put on my flashers, and dismounted. With the noise of the thunder and the traffic above shaking the bridge and the ground, I pulled out my phone and hit the weather radar icon. The front was long and skinny, stretching a good hundred miles to the north and south. The cells within it were intense, showing up as mostly yellow with some red, but the worst of them had already passed over the interstate to the east. And it was moving east. So if I turned north, I'd be safe all the way from South Carolina. But once I turned east again, towards the Island, I'd be chasing it down. Running the images again to get an idea of its speed of advance, I figured the timing might just work. It would take about forty-five minutes to get to my next turn. By that time, it would be close to the Island. With luck, by the time I'd close the distance to it again, it'd move offshore. As a last safety measure however, just in case, I decided to put on my rain gear. This time, thankfully, it went on easier.

The air behind the front was stiflingly warm and humid and for most of the ride up I-95, I questioned whether or not it was worth it to don my rain gear. The rain had stayed mostly to the east with just a few sprinkles and I was starting to cook under my plastic tarp. But a couple of miles from the South Carolina border something else began to bother me.

I'd been riding in the center lane, doing my standard speed of 72 mph, minding my own business when he'd passed me in the left lane doing about 80 mph. Not uncommon for traffic on I-95, I didn't give it much thought until he slowed again. It wasn't a hard deceleration, no taillights came on, but he must have taken his foot completely off of the gas because I closed the distance relatively quickly and passed him on the right. A few seconds later, when I was well ahead, he took off again in the same lane—the left—and bolted past me. As he pulled ahead, I could hear a bass reverberating inside his car, the kind that causes the rear window to pulse and its sheet metal to vibrate. Probably just a kid, I thought, listening to rap music—the kind that seems specially designed to irritate the shit out of middle-aged parents—but he was ahead of me and pulling away, so I didn't see him as much of a threat.

A moment later, however, I noticed I was closing the distance to him again. At first I thought of changing lanes to the right, but a big rig was blocking the road. So I rolled on, maintaining speed, and watched as I passed him again. Looking over with more curiosity this time, I could see that he was talking into a cell phone. But he was behind me and falling back further, so I didn't register much worry.

But that didn't last long. Glancing in my left mirror I noticed the car, an older style white Toyota Camry, was speeding up again. Checking my mirror to the right, I saw that the rig was still in the same spot, facing me. I was still too close to him to get over safely. So I decided to stay put in the center lane and maintain speed. And sure enough, moments later, he passed me again on the left, the car this time twitching from side to side as he bopped to the music. I could also see that he was looking up and to the right, scanning the road signs. He must be getting ready to exit, I thought, and snapped off the cruise control, momentarily slowing so I'd further open the distance.

A second later, his taillights came on and the car rapidly decelerated. For a moment, I thought he was going to slow down enough to slide in behind me and the truck. But when he was just about abreast of me, on the left, he unexpectedly put on more speed and pulled ahead, putting me directly in his blind spot. Realizing the danger with my front wheel directly across from his right rear wheel, I released the throttle, but when I saw his right shoulder dip and his left hand on the steering wheel suddenly jerk up, I knew I hadn't reacted fast enough. He'd made a snap decision to get off.

It all happened in a blur of action within a fraction of the second. My first instinct was to lean on the horn button, and for once I actually managed to hit it, but it was dead. I'd lost it when I'd crossed into Mississippi. But in any event, that wasn't going to stop him from coming over. I only had one chance and I knew it. And it totally went against every bit of road experience I'd garnered—in a car and on a motorcycle—for over thirty years and a half a million miles.

It was really the fault of my first car, the 1971 Pontiac Canyon Copper LeMans. Like most General Motors cars of its era, it was overpowered and under-braked. Part of that was my fault in that I did what most teenage kids did with a small block V8 powered car in those days, no matter what its original configuration. It was too easy. All you had to do was convert it to dual exhaust, advance the ignition timing, flip the air cleaner lid, and run it with premium fuel. And just like that, you'd gain GTO-like horsepower. But what we wouldn't do, of course, was change the braking system. Disc brakes cost money. So we'd put up with the standard drums and, over the years and miles, learn their weaknesses. They'd grab to one side unpredictably, particularly when wet, and once you stopped hard they were useless for another hour. My LeMans was so bad, especially with grabbing; I'd demonstrate it from time to time for my friends. After driving through a dark puddle, I'd say, "Watch this," take my hands off the steering wheel, hit the brake pedal with a quick, sharp tap, and look at the wheel instantly rotate as much as 180 degrees to one side or the other. They'd just shake their heads in disbelief.

So I learned with that car and a bunch of others after it to never trust brakes. Slow by using hills and downshifting the transmission. Look far ahead and take your foot off the gas as soon as you see brake lights. The same tricks that truckers use every day. And I carried those lessons into riding. The best way out of trouble was always to gently slow and steer your way to the danger, or accelerate hard and get out in front of it. It was, I recalled, the only part of my motorcycle license test where I'd lost points. During one part, riders are instructed to accelerate up to 40 mph and then, after crossing a start line, stop as quickly as possible without crossing a line further down the course. If you jam on the front and rear brakes, most people can do it, but I couldn't bring myself to lock it up.

Yet this time, I had to do it. It was life or death. If he clipped my front tire doing 70 mph with a truck close behind to my right, I was road kill. For the first time in my life, without any practice, I had to do an all-in, no-holds-barred, panic deceleration on an eight hundred and fifty pound motorcycle—on the partially wet pavement.

Without hesitation, I squeezed the front brake handle as hard as possible and slammed my right foot down on the brake pedal. Big Girl squatted down and slowed rapidly, much faster than I thought she would, but I'd never tested the rear anti-lock brakes that came as standard equipment in '08 and newer Harley touring bikes. Caught by surprise by the pulsing in the rear brake pedal, I did the one thing you're not supposed to do. I eased up. On any other bike, that one mistake could have been enough to kill me, but one of the nice things about Screamin' Eagle Road Kings is they come standard with upgraded front disc brake calipers. They made the difference. By the time I reapplied the rear brake, the rear bumper of his car had already passed my front tire. It missed me by about a foot. At 60 mph or 88 feet per second, that's about a hundredth of a second.

Stunned that I'd come that close, I raised my fist in a somewhat muted gesture of disapproval and shook my head. Without a horn, it was about all I could do. But a second later, from behind me, I heard a horn sound off. It was loud and mean, probably from a big car. As I craned my head to the right to look at me, I saw a silver Chevy pickup turn on its high beam headlights and start accelerating—fast. When it passed me on the right doing at least 85 mph, I noticed a Harley-Davidson sticker on the rear window of the cab. The driver was a biker. He must have seen the whole thing, become righteously pissed, and decided to go after the driver of the car in a fellowship driven bit of road rage. By the time the Camry exited, he was right on its tail. And I had to admit, it made me feel good. Somebody else had my back. I just hoped he didn't shoot the poor kid when he caught up with him.

When I crossed the border into South Carolina, my entire body relaxed, releasing, it seemed, a vast reservoir of stress. I put my feet up on the highway pegs, leaned as far back as possible and watched the pine forests flash by. The wind was at my back—the best possible riding condition—so I changed lanes effortlessly, hot-dogging a little, never worrying about speed. Big Girl seemed to be loafing, enjoying, for once, not having to fight anything. She'd never moved so effortlessly. Two miles from the exit on Highway 278, when I finally did look down at my speedometer, I was surprised to see that I was moving at well over 80 mph. Then again, I thought, it wasn't that surprising. She knew what I wanted and she wanted it too. She was pulling us home.

As I closed the distance to the storm, the sky became more threatening. In the distance, probably over the Island, a bulbous cloud bank had descended to ground level. Almost black at the edges, it was masking all of the vegetation and infrastructures to the east. So about the only things I could see were the taillights of the cars in front of me, the buildings to the immediate right and left, and the headlights of the oncoming cars.

Further ahead at the horizon, lightning bolts were cutting through the darkness and tasing the ground, probing, it seemed, for weaknesses. I wasn't going to be one of them.

A Panera Bread restaurant in one of the outlet malls was open, so I pulled into the parking lot just as the wind started swirling, dismounted and walked in. Holding my rain jacket in one hand and my helmet in the other, I found a table, pulled down the straps of my rain pants and sent a text to my wife.

"Stopped at Panera for lunch and for the storm to pass. Has it hit a house yet?"

While I was waiting for a reply, I quietly scanned the place. Several people were doing their best to ignore me, but it was evident I was making them uncomfortable. With my black riding gear covered in grime, a scraggly three-month-old goatee, and a strangely wind-burned face, I must have looked worse than a giant cockroach.

Just then, my phone buzzed with an incoming text.

"No, but coming soon," it read.

A quick check of the weather radar showed her to be correct. Based on the time-lapse images, I figured, it would take at least a half an hour for it to make my current location, move to the Island, and then out to sea. So I queued up in the line to order food and tapped out another message.

"Text me after it passes. Then I'll know it's safe to proceed."

Before I could even order anything, my phone buzzed again.

"K luv u. Take the time. Be careful."

Quietly slurping my soup, I watched the storm rage around me, peter out, and then march across the satellite images of the Island. I wanted desperately to get moving again, to close the final distance, but I patiently waited, knowing that it was the right thing to do.

Finally, my phone buzzed.

"Just passed. Come home."

My heart started pounding. This was it.

Sometime during the night before, during a restless on and off sleep, I'd had a vision of what it was going to be like to ride back onto the Island. Everything was dreamily perfect. The sky was clear except for some white, harmless cottony clouds. The air was comfortably warm and humid with scents of pine pitch, azaleas, and salt marsh grasses. The tide was ebbing, exposing the hundreds of inverted bowl-shaped mud flats in the sound. Fiddler crabs were hustling about their craggy surfaces, foraging for food. Up above, seagulls were spying for baitfish, occasionally drifting into place, resting in the warm updrafts. The surface of the sound was placid, its waters an inviting blue-green. A shrimp boat churned below the main bridge with a few pleasure boats passing it on either side. Their occupants, smiling and waving, were pointing at the dolphins jumping playfully in its bow wave. Further east, on the bridge over Broad Creek, a Haig Point ferry chugged by with a short blast of its air horn. A fishing charter followed, its mate rigging the lines for an anxious, excited family. It was their first trip offshore. Up the other way towards Shelter Cove, a line of jet skis snaked along the edges of the water—probably too close to shore according to the rules, but nobody cared. It was just too nice outside. Everything was in harmony: the trees, the flowers, the wildlife, the water and its creatures, all that was man-made, and, of course, man.

It was, of course, absolutely nothing like that. When I rolled onto the approach to the main bridge, the Sound was an angry snarl of razor-edged white caps, its waters browner than standard and cresting towards high tide. A final vicious blast of crosswinds did their best to try and blow me into the left lane as I reached the apex, with leftover drops of rain driving horizontally into my right side. By the time I rolled onto the Cross Island Expressway, the sky was darkening again, warning me that the storm was still lingering offshore. When I reached the top of the bridge over Broad Creek, the waters below were deserted. Nothing moved except the surface, driven by the wind and a fierce flood tide current. When I looked back up, a final lightning bolt shot out of the clouds and struck the ground to the south, no more than a mile away. Crooked and sinister looking, it hung in the air like a thin knife, flexing and twisting itself around the point of impact as if it was charging something. I could almost smell the residual ozone as I rolled down the southern slope of the bridge.

I should have taken that final lightning strike as a warning, but instead, I couldn't stop smirking. It would be so deliciously ironic, I thought, to have survived a five thousand mile cross-country motorcycle trip with so many close calls and wind up getting struck and killed by lightning less than a mile from my house. So, I figured, it couldn't possibly happen. I'd never get the laugh. No matter how bad the weather got, I was going to be fine. All I had to do was close the last distance.

My wife was outside in the driveway with the dogs when I pulled up. She was grinning, trying her best to suppress a smile, but I saw right through it. It was her signature "yeah I love you, but I can't show it too much or you'll get cocky on me" look. She'd left the right garage door open, so I pulled straight in, slowed to a stop, turned the front fork, and nudged Big Girl into the exact same spot she'd been eleven days earlier. A few seconds later, after a final blip of the throttle, I shut her down.

Resting for a moment in the silence, I took a deep breath, patted her tank, and whispered, "Nice job, Girl. You did it. You got us *home*."

And just like that, it was over.

The next sound I heard was the skitter-scatter of dog nails sliding across our concrete garage floor. Moving slowly so they wouldn't get too excited—as if that were even possible—I unbuckled my chin strap, removed my helmet, and quietly walked back out towards the driveway. The girl, a short haired miniature, was already doing her "Sweetie Doo" dance. The one where her tail wags so forcefully from side to side it spins her rear end halfway around and back again. The boy, a long-haired miniature who's even cuter, was doing his own routine. With his tail moving like a helicopter rotor, he was jumping up on my legs, desperately trying to beat his companion to the first kiss. Since Dachshunds are notorious leakers, we'd learned long ago not to greet them on any surface we cared about.

So when I finally emerged onto the driveway, I clapped both my hands together, reached down and shrieked, "Hellllloooo puppies!!"

When I touched the girl, she immediately flipped on her back, squirmed in delight, and started urinating. When I stroked the boy's back, he repeatedly jerked up to lick me and squirted all over my boots.

When my wife came around the corner and saw me, this time closer up, she said somewhat playfully, "I swear you love them more than me."

"Well Ma," I replied, "come on. When I get home, you don't smother me with kisses, fall on your back in ecstasy and start uncontrollably peeing. I mean—that's love."

"How about this," she said softly and planted a warm, sweet kiss on my cheek.

I had to admit, her kiss was better.

My daughter was next. Rounding the corner right after my wife, she pointed at my chin accusingly, scrunched up her face and blurted out, with typical eleven-year-old girl dramatic flair, "Yooooouuuuu promised!!"

"Well," I replied, trying to redeem myself, "all I said was that I'd shave it off after the trip. I never said when."

"Right now!" she fired back excitedly and grabbed my arm.

A moment later, tugging back against her pull to try and buy me a little more time, she led me up the garage stairs and into the house. When we were inside, she pulled me even harder, to the point where I was almost tripping over myself, straight into our master bathroom. My wife was right behind her. Standing in front of the mirror, I hesitated, hoping for a reprieve.

"Now?" I asked pleadingly.

"Yes," my wife said with some delight, "she's right. You promised."

It was two against one. Or in the case of mom and daughter versus dad matchups, more like a hundred against one. I was screwed.

It took a little longer than I thought it would, mainly because I didn't have a beard trimmer. But after several applications of shaving cream and a considerable amount of tugging, scraping, and rinsing, it was gone. Aside from wind-burned cheeks and an odd tan pattern caused by my sudden lack of facial hair, I looked like an average suburban Dad again. Yep, I thought, staring at myself in the mirror, an average suburban Dad. An ex-corporate executive. A white collar biker. Almost fifty years old, statistically over half dead, trapped in a big boxy house, chained to responsibilities, worrying about bills, leaky toilets, and so many other things. Living life like a schmuck again. I hadn't even left the bathroom and I was already depressed.

Later that night after some much needed—and appreciated—private time with my wife, I was lying in bed, wide awake, listening to the rhythmic ticking of our poorly balanced ceiling fan. The boy was between us, flipped over on his back with his paws cocked downward, softly cooing for more chest rubs (can they *ever* get enough?). The girl was curled up at my feet, snoring louder than my wife. But I wasn't really there. I was back on Big Girl, listening to the burble of her V-twin, crossing the country again. With the wind at my back and my feet up on the highway pegs, I was taking it all in. The rolling farmlands beauty, the scents of the summer wildflowers, the vastness of the sky, the rumbling of the thunder and the heavy rigs. Discovering and learning. Worried only about my next fuel stop or meal. Living life by incremental decisions. Tethered by love back to the ones sleeping under my roof, yet unchained. Above all else, free.

And as I focused harder, I actually started to feel her vibrations and the wind rushing across my neck. And I pondered, of everything I'd seen on the trip out and back, amongst so many interesting towns and stunningly beautiful landscapes—the bluegrasses of Kentucky; the emerald fields of Iowa; the wildflowers and the Black Hills of South Dakota; the mountains of Wyoming; the wheat fields of the plains states and so many dazzling waterfalls, rivers, and lakes—which one, which single scene, would sear itself the most into my memory. It came to me relatively quickly, and it surprised me. And as I finally trailed off to sleep, still gliding along on Big Girl, I couldn't shake it.

I was back in Northwest Nebraska, crossing the wheat fields, watching the coal trains.

Part V: Aftermath

For the next few days, I couldn't generate interest in anything. When I was at my desk, trying to work, I'd stare out the window, feeling left out of the world. Simple things I used to enjoy like walking the beach, riding bicycles, or washing my car became vapid chores. My wife put up with my melancholy, knowing that I'd gone through a lot, but I could tell that she was getting increasingly irritated. And she had every right to be. She'd missed me terribly and there was a lot to catch up on. When we'd walk the dogs, she'd be chatting away about this and that—school supply needs, an empty propane tank, the flowers she wanted to plant in the fall, her tennis teams, and a hundred other subjects—and I'd follow along, pretending to show interest. But I wasn't really listening. I was still coming down off of the high of the trip, and the withdrawal was worse than I expected. Almost as bad as coming home from an extended deployment in the Navy, particularly one that involved special operations. You get so addicted to the pace, to existing only to serve the mission. To being so singularly focused on doing your duty and what's necessary to survive, it's hard to adjust back to normal life. It seems foreign and unfulfilling, empty of purpose.

It finally came to a head a few days later. I was in my office, blankly staring out the window again, when she marched in, apparently a little peeved.

"It's Parent's Night tonight at Prep," she said sternly, "and we're going. Six thirty sharp. And no, you're not getting out of it."

It was always a sore subject with her, the fact that I hated to go to these things. In her mind, if you were a good parent and cared about your kids, you'd welcome the opportunity to get the information you needed for the upcoming school year, meet their teachers, and see what their day would be like. And as I always told her, I had no problem, per se, with those objectives. But what always bothered me, particularly in the years when I was an impatient, busy-as-hell business executive, were the inefficiencies. They'd always hand out a sheet of paper or two at the beginning that contained essential information about grading systems, lockers, fees, policies, etc. But then some boring-as-hell administrator would spend an hour going over the same bullet points on the papers, adding nothing. So I'd sit there wondering, OK, which is it? If you hand me some papers with the title "Everything You Need to Know" and you assume, for a moment, that I can actually *read,* why do you have to spend an hour of my evening saying the same damn things? Then they'd hand you a schedule of your kid's classes and you'd have to run around the school for ten-minute sessions with each of their teachers, simulating their day. Half of us would get pathetically lost, and if you actually managed to be in the right place at the right time, you spent five minutes helping the poor souls wandering the hallway. So you almost always got there late. Then you'd sit while the teacher crammed a thirty-minute presentation into five minutes, trying to absorb something before the next bell sounded. And because they'd typically run over, you'd have to dash out before you had a chance to meet. Then, when it was finally over, I'd escape to the car, only to endure the disapproving stare of my wife when she asked me how many of our kid's teachers I'd actually met. Because the answer was almost always zero. It was guaranteed, the failure. But it didn't matter. I knew I wasn't getting out of it.

When we arrived, she immediately started greeting the other parents she knew, some of them friends, and I did my best to play the happy, interested husband. I shook a few hands, said, "Hi, nice to see you again," a few times, and tried to feign interest, but it didn't last long. By the time we were sitting in the bleachers listening to the Principal's welcome speech, I was already somewhere else. Reliving the ride, thinking about the things I needed to do to get Big Girl back in fighting trim (change the oil, check the front tire, fix the horn). Most importantly, what I was going to do for the rest of my life, how I was going to get a sense of purpose back.

When the event was finally over, she asked for the car keys in a snarling tone and took off towards the parking lot, walking far ahead of me. I knew what that meant. She was seriously pissed.

About a mile from the school, she fired the first broadside.

"I was totally embarrassed," she said, "You didn't engage with our friends, you didn't ask any questions of the teachers, you didn't even listen to the Principal! I don't think you heard a single word he said!!"

Letting it sink in for a moment, I decided, stupidly, to be a smartass. "You're wrong," I said defiantly, "I actually heard two words: 'Welcome' and 'parents.'"

I paid for that one for a week.

After a while, however, things slowly settled back to normal. She still wasn't feeling right and felt depressed from time to time. But she was mostly happy and engaged, playing tennis, helping her friends, shuttling our daughter around to her various activities and the dozens of other things associated with being a stay-at-home mom. In the meantime, I was working on a new project that gave me a sense of purpose—this book. The idea to capture the story of my Sturgis trip on paper, or at least try to, had actually come to me on the way out of Tulsa on the second to the last day of the ride back. And I was making progress. But then, in late January, five months after I'd come back, our world changed.

I was in my office, quietly typing, when she called out and asked me to come into the bathroom. Wondering what she wanted, I walked lazily over to the entrance. When I saw her standing in front of the mirror, naked, bathed in sunlight from an overhead skylight, I thought, like so many times before but this time even more profoundly, how lucky I was. Somehow, after twenty-three years of marriage and four children, she'd become even more beautiful. Her skin, tan and lightly powdered after her shower, was smooth and radiant, almost glowing, while her curves, through the miracle of Motherhood, had become fuller and even more voluptuous. Being a guy, blood inevitably started rushing southward, but I could tell that wasn't going to happen. She was all business. Her left arm was stretched way overhead and she was probing her left breast, gingerly but methodically, with her right hand. Finally, she spoke.

"I'm pretty sure I feel a lump," she said, "and I want to show you."

"OK," I replied nervously and swung in beside her.

Taking my hand in hers, she placed in on the left side, in the fleshy part close to the base of the nipple, and showed me the spot. Sure enough, after some probing with my fingers, I felt it. About the size of a blueberry, hard and fibrous, it seemed strangely out of place, oddly foreign, in such a sensuous body.

"Yeah," I finally agreed, "I feel it. It's probably just a harmless cyst, but you better have it checked out."

She says she knew the day she found it, and based on the signals that her body was sending well before that, but I suspected when her doctor called after the MRI. They'd taken some biopsies and didn't have the lab report back, but she wanted to talk with us. On the way over to the hospital, I was more optimistic than she was, hoping that it would all turn out to be a giant false alarm, but as soon as I walked into the "Consult Room," I knew. A publication was on the table. It was one of those "So You've Got Breast Cancer" handbooks, and a counselor was already reaching for a box of tissues. When her doctor—one of the most highly respected specialists in the Southeast—entered, she got straight to the point.

"I'm ninety-eight percent sure," she began, "that you have invasive breast cancer. The tumor's about a centimeter in size and it's already spread into your lymphatic system."

"How can you be so sure?" I asked, "I mean, we don't even have the lab results back from the biopsies."

"I've seen enough of these to know," she answered gently, "so I think you ought to prepare yourselves."

Still somewhat in shock, my wife looked at me, longingly, searching for a connection, the one that only comes from sharing a life together, the one that reaches straight into a partner's soul. It didn't take long. And once we'd established it, I answered her silent question. Taking her hand, with tears slowly blurring my vision, I looked into her eyes and nodded gently. Of course, I'd be there.

On the ride back she asked me what I thought of her doctor.

"I have to admit," I said, "I was impressed. I expected to hear a bunch of medical professional cover-your-ass double-talk, like, 'It doesn't look good but let's wait to see the biopsy results.' But she had the guts to 'call the ball.' You don't do that unless you know what you're doing."

"Yeah," she replied, "I thought so too. But let's not tell the kids until we know for sure."

As usual, she wasn't thinking about herself, she'd already fast forwarded to our family.

It took a few more days, but as we suspected, her doctor was correct. It was breast cancer and an unusually aggressive one. About the only good news was that the type of tumors she had, while not receptive to hormone therapy, were particularly responsive to the miracle drug Herceptin. They wanted her to start treatment right away.

The older two boys took it hard but with grace, offering up feisty words of support like "You'll beat it, Ma," and, "We know you can do it."

Within a week or so they were even poking fun at her. Often after dinner, I'd hear her out on the porch talking to one of them, shrieking with laughter. Afterward, she'd tell me, with a Mother's pride, some of their best lines. Stuff like: "You get to take drugs now, Ma. Legally! How cool!" And, "You can get a wig with purple spikes and go punk!"

The younger two, however, were more worried. When she told our youngest son, the one who's always been the quietest and most sensitive, I was in the next room, secretly listening.

"Are you going to die, Ma?" he asked.

"No," she said with resolution, "but I'm going to need your help."

"With what?"

"Doing your job. Keeping up your grades, making the right choices and staying out of trouble."

"OK," he replied with his typical understated swagger, "I can do that."

And he did.

Interestingly enough, I turned out to be the biggest mess. It would hit me sometimes unpredictably and at other times with recognizable triggers. Her song was the worst. The one I'd ascribed to her when we were dating, the one that best encapsulated how I felt about her. Somehow it kept coming over the damn radio, an eighties hit by Genesis called "Invisible Touch." And when I'd listen to it, choking back tears, wondering if we'd still get to grow old together, I'd realize she hadn't changed. Still able, as the song says, to "reach in and grab straight hold of your heart." It got so bad that at one point, my oldest son shamed me back to manhood.

"I don't understand this," he said after one of my tear up episodes during dinner, "which one of you has cancer here?"

A call from Jim the next day presented another challenge. I'd forgotten that after Sturgis, around Thanksgiving time, we'd agreed to take another bike trip together. He and Hector were going to ride down from Philly in early March, meet me at the house, and we were all going to ride to Daytona for the annual spring rally. He knew about her diagnosis by this time, of course, and offered some additional kind words of support, but I could tell straight away where he was heading. He wanted to know if the trip was still on.

"No," I said, "I can't go anymore. I have to be here for her. But if you guys want to stop at the house on the way down or the way back, or both, I'm sure she'd love to see you."

"OK," he replied with a hint of disappointment, "I didn't think you'd be up to it. I'll let Hector know. But as a minimum, we'll definitely stop by and see you guys."

When I hung up, my wife was close by. I could tell she'd been listening to our conversation.

"So . . ." she began, "you're not going to go anymore?"

"No. I'm not leaving you."

"You sure? The timing is actually perfect. My chemo doesn't start until late March."

"No. I'm not going."

"OK. If that's what you really want."

"Yep. That's what I want."

Over the next couple of days, however, she kept bringing it up, quietly probing. I couldn't tell if she was playing the standard wife versus husband game, the one where the wife keeps asking the same question over and over because she hasn't heard the answer she wants to hear yet (in this case, I should change my mind and go), or if she was testing my commitment to her (I should stay). And the truth was, while I kind of wanted to go, I really did want to stay. The decision appeared to be a lot easier for me than for her. When she started offering justifications for why I should go, however, I began to change my mind. Her arguments made sense. We were about to embark on a long journey together, a tough one with an uncertain outcome, and she needed me to be rested and ready for it. Her job was to get through the treatments and stay as healthy as she could to maximize her chances, while I'd have to do everything else. Take care of her. Be "Mr. Mom." Plus keep up the house, manage the finances, and do all of the fix and repair jobs dads do. It would be a good way for me to recharge. Her last argument was more delicate, and she approached it with finesse. After some dancing around, however, I figured it out. My emotional instability was adding to her mood swings, so I wasn't really helping her to get mentally ready. A little time apart, she thought, might do us both some good.

Finally, reluctantly, I agreed. The only thing she asked, other than coming back again unharmed, was that I give up riding for the entire period of her treatment.

"We can't afford," she said, "to have both of us laid up. Somebody has to take care of the kids."

"No problem," I replied, "it's the right thing to do."

The ride down for Jim and Hector was a cold one, with temperatures in the thirties and forties most of the way, but a few days before the start of the rally they rumbled into my garage. I'd just gotten Big Girl back from being serviced, and Jim noticed her new front tire.

"Yeah," I said, pointing at it, "When I hit that pothole in Birmingham coming back from Sturgis I must have separated the plies in the tread. They said it was miles from blowing out. I'm amazed I made it home."

Jim shrugged his shoulders and let out a simple, "Bummer," but Hector captured what I was thinking best.

"Man," he said while inhaling through his teeth, "somebody was sure looking out for you."

A few days later, we were all on the road again, heading south. It was great to be riding again, feeling the wind on my skin, the warm sun on my back, and listening to Big Girl putter away while we passed the acres of pine forests, marshlands, and sea ports that define coastal Georgia. I'd like to say that I thought about my wife a lot on the way down, but I didn't. The demands of riding and watching the scenery were more than enough to keep me occupied. When we switched to the coast road south of Jacksonville, Florida, however, and I finally caught sight of the ocean, its deep blue waters washing up on a bright, polished sandy beach—she entered my mind.

Staring out at the serrated rows of breakers, I took a deep breath of the cool, misty salt air, smiled and said to myself, "You were right, Ma. This is just what I needed."

When we got to Daytona, everything, it seemed, fell into place. The weather was perfect, with warm days, cool nights, light winds, and almost no rain. The hotel was comfortable. Our favorite part was the giant outdoor gas fire pit off of the main patio. After dinner, we'd sit around it with our boots up, drinking scotch, smoking Hector's cigarette-style cigars, and listening to everyone's stories. During the days, we rode out to St. Augustine, the Kennedy Space Center, and took the scenic route around Daytona. We also liked the rally better. The crowd was younger, infused with spring break energy, and there was a much greater variety of bikes. At any given time, along with the Harleys, you'd see crotch rockets, European cruisers, and an incredible variety of custom trikes. Even the cops were laid back. As long as you weren't doing anything foolish, they left you alone. And, like Sturgis, there was a ton of variety in the nightlife. Small bars, boutique restaurants, and cafes intermixed with larger, temporary venues with live bands and multiple bar stands. Certainly enough to keep everyone entertained.

But sadly, our last night came. Deciding to ride into town before the worst of the crowds, we ate dinner early and found a couple of parking spaces along a side street close to the main drag. I was quieter than usual, with thoughts of my wife increasingly crowding my mind, so the guys tried to keep me occupied. We bounced from bar to bar downing shots, watched a few bar dances, and then, once the real party started, walked back onto Main Street to watch the bike parade. With only a single lane on either side, with the shops closer to the road, it seemed more personal than Sturgis, energetic, and fun. My favorite bike was a black Street Glide that had a small platform welded on the back with a tall, vertical pole sticking up from the center of it. A stripper was standing on the platform doing a pole dance as it rumbled by.

Jim and Hector pointed it out, roaring with laughter, and I agreed, saying, "Now *that*, boys, is *talent*."

After a few more stops and some pictures with busty barmaids, we wound up in a merchandise pavilion that sold jackets, vests, patches, and pins. Not seriously considering buying anything, feeling a little sad and homesick, I wandered around, killing time. Jim and Hector snapped me out of my funk. Approaching me from opposite sides, they suddenly closed towards my position. Feeling a little threatened, I looked up at Jim, wondering what was going on. With alarming seriousness, he cleared his throat and spoke up.

"If you're going to keep riding with me and Hector, you need to do something."

"What?" I asked innocently.

"You need to get a vest. It's time."

"Christ," I said with relief, "is that all?"

"It's important to us. We're not a club, but you have to at least look more the part."

"OK, fine," I said, "but I really wouldn't know where to start."

I hadn't noticed, but Hector had already moved off to the back of the store.

Jim pointed at him and said, "Over there. Hector's found one."

I got it now. It was all a set-up. While I was frivolously wasting time, they'd caucused, decided what I needed, and had already picked it out. It was sneaky and smart. I liked that.

When I got back to Hector, he was holding it up, beaming like a proud father. The vest was made of soft light brown leather and it had an inner fabric lining like a suit. I never did like the thick black leather jobs and I wasn't really a frayed denim guy, so I had to admit, at least at first sight, it looked like a winner. Taking it off the hanger, I gave him a preliminary nod of approval.

"It fits you, man," he said as I tried it on. "Different. Classy."

"Yeah," I replied laughingly, "good *sheait*."

It was one of Hector's favorite lines, always said with his thick Mexican accent, so Jim and I had long ago adopted it. In any event, he was right. It looked good on me. And it fit like a glove.

The hardest part, however, was the patches. The tables of inventory seemed endless, more than I'd ever seen in a single store. They had to have twenty thousand of them. Sensing that I was already overwhelmed, Jim moved to quell my anxiety.

"Don't worry," he said, "we'll help you. Step one is to find something with an HD logo on it that's pretty big. I'll work on that. We'll put it on the back in the center; maybe something above it and below. Not like the rockers that real clubs have because we're not one so we can't do that, but something that kind of defines you. Then, of course, 'I rode mine' patches from the Sturgis rally of eleven and Daytona this year. Hector can find those, and maybe a few other patches for the front. He's got a good sense of humor."

I had to admit, I was impressed. He'd put a lot of thought into it. So I grabbed my new vest and started searching, determined to get it done.

As Jim and Hector worked on their assignments, I carefully scanned each table. When I got to one that was military in nature, I found a "US Navy Veteran" patch. That'd work on the back above the main HD logo. Later, on a table with the state flag patches, I found the familiar South Carolina palm tree and crescent moon. That'd work on the bottom. When I hooked up with Jim again, he showed me several large HD patches. I immediately spotted one that I liked. The primary color of the large, block HD letters was a bronzy orange, close to the color of Big Girl. A black and white reflective Harley-Davidson banner ran through the center. About the time we were congratulating ourselves, muttering, "Yeah—this will all work," Hector walked up with the Sturgis and Daytona rally patches. It was coming together. All we had to do was find something for the front.

We fanned out again searching, and every now and then I'd look over at Hector and Jim to see what they were holding up. It was all stuff like, "DO I LOOK LIKE I GIVE A SHIT?" "HOLD MY BEER WHILE I KISS YOUR GIRLFRIEND," and "SHUTDEFUKUP." I was getting tired of frowning. Nothing seemed to fit. Finally, just when I was about to give up, I spotted something in the middle of a table I'd overlooked. Holding it between my fingers, fighting back a sudden wave of emotion, I looked over at Hector. Smiling warmly, he nodded his head. Jim saw his reaction and walked over to see what I'd discovered. When he saw it, he stopped dead in his tracks and bit his lower lip. Theresa had been through it too.

When the girl sewing the patches finally freed up, we placed the vest face down on her sewing table and arranged the patches where we thought they should be, at least on the back. When we were satisfied, she asked me if I had anything for the front. With trembling fingers, I handed her the pink breast cancer ribbon. A little surprised, she looked up, scanned me more carefully and spotted my wedding ring.

"Your wife?" she asked.

"Yeah," I replied. "Just diagnosed."

"Oh, I'm so sorry. I sure hope she'll be all right. Where would you like it?"

We'd been so meticulous with the placement of the other patches; I was embarrassed that I hadn't thought of it. Put on the spot, I wanted to go with the first thought that came into my mind, but I couldn't get it out.

Finally, with a breaking voice, I said, "On the left side . . . close to my heart."

"OK," she replied, adding with a sniffle, "This one's on me."

My new vest must have acted like an invisible force field because the ride back was pleasant and uneventful. No one even came close to bothering us. I led for most of the way and the traffic seemed to miraculously part whenever we approached. Even the bugs waved off. The only thing even remotely disconcerting was that I managed to put Big Girl into a slight fish tail once when I took off quickly from a stoplight. The pavement was a little wet from an earlier rain shower, so I had an excuse, but I made a mental note: her rear tire was probably shot.

The following morning, more than a little hungover from the aftereffects of Hector's tequila, we all said good-bye. Dour and anxious, I spent the remainder of the day preparing Big Girl for her upcoming slumber. By dinner, she was clean and resting comfortably on her battery charger, probably wondering, like me, when—or even if—we'd ever get to ride together again. But that didn't seem to matter much anymore. Something infinitely more important was at stake.

We called my wife's treatment regimen "the long slog." And right on schedule, in late March, it began. Three and a half months of chemotherapy with fun side effects like nausea, weight gain, and hair loss. Followed by surgery to remove the lump and the affected lymph nodes, recovery from surgery, physical therapy to regain full use of her arm, and then ten weeks of radiation treatments. They told us that each step would get successively easier, but it turned out to be exactly the opposite. She gained twenty pounds during chemo and lost every bit of her hair. Her pain after surgery was unexpectedly intense and lasted for six weeks. She didn't regain full use of her arm, especially in the movement of her head, for five months. Her skin broke down towards the end of radiation and her blood counts stayed frighteningly low, well after the time when they should have started to recover, triggering other false alarms. And, most surprisingly, near the end her cycle restarted, necessitating an emergency room visit.

When the ER doctor told her the cause of her heavy bleeding, she quipped, "You gotta' be kidding me. It was the one positive out of this—I finally got rid of it—and now it's coming back again. What's next? Acne?"

Yet she kept going. Normally a bit of a pessimist, I was amazed, week by week, by her ability to remain positive. She never once asked "why me?" or sank into depression. She never had a single thought of dying. It was all a test of some kind, happening for reasons that would ultimately prove to be positive. I doubted I'd have the same inner strength.

Her support network was also a significant help. I periodically sent out text updates to a short list of family and friends, but they usually weren't necessary. She must have spent two hours a day on the phone answering all manner of inquiries, gossiping, and cracking jokes. Often her friends knew more than me. Our neighbors were also terrific, particularly during the chemo phase. They picked up my daughter from school and had hot dinners waiting for us when we returned from the hospital. It made an enormous difference. Knowing that I didn't have to worry about anything domestic, I could focus on keeping her entertained as the drugs dripped. We played Battleship, card games, and watched movies. We met other patients and learned about their illnesses and families. And we watched, with a sense of awe, as virtually every major weather disturbance, including two tropical storms, magically dissipated right before hitting the Island.

"You see," she'd say when I'd play the time-lapse weather radar images on her iPad, "he knows better than to mess with me during chemo."

After a while, even the other patients felt comforted when "Ma" was there. Nothing bad was going to happen.

But in November, on an abnormally cold day in Savannah, Georgia, at the St. Joseph's/Candler Medical Center, her time came. It's an event that all cancer patients look forward to, a milestone of unparalleled relief: completing their last radiation treatment. And, as a symbol of their triumph and to honor everyone who's helped, they get to "ring the bell." In her case, it was especially meaningful. She was one of the lucky ones. The pathology reports after surgery had confirmed what we'd prayed for. The drugs had worked. She was cancer free. So for her, it was more than a second chance. It was a rebirth, and a very special one. A newborn comes out covered in goo, barely able to see, and wishing, probably, to be back inside where it's warm and comfortable. But a birth after nearly half a century is one that can indeed be comprehended—and appreciated. A gift of the best chapter of life, of future graduations, weddings, and grandchildren, shared with the ones you already love. A gift that makes every sunset, walk on the beach, new discovery, and minute with the people you care about, for the rest of your life, that much richer. Because you've been to the edge, have looked over, and know how good it is to be back.

Her sister and brother-in-law, wanting to share the moment with us, met me in the main lobby and we all gathered by the bell. It was mounted on the wall just inside the entrance. I'm not sure where they got it from, but it looked like it came from a large ship. Made of solid brass with one of those thick twisted ropes attached to the ringer, it had to weigh fifty pounds. To kill some time while we waited, I read the plaque that was mounted under it. "Ring this bell three times well," it said, "Its toll to clearly say . . . my treatments were done . . . or a milestone won . . . and I am on my way. [sic]" Seems simple enough, I thought, three rings . . .

When she walked through the double doors of the treatment wing and entered the lobby smiling with an enthusiastic thumbs-up, we knew the moment had arrived. Struggling to control my emotions, telling myself over and over, "Keep it together, keep it together," I handed her a bouquet of flowers. Seeing the pink roses, she gave me a kiss, hugged me in a way that was so tender I almost had to prop her up, and wiped away a tear.

"OK Ma," I said softly, "let it rip. You earned it."

And man did she let it rip. Grabbing the rope with the enthusiasm of a six-year-old girl, releasing nine months of stress, worry, and pain, she swung it from side to side so vigorously the ringing quickly became a clarion call. It reverberated through the lobby and into every nook of the hospital. It spilled out through the front doors and into the parking lot. Beckoned by the sound, people started coming. They poured out from the oncology center and the gift shop. They filed in from the chapel, the library, and the garden—doctors, nurses, technicians, and patients; employees and volunteers. And for a moment longer, as the ringing continued and intensified, I imagined it carrying out over the city, spreading out over the ocean and soaring into the upper atmosphere. With all living things stopping, turning, and wondering, like me, how a simple bell could sound so incredibly stirring and sweet.

When she was finally done and collapsed into my arms, giggling and crying, you could have heard a pin drop. Overcome with emotion, still telling myself to "keep it together," I managed not to completely break down, but it finally got to me. By the time I'd helped her to regain her footing, tears were literally squirting over my cheeks and onto the floor. Feeling a little embarrassed and self-conscious, knowing that so many people were watching us, I quickly wiped them onto my shirt. But there was nothing to be ashamed of. A quick scan of the lobby told me all I needed to know. There wasn't a dry eye in the place.

A few weeks later when everyone was home for Christmas, my wife and my oldest son were in the kitchen, bantering.

"So Ma," he teased, "Dad told me about the bell and your *three rings*. Excellent job following that instruction."

"Yeah well . . . [chuckle] . . . I definitely blew that one. But it was Daddy's fault. He didn't tell me."

"But even if he had, you wouldn't have followed it, right?"

"Of course not. After what I'd been through, I was going to ring that freaking bell until it cracked." [Hearty laugh]

"OK, Ma. That's fair. But now that you have a new lease on life, have you thought about taking any more risks? Doing more wild and crazy stuff . . . stepping out a little more . . . like maybe riding with Dad?"

I hadn't thought about it for a long time, but at that moment, it all came rushing back. How much I missed riding and how desperately, especially now, I wanted to share it with her. My heart stopped. Leaning in from the living room as far as I could without her spotting me, I blocked out the ambient sound, straining to hear her response, hoping that she'd at least offer up some thoughtful consideration, praying—though I knew it was a long shot—for her to change her mind. But she didn't waver.

"No," she said unequivocally, "I'm not doing that. *Somebody* has to be responsible."

Not sure if she was kidding, my son hesitated, but when he realized that she was serious, and, more importantly, that she never let cancer get to her and that she was still the same Mother he'd loved and admired for twenty-one years, he slammed his fist down hard on the counter and shouted, with obvious delight, "Ma's *back!!*"

Unbeknownst to them, still out of sight, I tiptoed back into the living room, smiled, and shook my head. Yep, I thought, walking away, she's back all right; never compromising her principles, stronger than ever.

A few days later, after our older kids had left, I was walking through the garage, taking the trash out, when Big Girl caught my eye. Sitting a little lower now and covered with fine dust, she looked dull, tired, and forgotten. The only sign of life was the red security light in her speedometer. After ten months, it was still blinking. I wonder, I thought, if she'll start . . .

Since I had the morning free, I quickly checked the weather. I couldn't have asked for a better Low Country winter day, especially for riding: sunny and dry with light winds and high temperatures approaching seventy degrees. Already excited, but still with a little trepidation, I walked back into our bedroom and opened my closet door. My riding boots were in the far corner nestled in dust devils. On the shelf above, just under the hangar that held my vest, I spotted my half-helmet. A single cobweb stretched from the crown to the buckle on the chin strap. Moving slowly, with my heart rate rising, I put on my vest, stuffed Big Girl's keys into my pocket, and slid on my boots. When I turned around, holding my helmet, my wife was standing a few feet from me. She must have snuck in when I wasn't looking.

For a long moment, as my heart raced, we just stared at each other. She was the first to start tearing up. She's never been big on compliments, but I sensed what was coming.

"You know," she said, struggling, "I just wanted you to know . . . how . . . *terrific* you've been through this."

Gulping to choke back another breakdown, recognizing in that one moment how much my support must have meant to her, I thought about what I'd done. It really hadn't been that hard. In fact, the Mr. Mom part had been kind of fun. I'd learned a lot. Not only about how to manage the domestic side of a household but how hard it is to devote yourself to other people for fourteen hours a day. I'd always wondered, during our most hectic years, after the kids went to sleep, why she often wanted nothing to do with me. I get that now. You don't wish to do anything with *anybody*. You just want to spend an hour or two with nobody *needing you*. But more importantly, I thought about what I'd done to help take care of her—being there during her chemo sessions and bringing her breakfast in bed, helping her shower after surgery and always running errands to fetch medicines and foods that she could stomach—and I realized how much I enjoyed it. It was never a chore or a burden, never just an obligation or duty. It was much more than that. So I took a deep breath, wiped away the tears that had already started to flow, and just said, earnestly, what I actually felt.

"It was . . . *an honor.*"

I couldn't remember a time when we hugged for so long.

Her approval, once she composed herself, was playful and swift. Stepping back, she swatted my helmet with her hand and said, "OK now. Go ride. You've earned it. Just—"

"—I know," I interjected, "be careful . . . and come back unharmed."

After a couple more mutual love taps, I was bounding back down the garage stairs.

Working carefully, I topped off Big Girl's tires with air, checked her oil, and assembled the rest of my riding gear. It was still a little chilly out, so full gloves were in order. When I was sure that everything was ready, I opened the garage door, pushed her back from her parking space, and mounted the saddle. A quick snap of the ignition switch confirmed that at least electrically, she was fine. Telling myself to go hard on the starter, that is, to keep it going until I was sure she was running, I flipped the "Stop/Run" switch. Her fuel pump whirred to life.

"OK Girl," I said, "show me you still got it."

When I hit the starter, I could tell straight away that it was going to be a tough wake-up call. Her strokes were longer, more strained, and spaced further apart—cheauuhh . . . cheauuhh . . . cheauuhh—and when she finally did catch, her "per pop!" was more of an earsplitting backfire. But she came back to life. Within a few minutes, after her idle had smoothed out, she was bouncing up and down like an excited puppy, eager to go.

I didn't know where I was going, but my ride from the Island that day was like the one I'd hoped for on the way back from Sturgis. The air was cool and dry, teasing me with scents of winter blossoms and freshly laid pine straw, while the sun, rising ever higher, erased the morning chill. The sound was glassy smooth, at slack current, lazily resting before the next flood tide. A squadron of seagulls made their way southward, probably trying, like me, to generate a little more body heat. Traffic was light. The tourists had long since departed and the commuters were already at work. I even had fuel, for once. I'd topped her off and put in some gas stabilizer when I got back from Daytona.

Deciding to take the back way to Savannah, I rode through the old town section of Bluffton, finding streets, parks, and boat landings that I never knew existed. After exploring some more, I pulled up to a local restaurant for an early lunch, a place I'd never been to before. The way it was supposed to be. And sitting at a table by the window, watching the sky turn ever bluer, it all started coming back. What I'd experienced over the eleven days of the Sturgis trip and as many months afterward, and how it had changed me.

I learned a lot, of course, about the art of riding a motorcycle. Important aspects like how to pack and load a bike, dress for the wet weather, pass-heavy trucks, manage crosswinds and where to ride in a lane. And slowly, day by day, mostly through the school of hard knocks, I bettered my technique. My biggest improvement was probably my ability to manage the wind. I can counter it more naturally now, with less anxiety, and I'm better able to predict the situations when it might become a problem (bridges and flat plains). I'm also, after my close call at the South Carolina border, more comfortable with hard braking. I'll still always lean towards steering or accelerating my way out of trouble, but if I ever have to lock her up again, I'll know what to expect.

But more importantly, I learned what it means to actually ride. What the "real deal" is. And it's not a local errand run, a day ride with a buddy, or even an overnight with your club. It's the long road trip. When you just pick a destination, pack a travel bag, head out across the country—and *wing it*. Navigate the old fashioned way, without turn by turn assistance. Stop whenever the need hits you, wherever you want, and discover, for better or worse, what each new location has to offer. Brave the elements and fight them when you have to, using all of your riding skills and instincts to survive. Meet new people that surprise you, in good ways and bad, but that add to your appreciation of the incredible diversity of our communities. And as the hours and miles tick away, as the sun crests above you and settles lower in the sky each day, appreciate the gift of having every sense in your body stimulated to the point of saturation, to the point when you can't see or smell or hear or even think about another thing.

Unfortunately, you can only experience that through the real deal. Anything less falls off exponentially. My wife, one day after I was home, saw me on the couch studiously working my Google Maps application and taking notes. Wondering what I was up to, she walked over and peered over my shoulder.

"You're not seriously thinking about another long motorcycle trip, are you?" she asked.

"No, no, honey," I fibbed, "I'm just playing around."

But I was scheming. Wondering how far it would be to Alaska and back. How long it would take. Whether or not to head back to the center of the country or make a giant counterclockwise loop. Maybe take the coast road down the Pacific Northwest, ride through California and come back across Route 66—seven thousand miles in six weeks. Or ride down to Key West, up the west coast of Florida, across the lower tier of states, up through California and the Pacific Northwest, across Canada and back down the East Coast (clockwise loop)—eleven thousand miles in three months. Now *that's* a ride.

A lot of people—including my wife—when I talk about going on long motorcycle trips, bring up the safety issue. Why not, they say, do the same thing, but in an open convertible car? Or tow the bike to the ultimate destination, like so many others do these days, and ride once you get there? Usually, I just say, "Well, it's not the same." And that's still true. But after Sturgis, I now have a much better understanding of *why*. When you drive a convertible, and I've owned two, about the best you can do is expose a quarter of your body to the elements. The windshield deflects just about all of the wind across your body and your feet, legs, and most of your torso are protected by the body of the car. So in effect, you're still significantly cut off from the environment. And *that's* what makes riding a motorcycle so special. You're *in* the environment—every bit of you. You see the road beneath your feet and experience the elements—the beauty of the earth, the fire of the sun, and the cooling effect of the wind—on every part of your body, all the time. Before air conditioned homes, office buildings, and malls, we actually spent most of our lives outdoors. We were hunters and gatherers, farmers and shepherds, fishermen and soldiers. We might have retreated to the shelter of a cave, a hut, or a simple cabin when the sky turned threatening, but we spent the best part of each day outside, braving the elements. We're meant to be connected to the life force of nature. When we plug into it, it recharges us. Riding a motorcycle infuses you, every minute, with a concentrated level of that force.

The risks, however, are considerable. There's no way around it. Even for an experienced middle-aged rider like myself, who doesn't ride while intoxicated or speed excessively. Riding a motorcycle is at least four times more likely to result in injury or death per passenger mile traveled than driving a car. It's pure physics. The average car weighs 3,200 pounds. The average motorcycle, with a rider, weighs maybe a quarter of that. So imagine if every time you drove a car, the traffic around you was all trucks weighing at least 12,000 pounds (the average garbage truck). Also, imagine that your vehicle had no engine compartment in front of you, no crumple zones, no safety cage, no airbags, and no restraints. Who's going to win if there's a collision? But we can't change the physics. So safe riders do everything they can to maximize their chances. The first step is to negate, as much as possible, the root cause of most motorcycle accidents (after speed and alcohol): not being seen. So we pour on lights and change out our pipes. I know that noisy pipes can be annoying, especially in quiet neighborhoods, but as long as they are within the law, personally, I'll ride with the shit-stinking loudest pipes I can find. If you can't see me, maybe you can hear me. They save lives.

The next step is proper protective gear. Like most riders, I assess the risks of the route I plan to take and adjust for the conditions. If I'm running an errand on back roads where the speed limits are low, I might just leave my helmet at home. For a ride on secondary roads where speeds rarely exceed 55 mph, I'll wear my half-helmet. But if I have to brave an interstate, particularly a busy one—unless it's so hot I'm at risk of heat stroke—I'll wear a full-faced helmet and a jacket with body armor. On colder days, I'll even wear riding pants with body armor. They keep you warm as toast.

The technique is probably more important than lights, pipes, and gear combined. It starts, at least for me, by assuming that everyone is pretty much out to kill me: the truck rumbling along beside me, the car coming up on my rear, the pickup waiting to make a left turn on a green light at the intersection ahead, and the minivan pulling out of a parking lot into my lane. So I do everything possible to minimize the risk. If I'm in somebody's blind spot, I'll drop back, change lanes, or quickly put on speed. If I'm coming up on an intersection when someone is waiting to make a left turn, I'll put myself in the best position within the lane to be seen (or even change lanes), place my left thumb on the horn button, slow a little, and be ready to brake hard. And when I ride on a road that has multiple entrances from parking lots and side streets, I'll either switch to the opposite lane or ride as far to the right as possible. During the Sturgis trip, I probably saved my can a dozen times with these techniques alone.

But I also learned something else on the Sturgis trip, related to safety, that I didn't expect: the importance of the design of the bike itself. My son Chris, through the years, has always razzed me about riding a Harley. To him, and many other motorcycle enthusiasts I suppose, there are better choices. Almost every time he's home, if I'm in the garage doing something to Big Girl and he happens to stroll in, he brings it up. The conversation usually goes something like this:

"Dad, come on. They're so heavy."

"Well, weight isn't necessarily bad."

"They don't corner as well."

"I don't slice through traffic. Only SQUIDs do that."

"They aren't as efficient as the Japanese and European bikes."

"I still get forty miles per gallon. That's good enough."

"They don't make as much horsepower."

"Horsepower gives you top speed. I don't ride flat out. Real riders want torque."

"A 110 cubic inch engine? Japanese bikes make twice the horsepower with half the displacement."

"Large displacement engines produce *torque*."

"But Dad, they're *air-cooled*. I mean, that technology is so *old*."

"It's less complex. Simple means reliable."

"They're expensive."

"You get what you pay for."

After a while, I just get tired and change the subject. But as I sat in the restaurant, staring at the reflections in Big Girl's chrome, I realized there's an entirely different dimension to them.

Before Sturgis, when people would ask me why I ride a Harley, I'd talk about the side that most people see. The rugged "tough guy" looks of the basic designs, the ability to customize just about everything, and the reputation of the brand. And I have to admit, even today, I like the reaction I get whenever I tell people I ride a Harley. You can always tell what they're thinking: Wow . . . he must be a *badass*. But the side that most people don't see, particularly weekend warriors, is that if you ever have to cross the country on a motorcycle and get back home again, unharmed, a Harley touring bike is the right tool for the job. A damn near the perfect tool, I thought. Heavy with wide tires so it'll track steadily through standing water. A low center of gravity to help fight crosswinds. A motor with enough grunt to pull you out of trouble without downshifting—because when the shit hits the fan, you're not going to have time. An electrical system that won't short out during a deluge. Wheels and suspension that can absorb potholes without breaking a sweat. A body that can deflect rocks, road debris, and hail as if they were gnats. The ability to stop on a dime. And that, I thought, more than anything else now, is why I ride one.

Then again, I thought, maybe I'll just keep it simple. And the next time Chris asks me why I ride a Harley-Davidson, I'll just answer the way I think Larry would: "Because they're fucking tough as nails."

I also discovered, in a way I'm still trying to grasp, the incredible beauty of this country. Prior to Sturgis, I'd considered myself to be reasonably well traveled. During my previous two careers, I'd had the opportunity to visit most of the major cities in the United States and plenty of smaller, surprisingly entertaining and charming towns. During the years when my sons were playing travel soccer and we vacationed with all of our kids, I traveled even more. But I never realized until I crossed the country on a motorcycle, that I actually hadn't *seen it*. Because to do that, you have to experience it the way our forefathers did: out in the open, exposed to the elements, with only a destination in mind and a compass to guide you, living day by day, discovering its wonders. And I thought about how lucky they were. To see it for the first time, raw and untouched, without buildings and roads and cell phone towers. Staggering mountains and sculpted canyons. Wild rivers and thundering waterfalls. Forests so thick you'd think it was evening. Open fields of wildflowers and mossy grasses, with the sky above another gorgeous canvas, impossibly big, always changing.

Some people would say we've managed, over two centuries of development, to irrevocably spoil the land, but I can attest, at least through my own experience, that it's still pretty spectacular. But you have to see it the way they did. Walking or riding. And since you can't ride a horse across the country anymore, about the only choice, if you want to make reasonably decent time, is to ride a motorcycle. Sure, you can look at the countryside through the windows of an aircraft, a train, a bus, or a car and see it. But to really appreciate it, to really understand its beauty and mystical, invigorating power, you have to *live it*.

That's why, after Sturgis, I'll never be the same. Because in those eleven days I lived, discovered, and learned more than during any other similar period in my life. And as I puttered along on Big Girl, heading west, marveling at the beauty of the Spanish moss dangling from the live oak trees, their branches long since clipped by passing trucks into a perfectly trimmed overhead the archway, I thought about something even more important.

I'd *loved* more. Not in the traditional sense, of course, because she wasn't there. But in a sense that matters more. What you do when you're *not* together—when time, distance, and circumstances test your commitment. The day when you stumble into an orchard flush with apples, you're tired, separated and hungry, and you only have to pick one and take a taste. But you know it's wrong, so you step back. Or you're on the road, during the lonely stretches when you're the most vulnerable, when you need a soulmate more than anything, and you reach out. And the person who comes to you first, your inner voice, your best friend and mentor, your guide and alternate conscious, is your life partner. It was, of course, her.

She was with me during that terrible ride across Missouri, she was with me during every discovery in and around Sturgis, and she was with me, guiding and protecting me, all the way home. Tucked away in the part of my mind that stores the warmest memories, the part of my heart that contains the greatest wellspring of admiration and affection, the spirit that comprises my soul. With a bond that transcended distance and time, that was stretched but never broken, and somehow, through the crucible of those eleven days and her terrible illness, became even stronger.

I know that someday she'll ride with me. But as I twisted on a little more throttle and upshifted into fifth, smiling at the "bada-bada-bwwwaaaaattt" coming from Big Girl's pipes, I thought, you know, I can wait. Because whether she's physically sitting on the back of my bike or not, I know she'll always be with me. And I'll always be with her—watching our children mature into wonderful adults, spoiling the grandkids when they come, walking on the beach with the puppies, and swapping stories with friends. Working when we have to, traveling when we can. Always discovering, always learning. Perhaps, at times, on the back of a motorcycle. Or maybe, just maybe, with some kind of compromise (a trailer Ma?), but riding together through the next chapter, wherever it takes us, laughing and loving, down every road.

Ann Marie
"Ringing of the Bell"

Last Chemotherapy
Treatment

November 2012

Robert McPherson is a native of the Washington D.C. area. He graduated from the University of Michigan in 1985 with a Bachelor of Science in Naval Architecture and Marine Engineering. After serving in the U.S. Navy ROTC he served as an officer on the USS Jacksonville (SSN-699) fast attack submarine. In 1992 Rob graduated with an MBA from George Washington University. In 1995 Rob joined Accenture where he quickly rose to Partner and was with the company for fifteen years. At Accenture he co-authored two white papers, "Achieving High Performance in U.S. Defense" and "Shaping the Navy's Future." And so began his love of writing.

Rob is a loving father of four children and resides in Hilton Head Island, South Carolina with his wife Ann Marie and daughter Emily.

Made in United States
Orlando, FL
06 April 2023